ATHENS AND ATTICA

Christopher Wordsworth in middle age

ATHENS AND ATTICA:

JOURNAL

OF

A RESIDENCE THERE

BY THE

REV. CHRISTOPHER WORDSWORTH, M.A.

FIRST PUBLISHED 1836

A new edition with additional material, edited by
Gerald Brisch

Also available as Archaeopress 3rdguides:

J. Theodore Bent, *The Cyclades, or Life Among the Insular Greeks*
Cecil Torr, *Rhodes in Modern Times*

Athens and Attica, first published by John Murray, 1836

This edition copyright Archaeopress and Gerald Brisch 2004

3rdguides is an imprint of
Archaeopress
Gordon House
276 Banbury Road
Oxford OX2 7ED
England

3rdguides series editor: Gerald Brisch

All rights reserved. No part of this publication may be reproduced, stored in a retrieval system, or transmitted, in any form or by any means, electronic, mechanical, photocopying, recording or otherwise, without the prior permission of the publishers.

ISBN 0 9539923 3 0

Printed in Great Britain by The Basingstoke Press

Acknowledgements

Portrait of Christopher Wordsworth (frontispiece) from *Christopher Wordsworth, Bishop of Lincoln* by Elizabeth Wordsworth, reproduced by permission of Bodleian Library, University of Oxford.
Cover photograph of the Theseíon by Nick Nacc.
With grateful thanks to Keith Bennett, Ianna Bitha and Brenda Stones.
For Holly Emma Dawes.

...nec non si forte lapides, inter quos vetustos quandoque effodiunt, epigramma comperis, rescribere velis. Cyriac of Ancona, *Later Travels*, Letter XXV

"Tourists", we are informed, is not how the group would refer to themselves. "Germans are tourists and Frenchmen are tourists but Englishmen are Greeks." Such was the sense of their discourse, and we must take their word for it that it was very good sense indeed... And to prove themselves duly inspired, they not only shared their wine flask with the escort of dirty Greek peasant boys but condescended so far as to address them in their own tongue as Plato would have spoken it had Plato learned Greek at Harrow. Virginia Woolf, *A Dialogue upon Mount Pentelicus*

The whole city is quiet. Looking over it from any of its hills the lights twinkle as abundantly as ever – an hour or two before the cocks start crowing. But in the very centre there is an unlit patch scooped out of that immense and sparkling sea; black as a cave-mouth – quite big – the cliff-edge indeterminate though darker than the night above it: an empty hole in human memory, more opaque than time. Kevin Andrews, *Athens*

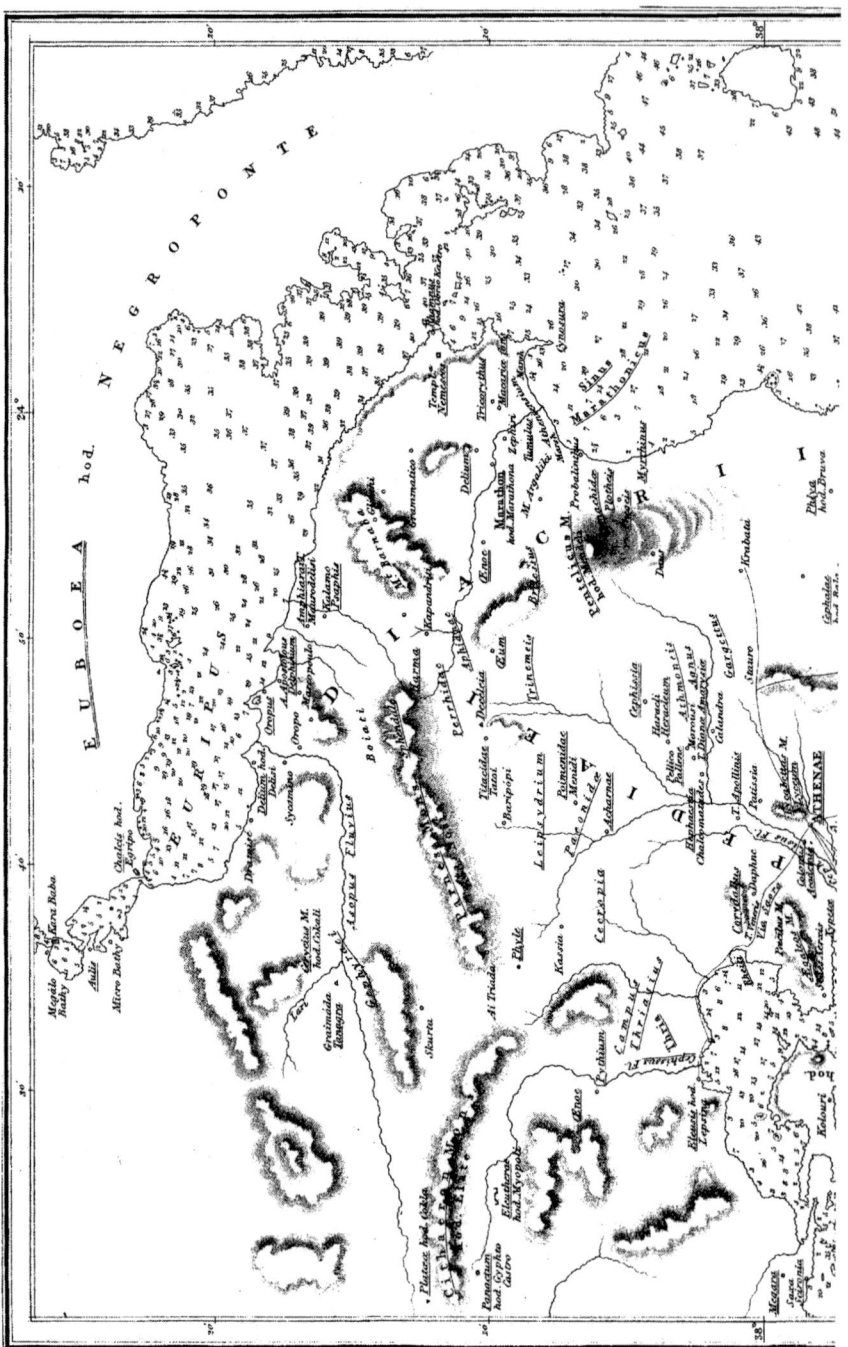

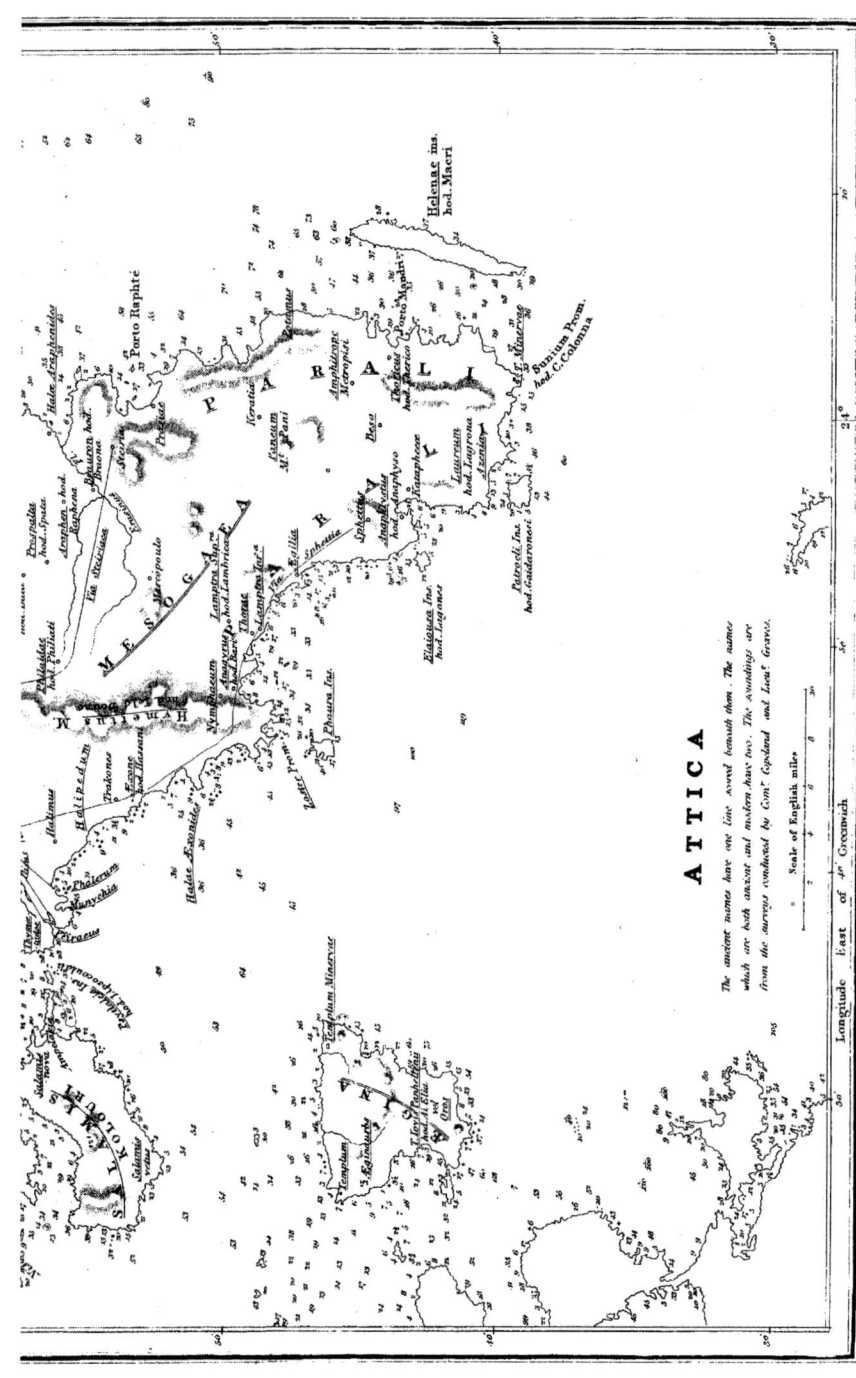

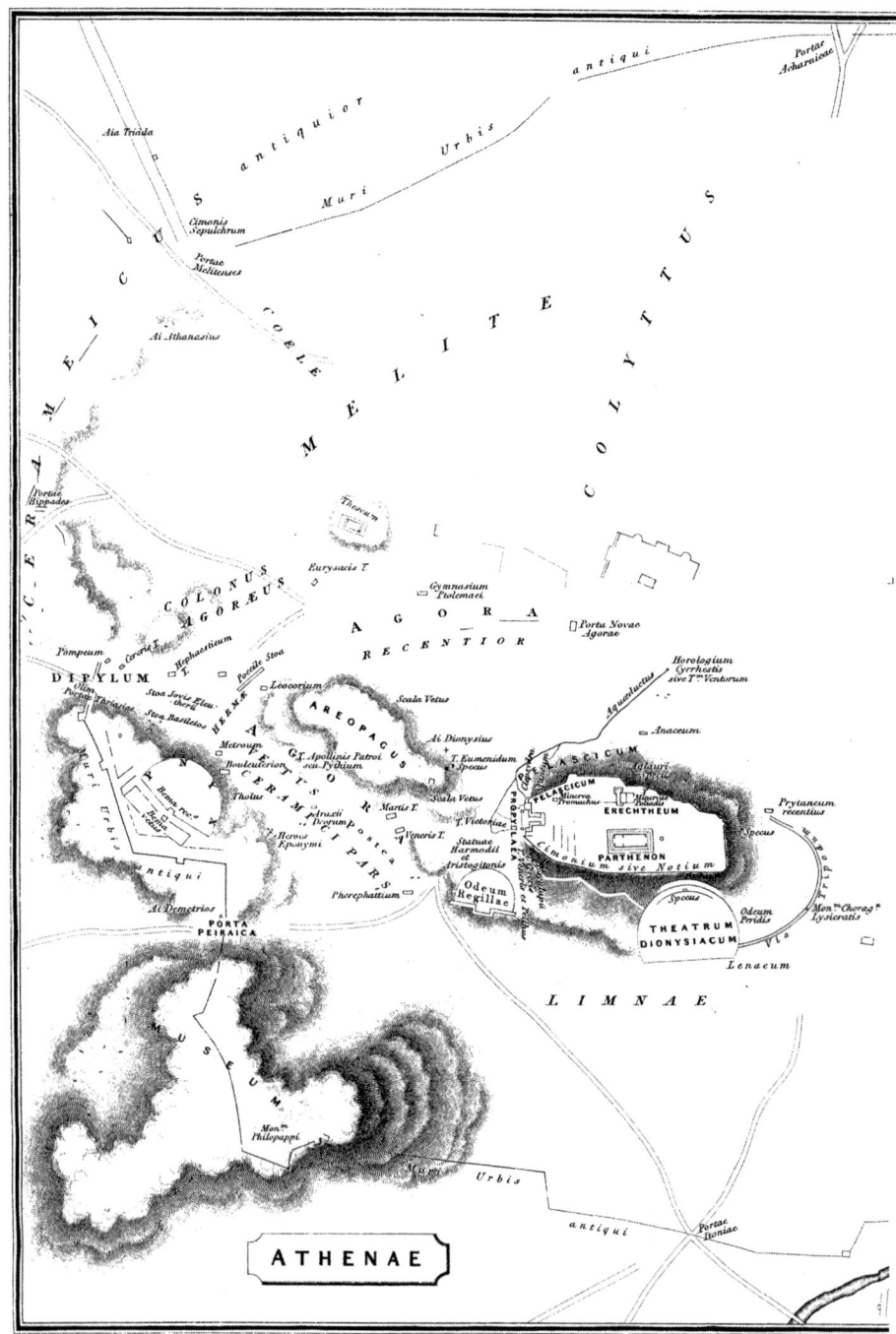

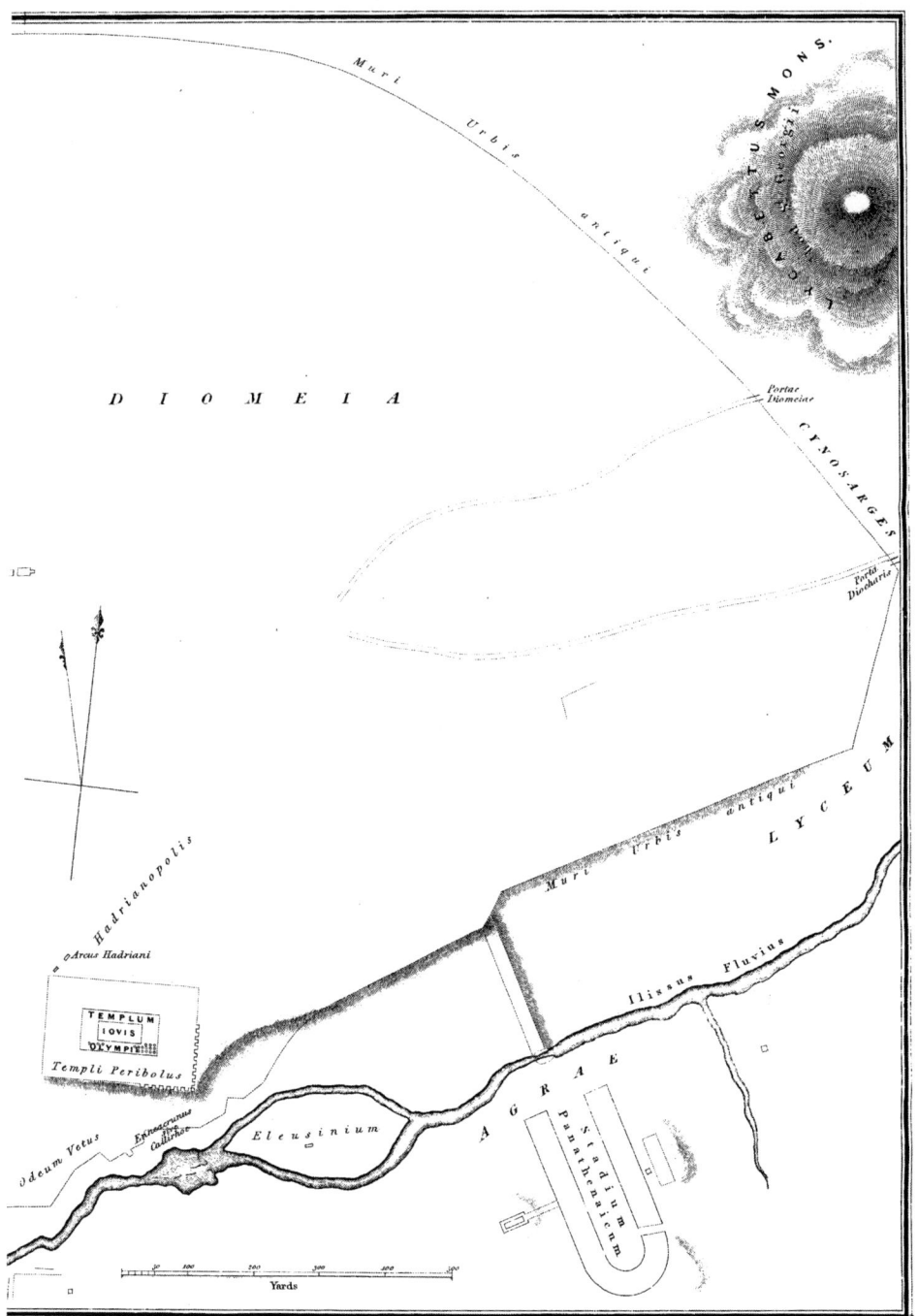

Athens from the Academy

Contents

Introduction	ix
Chronology	xxiv
Chapter headings	xxiv
Athens and Attica:	
Preface	I-IV
List of Plates	V
Contents	VI-VIII
Text	1
Appendix	157
Endnotes	165
Bibliography	221
Sidetrack 1: Itinerary	226
Sidetrack 2: Contexts	230
Sidetrack 3: Gazetteer	233
Index	238

Illustrations

Portrait of Christopher Wordsworth	facing title page
Map of Attica	ii-iii
Map of Athens	iv-v
Athens from the Academy	vi
The Pnyx from the Areopagus	viii
The Acropolis from the Pnyx	xxviii

The Pnyx from the Areopagus

INTRODUCTION

"The energy that went into discoveries about the natural world and its working during the first half of the 19th-century and the shaping and sharpening of critical tools to assist this, not only in the field of the physical sciences, but also in history and archaeology, was something that had excited Christopher himself as a young man." (V. Strudwick, *Christopher Wordsworth*)

Christopher Wordsworth, a member of an old and distinguished English family that included Christopher's illustrious uncle, the famous poet, chose to take his gap-year after graduation. In 1833, already a classics lecturer – he was 25 – at Trinity College, Cambridge (where his father was Master), he set out for Italy and Greece with a small group of companions. He returned a year later to resume his teaching post, became a priest, and in 1836 was appointed Public Orator for his university, a single honour for a brilliant academic still not yet 30. A few months later he was headmaster of Harrow School (Lewis Carroll's father being one of the other candidates to whom he was preferred) and busy courting Susanna Hatley Frere, second daughter of George Frere. In December 1838 they married (she 27, he 31) at Thorley Church near Bishop's Stortford. A little while before, from the headmaster's house at Harrow, he had sent his fiancée a small packet containing nine gold medals, all prizes from his triumphs in classical Latin and Greek at Winchester and Trinity:

"Harrow, 18th August, 1838.

If I can connect with you my <u>past</u> as well as my future life, both will have more value in my estimation. And, therefore, I beg you to accept the enclosed records of boyish honours, which would have had more charm for me than they possessed, even when first won, had I foreseen that they would ever, together with myself, have become yours."

As preoccupied as he was, Christopher (always "My Dear Chris" to uncle William) worked hard to complete three highly esteemed monographs relating to his Grand Tour for the publisher – Byron's publisher – John Murray. The full tour is encompassed in his two-volume edition of *Greece, Pictorial, Descriptive and Historical* (1839), with around 400 illustrations. This work contained many detailed topographical accounts of the young scholar's travels from Epiros to Attica and the Peloponnese; Wordsworth's model was the surveyor supreme, Colonel William Martin Leake, whose *Topography of Athens* first appeared in 1821.

The scope and production difficulties associated with the publication of *Greece, Pictorial, Descriptive and Historical* meant that the young headmaster had two other works of his with booksellers first. Before sailing to northern Greece, Christopher travelled to Sicily and southern Italy, by way of Rome, in the company of another Trinity Fellow, Mr Joddrell. Among the ruins of Pompeii, his attention was drawn to the many inscriptions traced by a hard stylus on the cement of the walls. Christopher set to work deciphering and translating them, and in his *Inscriptiones Pompeianæ* (1837) produced a monograph of great originality and influence. (The introduction starts, *"Let us then, my dear P., ascend once more, in fancy at least, our Neapolitan carratella, and drive off to Pompeii."* We may imagine the poor 'P' trying to look enthusiastic over breakfast before another day in the sun helping his friend untangle the spaghetti of 2000-year-old graffiti.)

However, the most accessible of the three travel accounts of the author (not least in terms of affordability and broader appeal) is *Athens and Attica* (1836); such was the book's popularity that it was reprinted the following year and went to three editions (1855). The work's contents represent the sections from Wordsworth's journals on Athens, and John Murray would have seen (while the full account of the author's *Greece* was still being prepared) the commercial advantage of a worthy guide at a time when the country was reshaping itself after independence. The result covers the winter months of 1832/3, and includes an anti-clockwise circuit of Attica, various excursions, a short cruise in the Saronic Gulf (and visit to the Aegina temples), and, of course, the great sites and sights of the new capital of a reborn Greece. (Murray's own *Guide to Greece* was still some years off, and Wordsworth's editor obviously had to keep an eye on their potential market.)

The scholar's style is, perhaps, best described as rigorous: there are few jokes and the few he does attempt are the sort that today might raise forced smiles and furtive eye contact between the party members of some conducted classical tour. But never mind, we are here in part to be instructed and can overlook any contemporary notions of "literary imperialism". There are, of course, Poussin-hued passages in a romantic style (no doubt he was conscious of his uncle), but the overall timbre is so authoritative and secure, and the writer throughout reflects such an awareness of all aspects of times past and present (he is no looter, although he does mention a gospel from Metéora among his later possessions; the Parthenon Marbles are in the British Museum already by 1815), that his company is a stimulating challenge. At times we are not so much tourists with Christopher as unfit cross-country runners, tearing through his pages with their thick runs of Latin and Greek inscriptions and quotations, the diacritics reaching up like impenetrable brambles. For Wordsworth, of course, these are to be leapt with ease (he was a great walker and runner) and he always assumes the reader's complete familiarity with classical languages and references (as well as ancient Greek and Latin, he spoke Italian, French, and Modern Greek) and you accompany him unprepared at your peril; one notes a trace of disdain in his Preface to *Athens and Attica* as he writes, *"At the desire of the Publisher,* [I have] *annexed a translation to the classical quotations in the text."*

Looking back, Christopher Wordsworth's first forty years are peopled with characters from *Tom Brown's Schooldays* and *Glittering Prizes*. Extraordinarily gifted (as were his two elder brothers, John (1805-1839) and Charles (1806-1892)), Christopher was born on 30th October 1807 in Lambeth, of father Christopher and mother Priscilla Lloyd, who died in 1815 when her youngest son was just eight. He was brought up in Bocking, Essex and Sundridge, Kent, before entering Winchester as a commoner in 1820. The young Wykehamist (known as "The Great Christopher" there) absorbs the classics under the strict gaze of Dr Henry Dison Gabell, learning Virgil and *"the Georgics by heart (and he never forgot them) in the beautiful meadows, watered by clear streams, close by which the school lies...It was considered an unpardonable offence (equal in enormity to a false concord or a false quantity) if a boy wrote 'Oh!' before a noun in the vocative instead of 'O'."*

After Winchester, in 1826, Christopher went up to Trinity and set about winning every classics award he set his cap at; and by his final year, the tutors had to dissuade him from entering competitions out of fairness for the other undergraduates. In 1830 he took his degree as Senior Classic in the Classical Tripos, 14th Senior Optime in the Mathematical Tripos, won the First Chancellor's Medal for Classical Studies, and was elected Fellow of Trinity College. It was all rather breathtaking and his achievements find a faint echo a hundred years later in the achievements of the archaeologist J.D.S. Pendlebury, also of Winchester and Cambridge, and the same mixture of intellect, athleticism, and emotional ties to the past.

In the biographies (pre-eminently by his daughter Elizabeth (1840-1932) and John Henry Overton, Canon of Lincoln and Rector of Epworth, whose quotations mostly illustrate this Introduction), there are conflicting accounts of Wordsworth's sporting achievements. One goes that he *"excelled more in the athletics of the mind than those of the body, but he was by no means deficient in the latter."* Another is more effusive, *"He was the best cricketer, the best football player, the best fives player with both the hand and bat, and the best runner in Winchester School."*

There was a strong competitive edge between the three Wordsworth brothers. The first cricket match (played at Lord's in 1825) between Winchester and Harrow finds Christopher and Charles gleefully on opposing sides, with Charles the Harrow captain. (Winchester won by 135 runs, with the young Wykehamist scoring 3 and 36. Charles was responsible for Christopher's low score in the first innings.)

This competitiveness between the three sons of Christopher Wordsworth senior (1774-1846), Master of Trinity College, Cambridge and youngest brother to the poet, may well have been the spur that drove the boys to achieve all they attempted, making the frustration of failure and disappointments in later life as painful as the successes were sweet in youth. Brother Charles strove to match his brother at every turn but seems to have had the more easy-going personality. He is most famous today for being one of the two founders of the annual Boat Race. The inspired prank to initiate a rowing race between the rival universities came from Charles Wordsworth (Harrow and Oxford) and a friend, Charles Merival (Harrow and Cambridge). Cambridge issued the challenge on 12th March 1829 and the first race took place at Henley-on-Thames three months later on 10th June, with Oxford the winner. (In the announcement, Charles sits at 4, *"Wordsworth (new oar) has neither words nor worth, action not utterance, &c., &c., &c. I only (row) right on; I tell you that, that you yourselves do know."*)

The 'new oar' (who advances to become Bishop of St Andrews in 1853) takes on Christopher again a little later when they are persuaded to write Greek and Latin grammars respectively. Christopher produces his

King Edward VI Latin Grammar (1841, and also with John Murray) which remains the most popular text for almost the next twenty years before being superseded by Kennedy's *Primer* in 1866. Charles's Greek volume on the other hand was less of a success. One pupil, later headmaster of Winchester, said in his memoirs that he would wake in the night with a start thinking of it and that he still shuddered at the "sight of p.75!"

For Christopher approaching 40, and on the verge of the high Victorian and establishment figure he was set to become, his world was viewed as if from the Acropolis of Athens, in the glow of some never-ending Panathenaic triumph – one of his favourite National Gallery paintings was Claude's golden *Embarkation of the Queen of Sheba*. Headmaster of Harrow, husband, and father to the first of his eventual seven children, respected scholar, future correspondent of Gladstone, Disraeli, Robert Peel, General Gordon, *et al.*, and nephew of the greatest poet England had produced to boot:

To the Rev. Christopher Wordsworth, D.D., Master of Harrow School

After the perusal of his "Theophilus Anglicanus", recently published:

> ENLIGHTENED *Teacher, gladly from thy hand*
> *Have I received this proof of pains bestowed*
> *By Thee to guide thy Pupils on the road*
> *That, in our native isle, and every land,*
> *The Church, when trusting in divine command*
> *And in her Catholic attributes, hath trod:*
> *O may these lessons be with profit scanned*
> *To thy heart's wish, thy labour blest by God!*
> *So the bright faces of the young and gay*
> *Shall look more bright – the happy, happier still;*
> *Catch, in the pauses of their keenest play,*
> *Motions of thought which elevate the will*
> *And, like the Spire that from your classic Hill*
> *Points heavenward, indicate the end and way.*

Rydal Mount, Dec. 11, 1843.

But things may fall apart, and Wordsworth embarks on the second half of his life, a phase characterized now more by Dickens and Trollope, that sees him metamorphosed from the good-looking young man of the frontispiece here into something of the elderly raptor (*"He carried his head erect and had something of that eagle eye"*) he was to resemble in later life, when described by Bishop Magee of Peterborough as that "Dear old man. Very little of his life in the nineteenth century: most of him is in the ninth and the rest of him is in heaven."

Long-sighted and remarkable for his rapid, horizontally darting eyes, even his friends and family admitted that the Bishop could be *"stiff, opinionated, sarcastic and stubborn"*, *"essentially of the stuff that martyrs are made of"*, and possessing *"the simplicity, the guilelessness, and the trustfulness of a little child...all through his career"*, very soon after his appointment at Harrow he began to clash with the governors and parents; it was the time of Arnold's root and branch reforms in public school education, of which Wordsworth was a keen proponent.

He began to regret his move from Cambridge don to Harrow; the numbers decreased greatly under his headmastership and his health suffered; he was prone to *"that sensitive state of nerves to which scholars and thinkers are peculiarly liable"*. His daughter Elizabeth (1840-1932), later Principal of Lady Margaret Hall (1879), Dame, and founder (1886) of St Hugh's, referred to the Harrow period as perhaps the most trying part of her father's life; the first plunge from the world of ideas into the world of experience. And also his first taste of failure. He applied on two occasions for the Regius Professorship of Divinity at Cambridge and was twice unsuccessful. Other misfortunes overtook him. His eldest brother John died in 1839, aged only 37, and his father a few years later. William Wordsworth died in 1850, leaving Christopher as literary executor and author of a memoir on his uncle (1851). And there was a major fire at Harrow School, in which the headmaster's house was burned to the ground; Christopher was able to save some personal treasures, including that Greek testament from Metéora.

The School governors were by now ready for another head, but Wordsworth was not a candidate for constructive dismissal. In the end, Sir Robert Peel stepped in to find a compromise acceptable to both parties and Wordsworth opted for fast-track preferment in the Church – having been thwarted in his hopes for a Cambridge Chair. He eventually resigned from Harrow in 1844, landing, with Peel's influence, the position as canon at the Collegiate Church of St Peter, Westminster (where he became famous for penning long sermons *"Just an hour, but not a moment too long"*, said one parishioner, and unmemorable hymns).

The move relieved the stress on his health; he was keen on regular exercise in the open air – morning and afternoon – a habit, along with good early starts and tea in bed, *"which he kept up to the very last week of his long and wonderfully energetic life"*.

His finances, too, began to improve. He was able later to give a set of his 6-volume Bible commentary to every assistant curate in his diocese, as well as commission Sir Gilbert Scott to design a new pulpit, altar rail, and reading desk for St James the Great, Thorley, where he and Susanna were married, and to provide for 25 Norham Road, Oxford, the first home of St Hugh's College.

In 1850, Wordsworth accepted a pastoral cure in the then Berkshire Diocese of 'Stanford-in-the-Vale-cum-Goosey', and for nearly twenty years would spend nine months out of twelve in rural seclusion. As archdeacon at Westminster (from 1865), Disraeli recommends him to Queen Victoria as Bishop of Lincoln, having *"confidence in your abilities, your learning, and the striking example you have set"*. He was duly consecrated on 24th February 1869 and there was no time for study-leave in Italy and Greece, of the kind he undertook in September 1832. But we are left with the three important volumes that were the results of his Grand Tour.

From the moment Wordsworth lands in Iphigeneia's Aulis from Euboea, until he leaves for the Peloponnese on the last page, the modern reader is treated to a demanding series of tutorials on Greek history (from Marathon to Navarino), almost every classical celebrity and literary figure, and on the then state-of-the-art 'archaeology' of the region, including reports on the known monuments, large and small – some of them still swaying from the final siege of Athens in 1827, just a handful of years before Christopher and his party arrive on their mules.

Not an archaeologist, of course (the modern science begins later), Wordsworth was part of an antiquarian tradition founded on the study of classical texts and inscriptions, topographical analyses, and detective work based on artefacts examined out of context. The work of these scholars – mostly English, French and German (and almost exclusively men) – towards the end of the 18th century and into the middle of the 19th century, undertook the early spade-work for the Schliemanns and Evanses, and the vast spectrum of today's archaeology industry.

And the young Cambridge don had a real genius for antiquarian research, aided by his ability to walk and ride all day; there are two detailed treks in *Athens and Attica*, timed to the minute (see notes on pages 167 and 204). Of particular interest is his walk, through field and marsh, to Pireaus, in the hope of tracing the Long Walls. There is a definite feeling of being in the company of an experienced, if quirky, tour-guide – a classics master working on his holiday; hard to keep up with, intellectually and physically. His tour around the monuments of Aegina is a *tour de force*; an indispensable accompaniment and unmatched in any guidebook in English.

With Pausanias, or Leake, or other commentary in hand, Wordsworth marches us from place to place, having sailed from Italy to the Ionian Islands and then northern Greece, fresh from his pioneering work on a *"new field of antiquarian discovery"* – as his daughter Elizabeth reminds us in her father's biography: *"In his work on Pompeian Inscriptions (1839) he broke ground hitherto untouched by scholars, in deciphering inscriptions traced by a hard stylus on the cement of the walls of Pompeii. The felicity with which some of these careless scratches of ill-taught slave or passer-by are thus illustrated after an interval of nearly 2000 years, has led to the works being spoken of in high terms by Garrucci, Lenormant, Mommsen, Zangermeister, and others."*

Christopher is now ready for further achievements. Fascinated by the efforts of Gell, Leake and others to locate the fabled northern site of Dodona and its famous oracle of Zeus, he arrives in Ioannina in September 1832 in the company then of Richard Monckton Milnes, later Lord Houghton, and hears of the remains nearby at Dramisus. The features there suggest to him an importance greater than the modest settlement he measures, and he is the first topographer to theorize that the ruined theatre and column drums there are, indeed, those of Homer's Dodona. His hypothesis is detailed in *Greece, Pictorial, Descriptive and Historical* (1839), but it was left to a pioneering Greek archaeologist to fully investigate the remains in the 1870s and find confirming evidence. The Bishop of Lincoln is understandably pleased to receive a letter *"dated Athens, 20th May, 1882 from M. Constantine Carapanos, the author of the magnificent work on 'Dodona and its Remains', and a member of the Greek Parliament: and in that letter M. Carapanos expresses a wish that he had been acquainted with the Bishop's volume on 'Greece' when he made his excavations at Dodona; which it is to be hoped may be continued by him, or by some other enterprising archaeologist – such as M. Schliemann – and may lead to other interesting discoveries at that place."*

The quotation is from the Bishop's *Where was Dodona? An Inaugural Address at the Lincoln Diocesan Architectural and Archaeological Society's meeting at Spalding, on Wednesday, June 14, 1882.* The entertaining pages include several sermonizing paragraphs that might well fit an archaeologist's T-shirt or tea mug today: *"Archaeological inquiries and investigations are not altogether barren and profitless but may produce some good fruit for the use and refreshment of those who labour in the ample fields of historical and geographical research, and in the noble cause of moral, social, and religious improvement."*

In the 1830s, and until much later, such expeditions to the wilder places of Greece were not without their dangers. On a return from Delphi, Christopher's party was attacked by bandits. His account of the robbery, modestly, does not reveal that he was the victim of his assailant's knife and had to rely upon the care of an English family in Athens for his recovery. There were other hardships enough for him to write: *"If any one requires to learn by a practical lesson what are the results which political disorganization will produce on his own personal freedom and convenience, he has only to spend a week in Greece. To a person who is content to remain stationary in one spot, the embarrassments resulting from this disastrous condition are not trivial; but to one who comes here for the purpose of exploring different districts, the difficulties which it involves cannot be enumerated."*

The Greek countryside was to remain unsafe for unwary travellers, as the infamous Dílessi murders of 1870 testified, for many years.

For their stay in Athens, Christopher and his party are put up *"…in a small house in that quarter of Athens which was once the inner Ceramicus: our abode is the nearest building to the Temple of Theseus. Formerly its site was the heart of the city: it is now on the extreme verge of the modern town, to the west of it. There are few other buildings near it. At a little distance to the south a peasant is now engaged in ploughing the earth with a team of two oxen: the soil along which he is driving his furrows was once a part of the Agora of Athens."*

Of course, the modern visitor will not expect to find everything as Wordsworth left it, or as he labelled or dated his sites and finds, but it is not difficult to locate his stones or inscriptions in quiet churches and only very little imagination is required to stand on the Mouseíon, with your back to the Parthenon, and see the modern accretions of Athens fade, and

Themistocles' walls stretch to out Phaleron and Pireaus; and beyond is Salamis.

At Sounion with Wordsworth in 1833 it is hard not think of Byron, who was famously there scratching his name on a column some twenty years before. The mention of Byron helps us to focus on the contemporary historical situation. Our guide cannot avoid the topical references; after all he was a boy of eight when Waterloo was fought. Scrambling over the Erechtheion, Christopher notes *"In the Caryatid portico one of the four marble beams of the roof has fallen...It fell during the siege of Athens, in 1827...three only of the six Caryatides remain..."* (Elgin's wife had removed one some years before...it was already in London.)

The struggle for independence against the Turks continued late into the 1820s and Athens retained an Ottoman presence right up until Wordsworth's visit: *"...the Athenian peasant, as he drives his laden mule from Hymettus through the eastern gate of the town, still flings his small bundle of thyme and brushwood, from the load which he brings on his mule's back, as a tribute to the Mussulman toll-gatherer, who sits at that entrance of the town; and a few days ago the cannon of the Acropolis fired the signal of the conclusion of the Turkish Ramazam – the last which will ever be celebrated in Athens."*

Christopher and his friends are in the soon to be reinstated capital when the new monarch, Otho of Bavaria (imposed by the European powers, anxious to maintain their influence in the politically fast-evolving eastern Mediterranean), is hailed in Athens; Wordsworth had the distinction of being the first Englishman to be presented to the king of Greece – a slowly expanding nation that was not to extend to its modern borders for another 120 years; Crete, for example, was not officially Greek again until 1913.

Most readers, of course, will be here with Christopher to walk around the classical sites, great and small. Archaeologists have since uncovered the vestiges of the past he sat on, peering over his notebooks and various literary sources ancient (Pausanias, Diodorus Siculus, Strabo, and Aristophanes' *Lysistrata* – *"the best topographical guidebook"* – to hand for Athens) and more modern (George Wheler, James Stuart, W.M. Leake, even John Milton and the Abbé Barthélèmy). The keen classicist today will find every famous, and most lesser known, authors referred to, as well as the learned asides of contemporary editors – Dr Thomas Arnold, B.H. Kennedy, and K.O. Müller.

In the landscapes he sees echoes of Poussin and Bassano and he is prone to a suitable introspection. Here we find him, for example, gazing over *"the beautiful ruin of the Æginetan Temple...Its site is sequestered and lonely. The ground is diversified by grey rocks overhung by tufted pines, and clusters of low shrubs, among which goats are feeding, some of them placing their fore feet on the boughs of the shrubs, and cropping the leaves with their bearded mouths. It is such a scene as this which proves that the religion of Greece knew how to avail itself of two things most conducive to a solemn and devotional effect, namely, Silence and Solitude."*

Athens and Attica is no less valuable for its contemporary descriptions of the capital and its environs: *"In this state of modern desolation, the grandeur of the ancient buildings which still survive here is more striking: their preservation is more wonderful. There is now scarcely any building at Athens in so perfect a state as the Temple of Theseus. The least ruined objects here, are some of the Ruins themselves."*

Athens was, in 1883, little more than a village in an impoverished rural setting – Greece's main harbour thrived in Cycladic Syros, Pireaus not establishing itself until the early 1900s. It was the arrival of Otho and his court that provided the means for the neo-Classical planning of Athens; for example the king's palace and gardens forming the foundations of the present-day parliament buildings and the surroundings of Síndagma Square.

In contrast to the material improvements that Otho and his Bavarian court were soon to bring to Athens, Wordsworth evokes the realities of rural Attica. His excursions often necessitate overnight stops in modest dwellings; he describes one such: *"...the interior of the Albanian cottage in which we are housed for the evening. Most of the objects which are grouped together in that picture are inmates of our present lodging. Our cottage consists of one room with a clay-floor, and thatched roof. At one end of it, near the middle of the wall, on the ground, a fire is blazing with ' a fresh supply of wood to welcome our arrival. At one side of the fire our páplomas are, which in the day-time serve for saddles, and couches by night. The fire is employed in boiling some rice for our repast. On the other side of it sit two Albanian women twirling their spindles, and uttering a few syllables, before they put between their teeth the flax which is to be wound on the spindle. Another is engaged in kneading cakes which are inserted among the wood-ashes of the fire, and thus baked. The master of the house stands at the door, with his scarlet scull-cap on his head, a belt girding his white cotton tunic, over which he wears a shorter vest of woollen, thick woollen gaiters, and sandals consisting merely of a sole of untanned leather tied with leathern thongs over the instep. About him are some children, whose necks glitter with gilded coins strung into a necklace."*

Wordsworth never returned to Greece. The gothic towers of his cathedral in the mists of Lincolnshire are a long way from the columns of the Parthenon, and the Bishop becomes a more remote character. Overton describes him as *"clear-headed and businesslike, yet he had a vein of mystic enthusiasm. In manner he was quick but courteous and dignified; his language was studiously refined, but rather full in its expression, after the manner of our older divines...A certain tendency to sarcasm and severity was kept under by rigorous self-discipline. To many he seemed the living embodiment of the spirit of the early fathers of the church..."* He writes to Gordon urging for converts, his fierce anti-Romanism never wavers, and he stands firm against the evolutionary sciences of his day (in particular against the heretical *Essays and Reviews* (1880), and his preference, even, for *"Ancient heathens – a thousand times better than the blindness and audacity of Atheism...I had rather have been among the votaries of Dodona* [than a] *secularist of Birmingham..."*

But at the end there is a view of Athens in the Bishop's rooms on his death and his children say that he often recalled his tour of Greece and that they would come down to *"dessert to be told stories from the Odyssey".* Although Christopher only spent a few months in the Mediterranean as a young man (and thereafter restricted himself to short visits to France, Italy and Germany and then on church business), few travellers of his generation to Greece were better qualified to present the classical past of the city of Theseus and Pericles, and his concise volume, *Athens and Attica*, very soon found itself among the best regarded of early 19th-century accounts.

In 1884 the Bishop's wife died, a blow from which he was not to recover. He survived her by four winter months, dying on 21 March 1885. He is buried next to Susanna Hatley in his church at Riseholme, Lincolnshire; his memorial is in the Cathedral, close by the north-east door, behind the choir. He rests beneath a suitably severe marble canopy, giving a blessing, Bible in hand. The inscription, not in Greek, is *Scriba Doctus* – Learned Scribe.

Some notes to this edition.

The indefatigable Christopher lands us near Aulis (see the Gazetteer for an index of place-names), in early October 1833, and it is not until the 13/14th of that month (Chapter VII) that we all reach Athens. On the way we accompany him to the already famous sites of Tanagra, Oropus, Rhamnous, and Marathon. Chapters VII to XXIII are needed to cover the monuments of Periclean Athens. Chapter XXIV has us following Themistocles and his Long Walls to the coast. We take to mules for Chapters XXV to XXIX and the anti-clockwise sea-side expedition that includes Sounion, Thorikos, Brauron, Porto Rafti, and then leads us back to the capital via Stavros and Markopoulo. Day-trips to Marousi, Kifissia, and Colonus follow in Chapter XXX, before Christopher reports on contemporary (i.e. 1832/33) Attika for the following four short chapters. We attend a lecture on the great sea-battle of Salamis (480 BC) in Chapter XXXV, before beginning the wonderful sightseeing tour around Aegina (Chapter XXXIV). (Our journeys are not recorded in chronological order; those interested may refer to the itinerary on page 229)

The two maps in the original are fold-outs and the three engravings are by the architect and draughtsman C.R. Cockerell R.A. He was himself a renowned traveller in Greece, and a witness, in 1811, to the discovery of the beautiful sculptures at the temples of Aegina and Bassae – now housed, principally, in Berlin, London and Munich.

As much as possible, the author's spellings, punctuation, and layout have been left. The original Chapter headings are reproduced on pages xxv-xxvii. Christopher's Footnotes have been consolidated to a concluding section as Endnotes.

Skill at the decipherment and transliteration of inscriptions was essential for the 18th- and 19th-century antiquary. Before the development of modern archaeological investigative techniques, writings on stones provided essential clues to society, monuments, personalities, and locations. Christopher's analytical eye and knowledge of ancient Greek and Latin made him a superb epigrapher. This volume contains many examples of his fascination in them and his transliterations have been reproduced. (Some have been reset in modern characters and some of the author's extended passages on fold-out pages have been transferred to the new section of Endnotes.) Where the scholar filled the lacunae he used red ink in the text, but this edition employs [square brackets]. (Epigraphy is today an arcane branch of archaeology, but hugely evocative still. There is a superb collection of inscriptions in the small and little known museum in Athens that is housed alongside the National Museum.)

The Appendix is in the form of a letter written to Wordsworth by his friend C.H. Bracebridge. It serves to update the reader to life in Greece, and recent archaeological discoveries in Attica, over the three years since Christopher's stay in Athens. There is an interesting reference to emigration (page 163); one of the earliest Englishmen to settle in the new country was Edward Noel in 1832. He created an estate at Achmetága (Prokópi), Euboea, which is still flourishing as a model farm and retreat.

The final note is reserved for the cover photograph. Of all the hundreds of possible options, the choice of the Theseíon/Temple of Theseus/Hephaestion (c.450 BC), in the Agora below the Acropolis, was straightforward. Although this, the oldest complete temple in Greece, has been reattributed since Wordsworth lived in its shadow, his own words explain why its columns grace this new edition of *Athens and Attica*.

"*To my companions and myself individually* [the Temple of Theseus] *has a personal interest which I cannot forbear recording here with a feeling of gratitude. We have now lodged near it, – almost beneath its shade, – for more than two months; during this time it has been our nearest neighbour.*

"*What a change has been wrought in this city, since the supposed relics of Theseus, the old Athenian king, were welcomed by the people of Athens with the sound of poetry and music to this very spot! and how little changed is the Temple, which once witnessed that scene, and now witnesses the present demonstrations of welcome to the New Monarch of Greece! Were this Temple endued with sense how must it marvel at these vicissitudes – how, having beheld that ancient pageant, must it wonder at the ceremony of to-day* [14th February 1833]; *how must it be astonished to hear a Bishop of Athens pronouncing that three Powers, England, France, and Russia, countries whose existence it never dreamt of before, have sent hither a King, from a strange and distant land, to be proclaimed to the Athenian people on that self-same spot, which was formerly believed to contain beneath its soil the venerable ashes of Theseus!*

"*Such is the integrity of its structure, and the distinctness of its details, that it requires no description beyond that which a few glances might supply. Its beauty defies all: its solid yet graceful form is indeed admirable; and the loveliness of its colouring is such, that, from the rich mellow hue which the marble has now assumed, it looks as if it had been quarried, not from the bed of a rocky mountain, but from the golden light of an Athenian sun-set."*

Gerald Brisch
February 2004

Oxford – Athens

Christopher Wordsworth - Chronology

The main biographical source is that of Wordsworth's daughter, Elizabeth. She was herself an important figure in the advancement of women's education in England. Elizabeth Wordsworth (later DBE) was Principal of Lady Margaret Hall, Oxford and founder of St Hugh's, 1886.

1805	Brother John born
1806	Brother Charles born
1807	(30 October) Christopher born at Lambeth
1815	Mother (Priscilla) dies
1820	Enters Winchester
1825	Plays in first Winchester v. Harrow cricket match
1826	Enters Trinity College, Cambridge
1830	Takes his degree
1832	(Autumn) Begins Grand Tour
1833	(February) First Englishman in Greece to be presented to King Otho
1833	(Spring) Returns to England
1833	MA and ordained deacon
1834	Takes up Classical Lectureship at Trinity
1835	Ordained priest
1836	Appointed Public Orator at Cambridge
1836	Publishes *Athens and Attica*
1836	Becomes Headmaster of Harrow School
1837	Publishes *Inscriptiones Pompeianæ*
1838	Fire destroys Headmaster's house at Harrow
1838	Marries Susanna Hatley Frere
1839	Publishes *Greece, Pictorial, Descriptive and Historical*
1839	Brother John dies
1840	Daughter Elizabeth born
1841	Publishes *King Edward VI Latin Grammar*
1843	Turned down for Chair of Divinity at Cambridge
1846	Father dies
1844	Appointed canon at Westminster
1850	Given the living of Stanford, Berkshire
1850	(23 April) William Wordsworth dies (CW is his literary executor)
1851	Publishes *Memoirs of William Wordsworth*
1853	Brother Charles appointed Bishop of St Andrews
1865	Made an archdeacon at Westminster
1869	(24 February) Consecrated Bishop of Lincoln
1884	Susanna Wordsworth dies
1885	(19 March) Dies

Wordsworth's original Chapter headings for *Athens and Attica*

Chapter I: Euripus–Aulis–Ancient City–Aulis–Dramisé–Delium–Battle of Delium.

Chapter II: Sycaminó–Tanagra–Pausanias–Tanagra.

Chapter III: Oropus–Delphinium–Earlier site of Oropus.

Chapter IV: Dicæarchus and Barthélèmy–Site of Aphidnæ found–Military Tower–Grammaticó.

Chapter V: Albanian cottage–Rhamnus–Two Temples–Temple of Nemesis–Larger Temple of Nemesis–Smaller Temple of Nemesis–Scenery of Rhamnus–Name of Rhamnus.

Chapter VI: Marshes–Battle of Marathon–Marathonian Tetrapolis–Arrival at Athens.

Chapter VII: Rome and Athens–Modern Athens.

Chapter VIII: General View of Athens–Mount St George is Lycabettus–Soil of Lycabettus.

Chapter IX: Architectural Results from Natural Elements.

Chapter X: Scenery of the Pnyx–Oratorical Results from Local Peculiarities–Effects of the Scenery and the size of the Pnyx–Antiquarian Illustrations from Local Properties–Change of Bema in site not in Aspect.

Chapter XI: St Paul Preaching–Analogy of Amazons with the Persians–Local and Political Union of the Areopagus and the Eumenides.

Chapter XII: Clepsydra–Lysistrata, Odysseus–The Cave of Agrauros–Subterranean Ascent from the Cave of Agraulus.

Chapter XIII: The Theatre Described–Dramatic Inscriptions–Site of the Theatre–Its Poetical Results–Suggestions to the Tragedians from its Local Scenery–Suggestions to Tragedians and to the Comic Poets–Local Illustration of the Theatre and the Pynx.

Chapter XIV: Character of the Acropolis–Ascent to the Acropolis–Local Illustration of the Hippolytus–Topography of Catullus–Temple of Wingless Victory–Local Illustration of the Lysistrata.

Chapter XV: Propylæa of the Citadel–The Propylæa–The Parthenon–Pediments of the Parthenon–Impressions of Shields–Euripides Illustrated from

	Architecture of the Parthenon–Divisions of the Parthenon–Prospect from the Parthenon.
Chapter XVI:	Triple Minerva–Promachus, Parthenos, Polias–The Peplus of Minerva Polias–Triple Minerva.
Chapter XVII:	Divisions of the Erectheum–Distribution of Erectheum–Its Present State–Olive and Trident–Erectheus of Euripides–Olive of Erectheum–Its Poetical Uses–Inscriptions in the Citadel–Oration against Leptines–Inscriptions Erased–Praxiteles–Canephori–Inscription in the Citadel.
Chapter XVIII:	Theseum and St Mark's–Hercules and Theseus–Temple of Theseus.
Chapter XIX:	Temple of the Winds–Athenian Winds–Dials–Street of Tripods–Jupiter Olympius.
Chapter XX:	Stadium and Plato–Dramatic Illustrations from the Stadium.
Chapter XXI:	Ilissus Unpoetical–Poetical Treatment of Ilissus and Cephisus–Fronto the Ilissus.
Chapter XXII:	Map of the City–The Agora–Route from the Citadel to the Western City Wall–Pausanias begins his Route from Dipylum–Old Agora absorbed by new Cerameicus–Colonus, Melite, Cœle, Collyttus–Diomeia, Lyceum–Pœcile in the Agora–Plan of Athens.
Chapter XXIII:	Panathenaic Procession–Santa Rosalia–Voyage of Peplos–Trojan Horse–Site of Pythium.
Chapter XXIV:	Three Walls–Two Long Walls–A Phaleric Wall–Long Walls.
Chapter XXV:	Nymphæum–Pastoral Offerings–The Inscriptions in the Cave–The Graces, Apollo and Hersus–Inscription Restored–Plato's Cave–Plato in this Grotto.
Chapter XXVI:	Road from Athens to Laureium–Sphettian Way, Anaphlystus–Lágrona.
Chapter XXVII:	Promontory of Sunium–Thoricis now Thoricó–Theatre at Thoricus–Ancient Gate and Port–Cephalus at Thoricus, and Œdipus at Colonus.
Chapter XXVIII:	Village of Keratiá–Ancient Epitaphs–Prasiæ–Steiria, Brauron–Iphigenia–Albanian Cottage–Albanian Character–Old Divisions of Attica–Ancient Inscription–Aristophanes.
Chapter XXIX:	Marble Lion.

Chapter XXX: Amarusian Artemis, and Marousi–Kalandra and Colænis–Hercules and Harakli–Hephæstus and Chalcomatades–Pallene and Pellico–Gargettus–Ancient Names–Colonus–Death of Œdipus–Where is the Scene of the Death of Œdipus?

Chapter XXXI: Climate of Athens–Other Districts Compared with Attica–Air of Athens.

Chapter XXXII: Present Appearance of Athens.

Chapter XXXIII: Feuds at Athens–Harangue of the Bishop–Assembly in the Open Air–Theseus and King Otto.

Chapter XXXIV: Present State of Attica.

Chapter XXXV: The Straits–Psyttaleia–Silver-Footed Throne–Bay of Salamis.

Chapter XXXVI: Port of Ægina–Western Temple–Date of Western Temple–Eastern Temple–Deity of Eastern Temple–Minerva–Panhellenium–Site of Panhellenium–Æacus and Elias–Ancient Inscription–Temple of Neptune–Leave Ægina.

The Acropolis from the Pnyx

ATHENS AND ATTICA:

JOURNAL

OF

A RESIDENCE THERE

BY THE

REV. CHRISTOPHER WORDSWORTH, M.A.

FELLOW OF TRINITY COLLEGE CAMBRIDGE,
CORRESPONDENT OF THE ARCHÆOLOGICAL INSTITUTE AT ROME,
AND HEAD MASTER OF HARROW SCHOOL.

M.DCCC.XXXVI.

TO THE

CHEVALIER CHARLES BUNSEN,

MINISTER OF

HIS MAJESTY THE KING OF PRUSSIA

AT ROME,

WITH FEELINGS

OF ADMIRATION AND GRATITUDE

THIS VOLUME IS INSCRIBED.

PREFACE

THE following pages are part of a Journal, written by the Author, of a tour which he made, during the years 1882 and 1833, in several of the provinces of Greece.

He has not thought fit to publish his entire narrative at once, for reasons which it is here unnecessary to state. He now publishes a part of it, relative to that particular district of Greece, which he supposes to be regarded generally with more interest than any other. The present volume commences a little before his entrance into Attica, and terminates soon after he has quitted it.

A word of explanation is requisite here, why he has been induced to adopt the system of orthography by which modern Greek names of places, which are often intimately connected with the ancient language, have been represented in this volume, while a different method of representation has been sanctioned by the authority, and recommended by the practice, of one of the ablest among the living topographers of Greece. He has done so for the following reasons.

He was addressing himself to the eyes of English readers, in some degree familiar with the ancient literature of Greece, and not to the ears either of modern Greeks themselves, or of those who are acquainted with their mode of pronunciation. He has therefore represented those words not according to the sound which they bear in the mouth of a modern Greek, but according to their strict grammatical orthography. The etymology of a name may often present interesting materials for topographical speculation. The name itself may frequently suggest a train of agreeable recollections. But if it be disguised in the dress to which he alludes, its genuine form will not be recognised by the generality of readers. All the previous associations with which, in their minds, it may be connected, and all the subsequent deductions which by them may be derived from it, will thus be utterly lost. In writing these words, therefore, he has endeavoured to suggest to the reader not their modern sound, but their ancient sense.

At the desire of the Publisher, he has annexed a translation to the classical quotations in the text.

His best thanks are due to Col. Leake, Capt. Beaufort, R.N. Hydrographer to the Admiralty, W.R. Hamilton, Esq., C.R. Cockerell, Esq., for the assistance they have severally rendered toward the publication of this Work.

Harrow, May 14, 1836.

THE AUTHOR'S DIRECTIONS FOR PLACING THE PLATES IN THE ORIGINAL EDITION

Athens from the Academy, to face the Title.

Map of Attica to face p.1

The Pnyx from the Areopagus p.64

Map of Athens, to face Chap.VII p.51

The Acropolis from the Pnyx p.111

CONTENTS

PAGE

Chapter	Page
CHAPTER I	1
II	7
III	12
IV	15
V	19
VI	26
VII	30
VIII	33
IX	37
X	39
XI	45
XII	49
XIII	53
XIV	59
XV	63

XVI	70
XVII	74
XVIII	81
XIX	83
XX	87
XXI	89
XXII	92
XXIII	100
XXIV	103
XXV	106
XXVI	112
XXVII	115
XXVIII	120
XXIX	126
XXX	128
XXXI	136
XXXII	139
XXXIII	141
XXXIV	143

XXXV	145
XXXVI	148
Appendix	157
Endnotes	165

CHAPTER I

From Chalcis he passes over to Aulis: thence to Oropus in Attica, where an ancient Seer (Amphiaraus) is adored as a God: thence to Athens, full of her old renown, yet having many objects deserving a visit, her Citadel, her Ports, and Walls which link the Peiræus to the City; Docks erected by great Commanders; the Statues of Gods and Men.[1]
T. Liv. xlv. 26.

Oct. 9, 1832.

HESIOD might have spared the only voyage which he informs[2] us he ever made, if this bridge which we cross this morning from Chalcis to the Bœotian shore had existed in his time. His love of glory overcame his antipathy to the sea, and tempted him across the Euripus. He returned from Chalcis to Ascra loaded with the poetic prize, which he dedicated to the Muses of his native Helicon; and he afterwards wrote to his brother Perses of the dangers of the sea, which it seems he knew too well ever to encounter.

We are now making on horseback the same passage which he made by sea. The narrow bridge which we are crossing has influenced the fortunes, altered the name[3], and changed the character of Eubœa. It was the policy of Bœotia[4], contrived with more than Bœotian shrewdness, to make "Eubœa an island to every one else but themselves." By its means the Bœotians blockaded against their southern enemies the Athenians these ancient Dardanelles of Greece. They locked the door of Athenian commerce, and kept themselves the key. This was the channel, by which the gold of Thasos, the horses of Thessaly, the timber of Macedonia, the corn of Thrace were carried into the Peiræus. Nor must we forget the vast importance of Eubœa itself, which from its position, and its produce, its quarries, its timber and its corn, was of inestimable value to Athens. Of the better part of this island her tenure was from that time precarious; and her communication with the northern markets was either dependent on the fear or amity of Bœotia, or it was exposed to the dangers of the open sea – the perils of the treacherous Coela, and the "vengeful Caphareus,"[5] which on a former occasion had rendered such signal service to Athens by the havoc they had made in the invading armada of Persia.

After passing the bridge of the Euripus we turn to the left. The road skirts the shore: the tracks of ancient wheels are visible in the rocky ledge which just rises above the sea. In a mile from the bridge we arrive at a flowing fountain. There are now some Greek peasants there, halting to give drink to their horses. They inquire of us, when the long-expected arrival of the new King of Greece will take place. They congratulate themselves on their recent liberation, on their being, as they style themselves, Independent Hellenes, and no longer the slaves of Turkey.

It was at a fountain near this spot – perhaps at this source –

Beneath the platane fair, whence gushed the shining stream.[6]

that Homer imagined a session of councillors and warriors assembled round the King of Greece, who then found as much difficulty in leaving his dominions as his modern successor does now in entering them.

We inquire of these peasants the name of the site in which we are: it is called Vliké. This is probably a modification of Αὐλική, which has the sound of Avliké to a modern Greek, and still preserves the recollection of the district of Aulis, when the name of Aulis itself has perished.

We ascend a high rugged hill which is on the right of our road, and on the western verge of a peninsula formed by two bays. At its summit there is a ruined Hellenic city, probably of the heroic age.

Its huge polygonal walls remain in their complete circuit. The interior of the city is strewed with broken pottery, and overgrown with wild plants. It is in an ancient city like this, that the traveller feels, I might almost say, an emotion of gratitude that the physical structure and inorganic elements of this country are such as they happen to be. Nature did well in forming Greece of hard imperishable limestone. For from this formation it results that the monuments here of the most remote times, constructed with the native stone, with all the severity of age combine the freshness of recent structure; thus appearing to appropriate the beholder to themselves, and not to be influenced by him. They exist not, it seems, in their age; but he lives in theirs. Their share in to-day seems greater than his own.

This is illustrated by the character of the place which we are now in. We enter the gate of this ancient town. The towers which flanked the old gateway still stand, on your right and left. The groove of the gate, the socket which received its bar, seem to have been recently chiselled. Within the city at the N.W. a large square cistern is hewn in the living calcareous rock: its clean sharp sides seem to have been lately carved to receive a shower, which is expected soon to fall. You advance to the eastern wall: a flight of stone steps invites you to mount from the area of the city to a tower projecting from the wall, in order, you might almost fancy, that from its lofty eminence you might look down on the valley, the shore, and the Euripus now lying below you, and in order that you might thus assure yourself whether or no the Grecian fleet of Agamemnon was still lingering in the port of Aulis.

To return from what might be, to what is. The hill on which we stand is called Μεγάλο Βουνὸ στὸ μικρὸ βαθὺ (*The Great Mountain, at the Small Deep*).

The name of our mountain is derived from its proximity to a small harbour, called μικρὸ βαθὺ in contradistinction to the port of larger dimension which begins at the south of the narrowest point of the Euripus, and spreads itself like an unfolded wing[7] from the side of Eubœa. This larger port is called μεγάλο βαθὺ. These its two titles are of great antiquity: for there can I think be no doubt that it is identical with the harbour, which is described by Strabo[8] under the same name, and in which he supposes the Greek fleet to have been moored. If so, the harbour to the south of it, now known by the name μικρὸ βαθὺ must have been the port which he describes as affording a roadstead for only fifty ships, and as more nearly connected with Aulis itself.

Hence a presumption arises that a city which is now referred in the language of the country to that smaller harbour, (στὸ μικρὸ βαθὺ), as is the case with the city in which we now are, is no other than Aulis itself, to which the smaller harbour immediately belonged.

The existence of a profusion of fictile fragments scattered over the area of this city, may have some little weight in identifying it with Aulis, which principally maintained itself in later times[9] by its produce of pottery. I pick up here the handle of a lamp among those broken relics of its former commerce: it is inscribed with the name ΤΛΕΠΟΛΕΜΟ (*of Tlepolemus*). Tlepolemus was perhaps the manufacturer at Aulis from whose fabric it issued.

The name of Aulis[10] itself would have tempted us to place it immediately on the *canal* of the Euripus; but knowing, as we do, that Aulis was *three miles*[11] distant from Chalcis, we are disposed to acquiesce in our present position, and to consider the name of Aulis to have been assumed by that city, not as expressive of its immediate contiguity to the Euripus, but of the priority of its foundation in the less restricted neighbourhood of that channel.

We meet a shepherd of the country in our descent on the S.E. side of this mountain. He informs us that there are ruins of Hellenic cities on two neighbouring hills to the N.W. They are called by him Κτύπα and Ανηφορῆτο (*the steep*). There is also an ancient citadel bordering on the sea, on a rocky peninsula to the S.W. of our present position. One of our companions who explored it describes its construction as very rude and strong.

Our road lies along the bare arable plain parallel to the sea, and bounded on the west by low hills. We leave two hamlets, Psaloútha (Ψαλοῦθα), and Gerilé (Γεριλὴ) on our left: to our right, at about ten miles distance from Egripo is the village of Dramisé (Δραμισή). It lies in a large plain below a small insulated hill on which is a modern tower. There is a small church here dedicated to St George. If any vestiges of antiquity exist at all in a Greek village, some in the shape of decorated or inscribed marbles will generally be found in its church, for the construction of which they have usually been employed. Thus the churches of Greek towns and hamlets have served the purpose of simple museums for the preservation of their local antiquities. At Dramisé, neither in its church nor in any of its buildings, can I find any evidence that it occupies, as has been supposed, the site of an ancient city. It has been identified with Delium.

There is indeed a tumulus on its shore, which might be considered an interesting relic of Delium[12], and of its field of battle; if there were better evidence than there is of its coincidence with that city. But to the site which Delium occupied another village has succeeded, similar to Delium in name. There can be no doubt that Δήλισι now covers the spot, which has been rendered famous by the intrepidity of Socrates, and the misfortunes of his country. Délisi is about seven miles from Oropó, the site of the ancient Oropus. It stands a little to the right of the road on a rising ground, which shelves down into the plain. The road soon divides into two branches; the path on the right hand, which we now pursue, leading over the shrubby hills to Oropus, that on the left skirting the seashore, and crossing the river Asopus at its entrance to the sea.

The site of Delisi has many advantages. It stands on the southern verge of the flat strip which fringes the sea from the Euripus, and now converges to a narrow margin running on southward from Délisi along the shore. It therefore commanded this avenue from Attica unto Bœotia along the coast. This was probably the reason why it was seized[13] and fortified by the Athenians as a post from which they might sally against their northern neighbours, and protect themselves from their aggression. In this sense Delium was a Bœotian Deceleia.

Its maritime position was also favourable. It is not close to the sea, but it no doubt possessed buildings on the shore. The sea makes here a reach in a south-easterly direction, so that a bay exists in the curve thus formed. By the possession of this bay Delium was made the emporium of the important city of Tanagra, which was five miles in the interior. The village of Délisi is now in ruins.

Our road bears to the right. We begin to ascend over wild and uncultivated hills, overgrown with low shrubs, and broken into deep furrows by the torrents which plough their way from the higher mountains on our right in their course into the sea. It was an evening in this season, at the beginning of winter, when the battle of Delium was fought[14]. It took place at about a mile[15] to the south of the village from which it was named[16]. One of these sloping hills covered the Bœotian forces from the sight of their Athenian antagonists. These abrupt gullies[17] channelled in the soil by the autumnal rain impeded the conflict of the two armies. They afforded less embarrassment to the manœuvres of the lighter troops; it was to their superiority in this species of force that the Bœotians were mainly indebted for their victory. Their success was complete. The darkness of the night, and his own good genius, preserved the Athenian Philosopher. He seems to have escaped in the first instance by following the bed of one of these deep[18] ravines into which the soil has been ploughed by the mountain streams. He returned home together with his pupil[19] and his friend by a particular road, which his guardian spirit prompted him to take, and which in vain he recommended to his other comrades, whom the enemy convinced too late of their unhappy error.

We cross the deep bed of the river Asopus at the village of Sycaminó, and then, in thirty minutes, arrive among the low cottages of Oropó.

CHAPTER II

From Oropus to Tanagra are 130 stadia. The road lies through a country planted with olives and well wooded, and is free from all apprehension of robbers.[1]
Dicæarchus, *(State of Greece,* p. 12, ed. Hudson.)

THIS extract from the Tour of Dicæarchus gives, with some exceptions, a fair idea of the route from Oropus to Tanagra[2] at the present time. It is still shaded by shrubs; but the olives which he noticed are now not so common there as plane-trees and pines. But the latter part of his description could not be applied now. The route is by no means free at present from all apprehension of klefts: or, in the words of our Greek Guides, it is far from being a στράτα παστρική.[3]

It might have been this difference of circumstances which induced the ancient Topographer to loiter longer on the road under the shade of these pleasant trees by the side of the Asopus, and thus, from the length of time which elapsed, to infer that the distance was greater, than they, who now are not so fortunate, are willing to allow. By us the distance from Oropus to Tanagra would be estimated at ten miles.

Of the trees which once overhung the river another record is probably preserved in the appellation of the little village which we traversed yesterday at dusk, and which we again pass this morning in our way to Tanagra. The mulberries (συκάμινοι) which once grew there have perhaps lent their name as well as their shade to this hamlet of Sycaminó. It is inhabited by Albanians. The women stand before their doors habited in a long white woollen coat, which was no doubt suggested by the exigencies of a colder climate than that in which they now live, and which therefore indicates not obscurely the northern extraction of these Albanian families. The braided hair of these women falls over the back in two long streaming folds – like that of the figures which are seen in the earliest sculptured representations of the Deities of Greece[4] –

With parted hair veiling the snowy neck (OVID)[5]

At Sycaminó the road turns to the left, and ascends the stream of the Asopus on its northern bank. The modern name of the Asopus here is Borién, of which appellation I cannot ascertain the meaning. It winds its way through low hills, in which it has made some romantic chasms. Beyond it on our left are the hills of Boiáti, and ascending above them the loftier ridge of Mount Parnes, at the foot of which Bœotia began. The modern name of Boiáti may be a record of this territorial starting-place.

The only habitation visible on our right is the tower of Staniáti and a small village of the same name.

The site of Tanagra is now called Graimáda (Γραιμάδα).[6] It is a large hill nearly circular in form, neither abrupt nor high. It rises from the north bank of the Asopus, and communicates by a bridge with the south side of the stream, where are also ancient remains. The proximity of the city to the Asopus supplies the reason why Tanagra was styled the daughter[7] of that river; and the ancient name[8] of the inhabitants themselves may perhaps have arisen from the requirements of that proximity, which are still provided for by the present bridge.

On the east of the city, separated from it by a small stream, which runs into the Asopus, there is another hill. There are some female peasants engaged in washing linen there, whilst they stand with their feet in the running stream. They call the torrent Lári, the hill above it Kokáli. This eminence[9] was consecrated to the minds of the ancient Tanagræans by the local tradition, which made it the birthplace of Mercury. There is no other eminence near it to dispute its right, and its present name may possibly be corrupted from that which it then bore.

The vestiges of Tanagra are not so considerable as the importance of the place had led us to expect. They are more remarkable for their extent than grandeur. There are some few remnants of polygonal masonry, and a gate of the city on the southern side of it, of which the lintel is more than six feet in length, and made of a single stone. The circuit of the walls can be traced, but there is little left of them but their foundations. The ground is thickly strewn with minute fragments of earthenware, which bespeak the existence here of a numerous population in former times, and remain an interesting relic of the domestic economy and social intercourse of private families and individuals, while the strong wall and towers of the citadel no longer survive to give any authentic evidence of the former power of the State.

This is probably owing not to the early destruction, but the prolonged existence of Tanagra[10]. It survived most of its confederate cities. In the Augustan age, Thespiæ and Tanagra were the only Bœotian towns which were preserved. Tanagra lingered on for a long time under the Roman sway in Greece. Its extant coins are many of them imperial. But its walls were then no appropriate condition of its dependent existence. Their materials were therefore destroyed, or converted to purposes of a more pacific character. Hence its vestiges are found to be what they are. In the degradation to which it was reduced under a Roman dynasty, the city of Tanagra might be said to exist rather in terra-cotta than in stone.

At the N.W. corner of the citadel, the outline is traceable of a semicircular building, probably a Theatre. It is scooped out in the slope on which the walls are built: it looks outwards on the plain below it. There is another site similar in shape to this, in the interior of the city, a little to the south of the present spot. In one of these two positions stood the Theatre at Tanagra, which Pausanias visited, and in which perhaps the minstrel of Tanagra, whose beauty[11], as he informs us, to judge by her statue, was equal to her poetical accomplishments, sung her strains which were so agreeable

> To white-stol'd Tanagræan maids;
> For deeply do they love the clear
> And plaintive roundelay to hear.[12]
> Corinna (in *Hephæstion*. p. 106. Gaisf.)

The former of these two localities commands an extensive view. Looking eastward, the plain of the Asopus stretches beneath us, from east to west. To the south of it is a range of mountains: of which Mount Elaté[13] is the western, and Mount Noziá, the ancient Parnes, is the eastern extremity.

A peasant here informs us that there are remains of an ancient city in the way from Tanagra to Thebes, to the N.W. of this spot, at an hour's distance from it, at a modern village called Bratchi. Which does this represent of the ancient members of the Tanagræan Tetrapolis?[14]

From the citadel of Tanagra we descend into the plain on the north, in the hope of finding some further vestiges of the ancient city. There are two churches in this plain, one to the west, the other to the east of the stream Lari: the one is dedicated to S. Nicolas, the other to S. George. They are at about a mile's distance from the city. From the blocks of hewn stone, and sculptured marble inserted in their plaster-walls, and lying near them, they may be supposed to have succeeded to the site of old Temples of Tanagra. The long distance which we traverse in passing to these Temples from the city of Tanagra, might still suggest the same reflection which was made by the Pagan[15] traveller, of whose peculiar temper it is very characteristic, that the idea which the inhabitants of Tanagra entertained of the Deities whom they adored, was of a more respectful character than was usually to be found in the devotional feelings of Greek cities. This idea, he observed, was expressively evinced by the free areas and fair sites, unembarrassed by surrounding edifices, and sequestered from the traffic of the city, which were by them selected for the abodes of their Deities. In these buildings there are no other remains than these fragments. Of inscriptions we find here only a few broken syllables. But there is an inscription[16] of some interest on a stone in the walls of another church. That church stands on the southern side of the Asopus, which we cross by the bridge above noticed. It is dedicated to St Theodore, and is built almost entirely of ancient massive blocks. The former part of this inscription records in elegiac verse the dedication of a statue by a victor in a gymnastic contest; the latter is a fragment of an honorary decree conferring the rights of citizenship on a native of Athens in consideration of the services which he had rendered to the state of Tanagra.

The inscription, it may be remarked, is also of importance as supplying conclusive evidence, if evidence were wanting, that the site of Graimáda is identical with that which was formerly occupied by Tanagra. We return to Oropó in the evening.

CHAPTER III

These ox-men from Boetia
With their olive-treading boots.
Cratinus (p. 80, *Runkel.*)

AN invitation has arrived this evening from Acharnæ, addressed to a neighbour of our Oropian host, requesting his presence at a wedding which is to take place in the neighbourhood of that Attic borough. His attendance is especially desired on account of the qualifications which he brings with him: he is reputed to be very skilful in his performances on the Bœotian pipe, which is an essential accompaniment of such a ceremony. It would seem that the character is still sustained of the ancient minstrels of this district, and that the pipers χαιριδῆς βομβαύλιοι² of Bœotia are still in request. But their courage seems to have diminished. On a former occasion³ they were represented on the Athenian stage as marching manfully with their instruments from Thebes to the Athenian market; and that in a time of international hostility. But now that minstrel cannot be prevailed to expose to the dangers of the road from Oropus to Acharnæ, although the person who invites him is no other than the wife of the Greek military chief, Captain Vassos, whose soldiers are now in uncontrolled possession of this whole province. The character of a bard is no longer sufficiently sacred, nor is the passport of their chief enough respected, to procure him protection from these bandits. Some of them are known to be at no great distance from this place. Last night a neighbouring sheepfold suffered from their depredations. He therefore declines the invitation. He informs the wife of the Acharnian chief that she must find herself a minstrel nearer her own home.

To her of Pipers twain one shall Acharnæ send.[4]

There are few remains of antiquity at Oropó. The modern cottages are built round a low hill. Some large blocks of hewn stone are all that remain of the fortifications of a town which was, on account of its site, so long the object of military contention to its two powerful neighbours. A few mutilated inscriptions[5] are all that survive of the literature of a city, which formerly occasioned by its misfortunes[6] the introduction of Greek philosophy into the schools and palaces of Rome.

We descend from Oropus to the sea. The road terminates after two miles at the small bay called Ai Apostólus (ἐς τοὺς ἁγίους ’Αποστόλους, at the Holy Apostles), most probably the site of Delphinium, which was once the harbour of Oropus. Of this identity we have some evidence in the modern usage of the place for the same commercial purposes. Apostólus is now the wharf of Oropó (σκᾶλα τοῦ ’Ωροποῦ): it is the port from which passengers embark for Eubœa. This was the case with Delphinium. The name itself of Apostólus was, I conceive, chosen from reference to this its maritime character. The vessels[7] which left its harbour, the voyages which were here commenced, suggested, from the very terms in the language by which they were described, the present appropriate dedication of the place to the Holy Apostles; which the pious ingenuity, by which the Greek Church has always been distinguished, has not allowed to be suggested in vain.

At Apostólus there are few vestiges: there is a tumulus with a sarcophagus near it, and an uncut well. On our right is a hill with a middle-age tower, probably erected to command the harbour. The convenience of the place has induced Vassos the Greek Capitano mentioned above, to select it as the site of a large ill-shapen house, which he is now erecting on the spot.

It seems to me highly probable that Oropus itself occupied in earlier times a site on the sea-shore[8]. The founders of Greek cities very frequently chose a maritime situation; or if an inland one was selected, it had those recommendations of natural strength, which though affording less facility for acquiring wealth, supplied security for maintaining it. But the site of the modern Oropó has neither the strength of an inland nor the opportunities of a maritime position. Yet choice of both was offered at no great distance. That offer was not I think declined. Oropus I believe stood on the sea-shore at the time of the Peloponnesian war. The historian[9] of that war seems to refer to such a position. There is distinct testimony[10] of its removal from the coast to an inland position; that transfer was probably not permanent; for the inhabitants of Oropus were renowned in later times for their grasping exactions levied on all imports into their country; a character which seems to imply that their city was a sea-port.[11]

CHAPTER IV

Where are my Bay-trees vanish'd?[1]

Theocr. ii. 1.

THE Abbé Barthélèmy, whose Voyage du Jeune Anacharsis[2] we find an agreeable companion in Attica, promises us on the road from Oropus to Athens, on a part of which we now are, some pleasant objects, which we cannot discover on the spot where they are said by him to exist. His party of travellers, in their journey from Athens to Oropus at the beginning of spring, found, as he tells us, the road sheltered by the green foliage of bay-tree groves. Before their arrival at Oropus they visit the temple of Amphiaraus, which was agreeably situated in the neighbourhood of limpid streams.

Now the promise of this scenery on the wayside rests solely on the supposed assurance of Aristotle's scholar Dicæarchus, some leaves of whose journal of his tour in Greece are still preserved to us. From Athens, says Dicæarchus, "*From Athens to Oropus is an ascending road of about a day's journey to an expeditious pedestrian, which passes through bay-tree groves, and the Temple of Zeus Amphiaraus.*"[3] With respect to this Temple of Amphiaraus, its site has been fixed, by aid of inscriptions found on the spot, at about three miles from Apostólus, near a stream in a deep valley which we cross in our ascent to the modern village of Calamo.[4] And first it may be remarked, that this Oracle of Amphiaraus[5] would hardly have occurred in the road from Athens to Oropus, had Oropus been on the site of Oropó, and not, as has been above suggested, on the sea. The road would then have passed at some distance to the west of the Temple, and not, as it did, immediately by it. But however this may be – with respect to the other features of the route – the bay-tree groves can hardly plead as an excuse for their own absence, that Time, which has ruined the Temple, has also uprooted them. They in fact never really existed here. They have been planted in such abundance upon these hills by geographers[6], out of the fertile nursery-garden of a false print. The word δαφνίδων in the text of Dicæarchus is an error of his transcribers: it is not Greek. And besides, what topographer would have ever described a route of about thirty miles, which is the distance of Athens to Oropus, by telling his readers that it passed through "bay-trees and a temple?" To give his description any value some known place or town would have been specified in it. The passage is therefore corrupt. And how is this corruption to be removed? It is evident to me that in the text of Dicæarchus the expression ΔΙΑ ΔΑΦΝΙΔΩΝ should be corrected to ΔΙ' ΑΦΙΔΝΩΝ. The Attic borough APHIDNÆ may be inferred from a passage in Herodotus[7] to have been near Deceleia. Now Deceleia was in the direct road from Athens to Oropus[8], that is, on the precise road which Dicæarchus is here describing. Again, the verbal confusion of ΑΦΙΔΝΩΝ with ΔΑΦΝΙΔΩΝ, which I here suspect to have occurred in the text of Dicæarchus, is both easy for transcribers to make, and was in fact frequently made[9]. The inference therefore before suggested by Herodotus becomes almost a certainty. Deceleia was 120 stadia from Athens[10]. Hence assuming, – what from Herodotus compared with Dicæarchus we may now safely do, – that Aphidnæ was near to Deceleia, whose direction and distance from Athens are known, we are now enabled to assign the site of the important fortress Aphidnæ; which was the borough of the poet Tyrtæus[11], and of the two illustrious friends, Harmodius[12] and Aristogeiton. Other topographical consequences may he deduced from this result. The two Attic villages of Perrhidæ[13] and Titacidæ[14] were connected by relationship and vicinity with the town of Aphidnæ. The determination of their positions hangs as a corollary on that, which is now ascertained, of Aphidnæ their more important and illustrious neighbour.

We do not now proceed further in the direct road to Athens, but wishing to take Rhamnus and Marathon in our way, we diverge from Kalamo in a south-easterly direction. The route lies over mountain-tract broken into frequent ravines by the torrents which fall from the higher summits on our right. It ascends with more or less rapidity, till we arrive near a spot called Gliáthi, on the broad tops of Mount Barnaba. Here is a magnificent view, which extends on the west over the highest ridge of Mount Parnes (Noseá), and catches a glimpse of the shining waters of the Saronic gulf. To the south of us at a small distance are the high peaks of Tirlos. They are probably those of the ancient Brilessus[15]. Beneath us on our left is the strait of the Eubœan sea.

The surface of these hills is here and there clothed with low shrubs. But there are no timber-trees. We must, I suppose, console ourselves for the dreary barrenness which is spread over this whole country, by adopting Plato's belief, that in better days it was shaded by stately trees which are now no more[16].

At Gliáthi, a little to the right of the road, are some well-preserved remains of an ancient military tower[17]. It is constructed with well-joined polygonal stones. It had one entrance looking to the west: this entrance was defended by two doors, one opening inwards, the other outwards. There are also two loopholes in the walls.

This building is an interesting illustration of the importance of the line of communication over these mountains to Athens, the value of which was best proved by its loss. A little to the west of the tower is a spring of water, with the remains of ancient substructions, and a bas-relief lying near it of very good execution, but too much mutilated to warrant a conjecture on its subject.

We proceed for about three miles till we arrive at the verge of this broad mountain area. It begins now to descend towards a plain which communicates with the field of Marathon, and then terminates in the sea.

After a descent of half an hour we arrive to pass the night in the Albanian village of Grammaticó.

CHAPTER V

In their houses were goats, sheep, kine, fouls, and their offspring: their cattle were foddered with provender within: here was wheat and barley in bowls: in this way, having taken up our quarters, we passed the night.[1]

Xenoph. *Exped. Cyr.* iv. 5.

THIS picture, originally drawn from an Armenian dwelling, represents very accurately the interior of the Albanian cottage in which we are housed for the evening. Most of the objects which are grouped together in that picture are inmates of our present lodging. Our cottage consists of one room with a clay-floor, and thatched roof. At one end of it, near the middle of the wall, on the ground, a fire is blazing with a fresh supply of wood to welcome our arrival. At one side of the fire our páplomas[2] are, which in the day-time serve for saddles, and couches by night. The fire is employed in boiling some rice for our repast. On the other side of it sit two Albanian women twirling their spindles, and uttering a few syllables, before they put between their teeth the flax which is to be wound on the spindle. Another is engaged in kneading cakes which are inserted among the wood-ashes of the fire, and thus baked. The master of the house stands at the door, with his scarlet scull-cap on his head, a belt girding his white cotton tunic, over which he wears a shorter vest of woollen, thick woollen gaiters, and sandals consisting merely of a sole of untanned leather tied with leathern thongs over the instep. About him are some children, whose necks glitter with gilded coins strung into a necklace.

On the wall of a cottage hangs a loom (ἐργαλεῖον), which has probably not altered its form since the contest of Minerva with Adrachne: near it are some bins filled with the acorns of the Balaniá oak, which are exported for dyeing. There are also lying near them some silk-works (κουκουλιὰ) from which the silk (μεταξὶ) is soon to be unwound, and some husks of the cotton-plant (bambáki) bursting with their snow-white contents.

As the night comes on, these objects about us are dimly illumined by the light of our fire: no other light is provided. Ere long, all the children are laid side by side on one mantle on the floor, at the more distant end of the apartment. The master of the house terminates this domestic series, which consists of ten persons. Sleep soon comes and strings the whole family together like a row of beads in one common slumber. Further beyond them, and separated from the family by a low partition, is the place allotted to the irrational members of the household. The fowls come there from the open air to roost on the transverse rafters of the roof: the ox stands there at his manger, and eats his evening meal: and the white faces of three asses belonging to the family are seen peering out of the darkness, and bending nearly over their sleeping master and his children.

The time and place, the group and the glimmering light, remind one of a more solemn scene – of a Christmas præsepe, such for instance as would have come from the vigorous and rustic pencil of Bassano.

Our host conducts us the next morning from Grammaticó to some ruins to the east of the village. They are the remains of the ancient Rhamnus. The path lies over some low hills sprinkled with groups of wild pear (ἄγρια ἀπίδια), heath (ἐρείκη) and arbutus (κομαριὰ). In an hour and a half we arrive at the site of the ruins.

Their position is remarkable. The ground is covered with dense clumps of lentisk (σχοῖνο). There is no house visible. Our position is on a woody ridge which runs eastward to the sea: on each side of it is a ravine running parallel to it. On the eastern extremity of this ridge is a small rocky peninsula. This was the site of the town of Rhamnus. The ruins first mentioned are those of its two Temples. They stand at a few minutes' walk to the west of this peninsula on the higher ground, at which we first arrived.

Among the lentisk-bushes which entangle the path there, you are suddenly surprised with the sight of a long wall of pure white marble, the blocks of which, though of irregular forms, are joined with the most exquisite symmetry. This wall runs eastward, and meets another of similar masonry abutting it at right angles. They form two sides of a platform. On this platform are heaps of scattered fragments of columns, mouldings, statues and reliefs, lying in wild confusion. The outlines of two edifices standing nearly from north to south are distinctly traceable, which are almost contiguous, and nearly though not quite parallel to each other. These two edifices were temples; this terraced platform was their τέμενος or sacred enclosure. The temples, to judge from its diminutive size and ruder architecture, was of much earlier date than the other. It consisted of a simple cella being constructed *in antis*: whereas the remains of its neighbour show that it possessed a double portico and a splendid peristyle. There were here twelve columns on the flank, and six on each front.

As the modern towns of Italy have their patron saint, so the villages of Attica had in most cases their tutelary deity. Hercules was the hero of Marathon: Amphiaraus was supreme at Oropus: Diana in the villages of Brauron, Athmonum, and Myrrhinus: and Rhamnus gave a name as well as its homage to the goddess Nemesis. Which of these two temples was consecrated to that deity?

The Rhamnusian goddess, so Nemesis was called, seems to have a natural claim to the noblest edifice in her own city. The larger and more modern of these temples has therefore been assigned to her.

This opinion seems reasonable. The following is an evidence of its truth. In rambling among the ruined blocks of building I happen to light upon a large slab lying on its face. On turning it over, I find it to be traced with an ancient inscription: a part is broken off, the rest is much corroded by the damp earth upon which it lay: it runs thus, with the conjectural supplements which seem to me most probable:

A decree of the Senate and People of Rhamnus: Herodes dedicates a statue of Vibullius Polyducion an Eques, whom he reared and loved as his own son, at his own cost to Nemesis, to whom he used to sacrifice in company with him, his own affectionate and ever-remembered foster child.[3]

This inscription records the dedication by Herodes Atticus, who had a villa in this neighbourhood, of a statue of one of his adopted children, Polydeucion, to the goddess Nemesis.

From this inscription confirming the previous presumption, it is clear that the *larger* of the two temples, in which the inscription now lies, was dedicated to Nemesis. The question now arises, to whom was the smaller temple inscribed, which nearly touches the former.

It has been inferred, from the discrepancy of age of these two buildings, together with their very unsymmetrical local combination, that they never existed as contemporaneous temples for worship, but that the smaller of the two was either destroyed or fell into decay, before the larger was erected.

The Persians are known to have destroyed the Greek temples of which they acquired possession. When they landed at Marathon they probably employed some of their large force in this work of demolition. The earlier temple at Rhamnus is supposed to have been one of their victims. After the battle a statue, we are told, was wrought from the Parian[4] marble which the Persians brought as materials for a trophy of their anticipated victory, dedicated to the Rhamnusian Nemesis. This was, perhaps, one of the ornaments of the second more magnificent temple, which the Athenians erected in honour of the goddess, who had exercised in their favour her functions of chastising the insolence of presumptuous men, who in this case outraged the sanctity of her worship.

Such is the supposition[5] by which the awkward collocation of these two temples has been explained. It seems to be partially true, but not in its full extent. The earlier temple was probably destroyed, not at the time here assigned. This may be shown from the two interesting monuments which still stand in the vestibule of the earlier and smaller temple. They are two chairs (θρόνοι) of white marble, which stand one on each side of the entrance to it. Now, we see inscribed on the plinth of the chair which is on the *right* of the door of the temple,

To Nemesis Sostratus dedicates this.[6]

But it surely will not be contended that these chairs were dedicated in this temple *after* its destruction. And what example can be found of a Greek inscription written in such characters as these, and belonging to an era *antecedent* to the battle of Marathon? Its *long vowels* preclude that: this inscription is evidently much later than even the age of Pericles.

The destruction therefore of the earlier temple could not have taken place at the time supposed.

Both these temples were dedicated to Nemesis. This is proved by the two inscriptions above cited. It must, I think, be granted that the former temple was in ruins before the latter was erected, on the grounds before stated. An Athenian temple would not have been demolished by Athenians. At what period, then, did *foreigners* possess the inclination and the power to destroy a temple of Attica? The range of time in which this period is to be sought is defined by two limits. The earlier limit is furnished by the probable date of the inscription on these chairs: the later by that to which, from its style, the second temple may be assigned. In looking between these two limits for an occasion in which such an event as the destruction of the earlier temple might have taken place, we are naturally attracted to the close of the Peloponnesian war.

It seems not improbable that the victorious antagonists of Athens wreaked their vengeance at that time on the public buildings of their vanquished rival. The Long Walls of Athens were not the sole sufferers. But the *sacred* buildings, it may objected, would have been protected from their outrages by the respect for national religion which a Greek victor would feel. This is admitted. But a Greek victor was then leagued with a Persian ally[7]. The Temple of Nemesis at Rhamnus was a signal monument of Persian ignominy. It was a memorial of Athenian glory won from Persia on the field of Marathon. It would be regarded by the Persian with the same exasperation with which a French soldier would look on the Belgian Lion on the field of Waterloo. The feeling of indignation would not be idle, when an occasion was given, such we have supposed, for its exercise. Nemesis, I am inclined to think, suffered then from the exercise, in the hands of others, of her own functions. Such is our conjecture.

We leave the temples, and walk eastward down a narrow glen to the rocky peninsula on which the town of Rhamnus stood. Its remains are considerable. We enter the western gate, flanked by towers, and follow the line of the southern wall toward the sea. This wall is well preserved; it is about twenty feet in height: the part of the town which borders on the sea is rendered very strong by its position on the edge of high perpendicular rocks. Though not large, it was thus well adapted to answer the purposes for which it was used, as one of the main maritime keys of Attica.

The beauty of its site and natural features, enhanced as it is by the interest attached to the spot, is the most striking characteristic of Rhamnus. Standing on this peninsular knoll, the site of the ancient city, among walls and towers grey with age, with the sea behind you, and Attica before, you look up a woody glen towards its termination in an elevated platform, where, as on a natural basement, the Temples stood, of which even the ruined walls, of white shining marble, now show so fairly to the eye through the veil of green shade that screens them.

If Nicolas Poussin had ever left Italy to travel in Greece, and given himself to the delineation of Greek landscape, he would have chosen Rhamnus as one of the first scenes to exercise his pencil. He would then perhaps have introduced into this his landscape a person who was connected with this place, who derived his name from it, and was alike remarkable for his genius, his actions, and his misfortunes. Antipho the Rhamnusian would have been in his place here. And if the painter might have been allowed further license, he would perhaps have imagined as appearing at the verge of this glen and descending from it, the scholar of Antipho, the historian of the Peloponnesian war. But he must have left it to the spectators of his landscape, to imagine that Thucydides was then arriving from Athens, having crossed, as he would have done, the field of Marathon, to come and listen here, in such a scene as this, to the words of such a master.

We return toward the temple by the ridge above mentioned; it was fortified by walls parallel to itself both on the north and south. Their bearings it is not easy to explore, the whole surface being overgrown with a very thick prickly shrub, which prevents our progress. It at the same time suggests the reason for the ancient name by which the city was called. On this hill the propriety of the name of Ραμνοῦς is felt[8].

For the sharp rhamnus mantles o'er the hills.

CHAPTER VI

Miltiades! from thy sword the East did flee;
And Marathon a Temple is to Thee.[1]
                    Inscript. Ap. Grut. p. 438.

Oct. 12.

AFTER an hour and a half from Rhamnus we reach the plain of Marathon. It is a still afternoon, and the sky is gloomy. The place looks very dreary. The plain extends in length six miles along the shore, and rather more than two inland. It looks brown and dry: it has no hedges, and few prominent objects of any kind: here and there is a stunted wild pear-tree, and there are some low pines by the sea-shore; and occasionally there is a small solitary chapel in ruins rising out of the plain. There is no house visible except on the inland skirts of the plain; and a few peasants ploughing at a distance with their slow teams of small oxen are the only living creatures to be seen.

In this level solitary place the eye is naturally arrested by one object, which raises itself above the surface of the plain more conspicuously than any thing else. That object is the Tumulus which covers the ashes of those Athenians who fell in the battle of Marathon. It produces a sensation of awe to find oneself alone with such an object as this. It was a wise design which buried these Athenians together under such a tomb in the place they fell.

The plain is hemmed in near the sea by a marsh[2] on each side. It was fortunate for Athens that the battle was not fought in the summer, but in the autumn; particularly if that autumn was a rainy one. Pressed in on both sides by these morasses, which then would have been inundated, the Persian force had not free scope to bring its vast numbers to bear. Here they were embarrassed by their own power: hence it was, that at these morasses the greatest slaughter of the Persians took place[3]. Hence too these marshes themselves were honoured with a place in the Athenian pictures of the battle of Marathon: while the figures of Minerva and Hercules were exhibited in the frescoes on the walls of the Pœcile at Athens in the front of the fight[4], the water of these marshes was seen gleaming in the background of the picture.

The time of the day, as well as of the year in which the battle was fought, deserves notice. It is mentioned incidentally – and the expression seems to be one of traditional gratitude, – that the crisis of the victory was in the *evening*.

Heav'n be thank'd! we routed them, when first the day began to wane.[5]

That evening was introduced into the scenery of the Athenian recollections of Marathon, just as the Aurora and Hesperus sculptured on the column of Trajan enter into the representations of his victories, being the symbols of times of day in which those victories were achieved. The hour of the day, combined with the local bearings of the plain of Marathon, may have conduced much to the success of the Athenians. The sun would then have streamed in full dazzling radiance, so remarkable in the sunsets of Greece, on the faces of their adversaries, and against it the conical tiara of the Persians would have offered little protection.

The ancient topography of the plain has been illustrated. The northern marsh[6] (Δρακονερὰ) is fed mainly by a source anciently called Macaria, from the daughter of Hercules[7], who devoted herself to death in behalf of the Heracleidæ, before the victory which they gained over the Argive Eurystheus on this plain. Near this fountain was the marshy village of Tricorythus[8], one of the members of the Marathonian tetrapolis. It seems to have stood on the forked hills above the hamlet of Kato-Suli. It was probably so called from the triple peak⁹ on which its citadel was built.

Skirting westward the inland margin of the plain from its N.W. angle, under the mountain of Staurokoráki, we come to a stream which flows from a valley on our right: on its right bank are two Albanian villages; on its left, rather higher up, is the modern hamlet of Marathóna. This is probably the site of the ancient village of Marathon. The coincidence of the name is a strong argument. There is also a hill above it, part of Staurokoráki, which on the spot I hear called Δήλι and which suggests a question whether it does not preserve a record of the Temple at Marathon[10], called Δήλιου, at which sacrifices were offered, before sacred processions embarked for the island of Delos. Further up the same valley is Œnoe, still known by its ancient name.

Returning down the valley, and following the roots of the hills, Kotróni and Argalíki[11], the former of which is the southern boundary of the valley of Marathóna, the latter of the plain of Marathon, we end our circuit at the south-east angle of the πμαιξ.

This marsh is now called βάλτος[12] and βρεξίσι; terms both indicative of the humidity of the soil. A herdsman here informs us, that the water of the marsh is salt at its eastern extremity, and that saltwater fish come up the stream there in the winter: the upper bank of it affords pasturage for his own cattle. Pausanias[13] heard nearly the same account of it when he was here.

Probalinthus, the fourth village of the Marathonian tetrapolis was in this immediate neighbourhood. It is the first of the four mentioned by Strabo in his voyage northward. It is also in a different tribe than the other three; and that tribe comprised a district to the south of Marathon. Too much stress cannot indeed be laid on this circumstance; but perhaps more topographical[14] inferences might be drawn from the arrangement of the Demi in their respective tribes than have yet been attempted.

Oct. 13.

The husband of our Albanian hostess at Zephíri, where we pass the night, was carried off a few nights ago by the klefts into the mountains, and they now demand for his ransom a thousand Turkish piastres, which are to be paid within a stated number of days. Such is now the state to which the inhabitants of the Marathonian plain are reduced. It is impossible, without incurring great risk, to pass over Mount Pentelicus by the usual road from Marathon to Athens. After visiting a second time the plain this morning, we proceed therefore along the lower grounds, near the sea. This is said to be the safer[15] road.

Our way lies along a plain covered with arbutus, pines, and lentisk. We pass a stream, and arrive at the village of Epikeráta, in about an hour, from Marathon. Further on is the village of Κραβάτα where, in the church of the Madonna (Παναγία) are some sepulchral inscriptions:

ΝΙΚΩΝ
ΤΕΩΝΟΣ
ΓΑΡΓΗΤΤΙΟΣ

Nicon the Son of Teon, of Gargettus.

ΤΕΩΝ
ΝΙΚΩΝΟΣ
ΓΑΡΓΗΤΤΙΟΣ.

ΦΑΝΟΣΤΡΑΤΟΣ

These are the only villages on the road. After a ride of eight hours and a half, we arrive in the dark at the eastern gate of Athens.

CHAPTER VII

This Athens is, the antique town of Theseus.[1]
Inscription on Hadrian's Gate at Athens.

THE town of Athens is now lying in ruins. The streets are almost deserted: nearly all the houses are without roofs. The churches are reduced to bare walls and heaps of stones and mortar. There is but one church in which the service is performed. A few new wooden houses, one or two of more solid structure, and the two lines of planked sheds which form the bazaar are all the inhabited dwellings that Athens can now boast. So slowly does it recover front the effects of the late war.

In this state of *modern* desolation, the grandeur of the ancient buildings which still survive here is more striking: their preservation is more wonderful. There is now scarcely any building at Athens in so perfect a state as the Temple of Theseus. The least ruined objects here, are some of the Ruins themselves.

This being the actual state of the place, however melancholy may be the aspect of objects about us, it cannot but be felt that this very desolation itself has its value. It simplifies the picture. It makes an abstraction of all other features, and leaves the spectator alone with Antiquity. In this consists, particularly at the present period, the superiority of Athens over Rome, as a reflection of the ancient world. At Athens the ancient world is everything; at Rome it is only a part, and a very small one, of a very great and varied whole. 'Romam *sub* Româ quærito,' said Aringhi of the vast remains of the Imperial City which were to be found in the catacombs beneath it; the same expression may be repeated of ancient Rome generally; for ancient Rome is to be sought beneath the Rome of the middle ages, and still further beneath the Rome of the present day. How rarely therefore is it found! On the Quirinal hill few people think of the legend of Quirinus, while the Palazzo Quirinale dazzles them with its splendour. If we may use the illustration, the ancient characters impressed on the Roman soil can only be descried with great labour through the modern surface of the illuminated missal of papal splendour, which has been superscribed over them. Athens on the other hand, though a very tattered manuscript, is not yet, like Rome, a Palimpsest.

Since our first arrival here on the thirteenth of October, we have been engaged in an excursion to Ægina, Nauplia, and some of the Islands of the Ægean; and we are now at Athens for the second time. Remaining here for a considerable period, we begin to regard Athens as a temporary home. It is now, which is of much consequence in the very troubled state of affairs in this country, not merely the most agreeable but also the most secure residence in Greece.

We are in a small house in that quarter of Athens which was once the inner Ceramicus: our abode is the nearest building to the Temple of Theseus. Formerly its site was the heart of the city: it is now on the extreme verge of the modern town, to the west of it. There are few other buildings near it. At a little distance to the south a peasant is now engaged in ploughing the earth with a team of two oxen: the soil along which he is driving his furrows was once a part of the Agora of Athens.

There is not a single volume of any kind, ancient or modern, now to be purchased here. We have however been supplied with some assistance of this kind from the private libraries of the modern μέτοικοι of the place. The Athenians themselves are not very wealthy in resources of this kind. There is one copy of a book here, which is of great service to us. This is Colonel Leake's very valuable work on the Ancient Topography of Athens.[2] That I now add any thing on the same subject, after his labours upon it, is in a great measure owing to his labours themselves.

———

CHAPTER VIII

―――

*They climb the ample hill which looking down
Upon the Citadel, o'erhangs the shaded town.*[1]

Virg. Æn. 421.

―――

WE ascend today the peaked hill of St George, which is about a thousand yards to the N.E. of the modern walls. This is one of the most remarkable points in Athenian Topography. This hill is to Athens what Monte Mario is to Rome. From its summit the site and neighbourhood of Athens lie unrolled before the eye as in a map. Here the peculiarities of its physical form which distinguish Athens so remarkably from all other places are more strikingly exhibited than in any site.

This peculiar form might here be imagined to have been produced by some such process as this. It looks as if the surface of the country had once been in a fluid state, swelling in huge waves, and that then some of these waves had been suddenly fixed in their places into solid and compact rock, while the rest were permitted to subside away into a wide plain. By some such agency as this we might fancy that the objects now before us had been produced. Hence we might suppose to have been formed the insulated rocky peak on which we now are: hence the tabular rock of the Acropolis rising from the plain, in the centre of the city, as the large natural Pedestal on which its future Statues and Temples were to be supported: and hence the lower and longer ridge at the S.W. verge of Athens, which commences a little to the north of the Pnyx, and terminates in the eminence of the Museum.

Nor is the hill of St George a favourable position merely for considering the *forms* impressed upon the surface of the soil. It is one of the best stations for tracing with the eye the natural limits by which the ancient city of Athens was bounded.

On the S.W. of the ancient city, the ridge of low hills, on one of which was the Pnyx: Mount Lycabettus on the opposite side; the bed of Ilissus on the south, appeared to the mind of Plato[2] to be the legitimate boundaries of his own city. In his Utopian vision of its happier state, he assigns those limits even to the citadel itself. Concerning the actual site of these three important points, the Pnyx, the Ilissus, and Mount Lycabettus, there can no doubt be entertained, with the exception of that of Lycabettus. This we believe for the following reasons to be identical with the hill on which we now are; namely, with the hill of St George.

First of all, it must be conceded, that such a remarkable hill as the present, and one immediately overhanging the city, could not long have remained without a name. It is also an isolated hill; therefore its name would have been limited to itself.

Now of all the earlier names of Attic mountains, there is not one, either that must not be applied to some other hill, or that can be applied to this remarkable hill of St George. The names Pentelicus, Brilessus, Hymettus, and others, have all been occupied by other mountains: that of Lycabettus alone remains to be disposed of. Hence we infer that St George and Lycabettus are the same.

The same inference must be derived from the passage of Plato[3] above noticed. To give an idea of the extent of the place, it is natural to specify the limits by which it is bounded: and those limits, to answer this purpose, must be at opposite extremes; they must be, as it were, the poles of the place in question. Plato assigns the Pnyx and Mount Lycabettus as the limits of Athens. Hence the Pnyx, being comprised within the walls at the S.W., Mount Lycabettus must be the limit at the N.E.; that is, Mount Lycabettus coincides with the hill of St George.

One proof more may be added. The Clouds, in the extant play of Aristophanes, to which they give their name, are very naturally represented as coming to the theatre at Athens from the N.N.E., from the hazy ridges of Mount Parnes. Now in the edition of that play, which is now lost, we know from a surviving fragment of it, that they were represented as irritated by the discourteous reception which they met with on the Athenian stage, and that they resented this provocation by threatening to quit the theatre, and to fly off to the heights of Mount Parnes, from which they had come. We are informed of the route which they intend to take, in their way from Athens thither. They are sailing, off, we are told,

> *To the summit of Parnes, swelling with rage, and have vanish'd tow'rds Lycabettus.*[4]

They are vanishing towards Mount Parnes, and they are taking *Lycabettus* in their way. Lycabettus is their first object in their way thither. The first, and indeed the only mountain that they would pass in their way from Athens to Mount Parnes, is that which is now called St George. Therefore, St George is Lycabettus.

But it is alleged that the hill of St George is the Anchesmus of Pausanias: and Sig. Petaki, a resident Athenian antiquary, informs me that he found a few days ago, the words ΔΙΟΣ ΟΡΟΣ, *Mount of Jove*, inscribed on a rock here in very ancient characters: by which he proves that this mountain is Anchesmus which was consecrated to Jove[5]. We requested him to point out the site of this inscription; but in vain. However, the identity of St George with the Anchesmus of Pausanias, need not, I think, be disputed. But it does not therefore follow, that the same mountain is not Lycabettus of *earlier writers*. These two names never both occur in the same author. The name of Anchesmus is found in no writer before Pausanias. The discovery therefore of the inscription above-mentioned can only prove, what would *a priori* be not unlikely, that Anchesmus was a more recent name for Lycabettus.

Socrates, in his conversation on domestic economy with Ischomachus, which was carried on in the portico of Zeus Eleutherius, in the Agora, at Athens[6], selects Lycabettus as a specimen of thin and arid soil; and in another dialogue, conducted beneath the same portico[7], he compares the possession of superfluous wealth with that of a freehold on the slopes of this mountain. We may imagine him pointing to its bare sides of thinly covered grey lime-stone, in confirmation of his argument, from the place in which he is represented as conversing, whence it was distinctly visible. This mountain was probably a sheep-walk. A rude inscription, graven on one of its rocks beneath a small cave in them, and immediately facing Athens, seems to indicate this. The word OPOC (or land-mark) written vertically, is there inscribed[8]. And I find the same word written, in the same direction and characters, on the face looking towards Lycabettus, of the small rock now called σχιστὴ πέτρα (cleft-rock) which lies between Lycabettus and Athens. A line drawn between these two inscriptions no doubt determined the range of pasture allowed to the flocks of some Athenian proprietor, whose occupation of land on the barren slope of this mountain was little envied by the Athenian philosopher.

CHAPTER IX

Here Earth supplies the primal elements.[1]

Luret. ii. 590.

OF the earliest public buildings at Athens, the simplicity is very remarkable. Whatever their object, religious, political, judicial or social, their character in this respect was the same. In these buildings this character particularly expressed itself by two properties, the one resulting from the nature of the Athenian climate, the other from that of the soil. The beauty and softness of the former, brightened by the colour of the atmosphere, and refreshed by the breezes of the neighbouring sea, naturally allured the inhabitants of Athens to pass much of their time in the open air. Not poetically alone, but literally, were Athenians described as

For ever delicately marching
Through pellucid air.[2]

Hence also we may in part account for the practical defects of their domestic architecture, the badness of their streets, and the proverbial meanness of the houses of the noblest individuals among them. Hence certainly it was that in the best days of Athens, the Athenians worshipped, they legislated, they saw dramatic representations, under the open sky.

Again, these buildings, if buildings they can be called, possessed a property produced immediately by the Athenian soil. Athens stands on a bed of hard limestone rock, in most places thinly covered by a meagre surface of soil. From this surface the rock itself frequently projects, and almost always is visible, protruded like the bones under the integuments of an emaciated body, to which Plato has compared it[3]. Athenian ingenuity suggested, and Athenian dexterity has realized, the adaptation of such a soil to architectural purposes. Of this there remains the fullest evidence. In the rocky soil itself walls have been hewn, pavements levelled, steps and seats chiselled, cisterns[4] excavated, and niches scooped; almost every object that in a simpler state of society would be necessary either for public or private fabrics, was thus, as it were, quarried in the soil of the city itself. Thus the city itself was αὐτόχθων, indigenous, as its earliest inhabitants were supposed to be. Thus too, the earliest buildings of Athens might be said to be the works of the sculptor rather than of the architect.

These assertions will best be illustrated by a reference to some of the public buildings most remarkable for their antiquity, and for the important objects of various kinds for which they were designed.

The most remarkable of these is the Pnyx.

CHAPTER X

*He gladly visits that Spot which was the scene of the contests
of Demosthenes and Æschines.*[1]

Cic. de Fin. v. 2.

THE Pnyx was part of the surface of a low rocky hill, at the distance of a quarter of a mile to the west of the central rock of the Acropolis: and at about half that distance to S.W. of the centre of the Areopagus hill. The Pnyx may be best described as an area formed by the segment of a circle, which, as it is very nearly equal to a semicircle, for the sake of conciseness we shall assume to be such. The radius of this semicircle varies from about sixty to eighty yards. It is on a sloping ground, which shelves down very gently toward the hollow of the ancient Agora, which was at its foot on the N.E. The chord of this semicircle is the highest part of this slope: the middle of its arc is the lowest: and this last point of the curve is eased by a terrace wall of huge polygonal blocks, and of about fifteen feet in depth at the centre: this terrace wall prevents the soil of the slope from lapsing down into the valley of the Agora beneath it. From its being thus consolidated, and, as it were, *condensed*, (πυκνουμένη) by the upward pressure of these massive stones, the Pnyx derived its name. This massive wall is probably coeval with the birth of oratory at Athens. The chord of this semicircle is formed by a line of rock vertically hewn, so as to present to the spectator, standing in the area, the face of a flat wall. In the middle point of this wall of rock, and projecting from, and applied to it, is a solid rectangular block hewn from the same rock. This is the Bema or rostra from which the speakers in the Assembly of the Pnyx addressed the audience who occupied the semicircle area before them. The Bema looks towards the N.E.; that is, toward the ancient Agora.

Steps are hewn on either side of this rostrum, by which the speaker mounted it: and at its base, on the three sides of it, is a tier of three seats cut from the same rock.

This was the place provided for the public assemblies at Athens in its most glorious times[2]; and nearly as it was then, is it seen now. The Athenian orator spoke from a block of bare stone: his audience sat before him on a blank and open field.

In this spot it is impossible to resist the impulse of reflections arising from the place itself, upon some of the distinguishing characteristics supplied to Athenian oratory by the very locality in which it was exerted.

The Pnyx from its position, and its openness, supplied the orator who spoke there, with sources of eloquence influencing himself, and objects of appeal acting on his audience, which no other place of a similar object, not even the Roman Forum itself, has ever paralleled in number or interest.

First of all the Athenian orator standing on the Bema of the Pnyx had the natural elements at his service. There was the sky of Attica above his head, the soil of Attica beneath his feet, and above all, the sea of Attica visible behind him. Appeals to the Ruling Powers of these elements in other places vague and unmeaning, here were generally just, and sometimes necessary. Here, without any unnatural constraint, he could fetch the deities from those elements, and place them as it were on this platform before him. They would appear to answer his call, not like stage-deities, let down *ex machinâ*, but as stepping spontaneously from those visible elements, in which they were believed to dwell. There must therefore have been something inexpressibly solemn in the ejaculation Ω Γῦ καὶ Θεοὶ! *O Earth and Gods!* uttered in his most sublime periods by Demosthenes in this place.

Nor was it merely that the sea and the sky, the vales and mountains of his native land, by which he was immediately

CHAP. X.] ATHENS AND ATTICA 41

surrounded, gave nerve and energy to the eloquence of the speaker here, which no other excitement could so well supply: so that we seem, as it were, still to inhale the air of Attica from the pages of Demosthenes; he had not merely the natural elements in his favour, but he had also those historical objects, both of nature and art, immediately around him, by which the imagination of his audience was most forcibly excited, and in which their affections were most deeply interested.

Visible behind him at no great distance was the scene of Athenian glory, the island of Salamis. Nearer, was the Peiræus, with its arsenals lining the shore, and its fleets floating upon its bosom. Before him was the crowded city itself. In the city, immediately below him was the circle[3] of the Agora, planted with plane trees[4], adorned with statues of marble, bronze and gilded, with painted porticoes, and stately edifices, monuments of Athenian gratitude and glory: a little beyond it, was the Areopagus; and above all, towering to his right, rose the Acropolis itself, faced with its Propylæa as a frontlet[5], and surmounted with the Parthenon as a crown. Therefore, the Athenian orator was enabled to speak with a power and almost an exultation which the presence of such objects alone could give either to himself or his hearers. Thence be could thus extol the generous sacrifices made by his and their common State, as being the efficient causes ...*Whence there still survive to her, everlasting possessions; on the one hand, the memory of her exploits; on the other, the splendour of the monuments consecrated in their days; that Propylæa there, the Parthenon, Porticoes and Docks.*[6] These objects were all present before their eyes to witness the truth of this appeal.

It is evident from the productions of eloquence of which this passage is a specimen[7], and from the considerations above suggested, that much of the peculiar spirit which distinguishes Athenian oratory is to be ascribed not merely to the character of the speaker, and the physical quickness of his audience, but also, if we may so say, to the natural scenery of that theatre on which that eloquence was displayed. What was said of their warriors in the field, might therefore be repeated of their statesmen in the Assembly, that they were supplied by a focal power with peculiar resources which rendered them matchless,

For on their side the Earth herself did fight.[8]

We have not yet spoken of the vast *size* of the place provided for the meetings of the Athenian Assembly. In its area of more than twelve thousand square yards it could accommodate with ease the whole free civic population of Athens. The orator from this Bema often addressed an audience of six thousand Athenians[9]. The peculiar character of such an audience is not to be neglected by one who would consider what part that man had to play who *held the reins of the Pnyx*.[10] Before Demosthenes ventured to meet such an audience, remarkable alike for the enormity of its numbers and the impetuosity of its passions, well might he have gone day by day down to the beach of Phalerum, and there have paced along the shore in order to prepare himself, by practising, as he there did, upon the Ægean Sea, to face with less apprehension and alarm the winds and storms of the Athenian Assembly.[11]

We pass for a moment to a subject of a more technical character, in which a consideration of the objects before us may afford some interest. The scenes which are described as taking place on this spot gain much in distinctness from local illustration. Placed where we are now, we may imagine Dicæopolis in the Aristophanic play of the Acharnians arriving here early in the morning, taking his seat on one of these lime-stone[12] steps, and speculating on the Agora beneath him, where the logistæ are chasing the stragglers with their vermilion-coloured rope. The Prytanes appear from the Agora; they ascend the slope of the Pnyx; a contest takes place for the first seats, covered with planks and perhaps with cushions at the base of the stone rostrum, around which are ranged the bowmen of the Scythian police. The citizens, equipped with staff and cloak, are seated on this elevated[13] area of the Pnyx. The lustrations are performed. The herald comes forward to invite the future orator to speak; and questions circulate among the audience, what orator will put on the crown, and who now enjoys the sway of the bema[14], of that simple block of stone, the political ὀμφαλὸς of Greece; what will be the object of his harangue, to recommend a war, or a new tribute, and

From the rocks to watch the taxes swimming in like tunny-shoals.[15]

All which speculations, being made under the open sky, may be in a moment terminated by a single drop of rain producing the announcement

A portent! .... and I felt a drop of rain:[16]

and thus the assembly be dissolved, more rapidly than it met.

A question remains to be asked here. Should we be justified in assigning the principal object in the Pnyx, as it is now seen, to so early a period as the time of the Peloponnesian war? As far as the present bema is concerned, I think we should not.

It is asserted, on the supposed authority of Plutarch, that the bema of that age looked towards the sea; that it was afterwards turned toward the land by the Thirty Tyrants, who thus are thought to have intimated their antipathy to a popular government; a maritime and democratic power being in their opinion identical.

Now the *present* bema looks in an *inland* direction: it is not *therefore* the bema from which Pericles spoke. It has been attempted to obviate this conclusion by different expedients. The veracity of Plutarch has been questioned – his assertion rejected as false. It is impossible, as is alleged, that the aspect of the bema should ever have been such, that an orator standing upon it must have turned his back on the Agora and city of Athens. This seems to be a cogent argument, but it is not a pertinent one. The words of Plutarch[17] require, I conceive, not so much to be refuted as explained. Their meaning seems to be this. According to its original structure, from the bema in the Pnyx the sea *was visible*; the Thirty Tyrants altered it in such a manner that it should not command a view of the sea, but of the land only. Now this might be done in two ways; either the position of the bema might be altered, or its height reduced: its *aspect* in either case might, and I believe in reality did, remain precisely the same as before. From the existing indications on the spot, the former of these two alternatives seems to have been adopted.

There are very distinct remains of another solid rectangular rock, in short, of another bema, which has evidently been mutilated by design, at a distance of about twenty-five yards immediately behind the existing one. From the former the sea is distinctly visible; from the latter it is not. The former, therefore, I am inclined to believe to be the spot from which Themistocles, Cimon and Pericles, the latter to be that from which Demosthenes, addressed the Athenian assembly.

CHAPTER XI

The Court of Mars at Athens. [1]

Juvenal.

SIXTEEN stone steps cut in the rock, at its southeast angle, lead up to the hill of the Areopagus from the valley of the Agora, which lies between it and the Pnyx. This angle seems to be the point of the hill on which the Council of the Areopagus sat. Immediately above the steps, on the level of the hill, is a bench of stone excavated in the limestone rock, forming three sides of a quadrangle, like a triclinium: it faces the south: on its east and west side is a raised block: the former may perhaps have been the tribunal, the two latter the rude stones which Pausanias saw here, and which are described by Euripides[2] as assigned, the one to the accuser the other to the criminal, in the causes which were tried in this court. There the Areopagites, distinguished alike for their character, rank, and official dignity, sat as judges, on a rocky hill in the open air[3].

There are the ruins of a small church on the Areopagus dedicated to S. Dionysius the Areopagite, and commemorating his conversion here by S. Paul[4]. S. Paul stood in the centre of this platform. He was brought, perhaps up these steps of rock which are the natural access to the summit, from the Agora below, in which he had been conversing, to give an account of the doctrines which he preached, to the Areopagus, as the religious tribunal at Athens. Here, placed as he was, he might well describe the city of Athens as he did. With the city at his feet, and its statues and temples around him, he might well feel from ocular demonstration that the city was crowded with idols[5].

The temple of the Eumenides was immediately below him: the Parthenon of Minerva facing him above. Their presence seemed to challenge the assertion in which he declared here, *that in temples made by hands the Deity does not dwell.*[6] In front of him, towering over the city from its pedestal on the rock of the Acropolis, – as the Borromean Colossus, which at this day with outstretched hand gives its benediction to the low village of Arona, or as the brazen statue of the armed angel, which, from the summit of the Castel S. Angelo, spreads its wings over the city of Rome, – was the bronze Colossus of Minerva, armed with spear, shield and helmet, as the Champion of Athens. Standing almost beneath its shade, he pronounced, that neither to that, the work of Phidias, nor to other forms in gold, silver, or stone, graven by art and man's device, which peopled the scene before him, the Deity was like.

The remark therefore which has been well made[7] on the skilful adaptation of S. Paul's oration to the *audience* which he was addressing, may be applied to describe its perfect congruity with the *place* in which he was addressing them. Nothing could present a grander, and, if we may so speak, a more *picturesque* and *scenic* illustration of his subject than the objects with which he was surrounded. In this respect, Nature and Reality painted, at the time and on the spot, a nobler cartoon of S. Paul's preaching at Athens than the immortal Raffaelle afterwards has done.

On the eastern extremity of the Areopagus the Persians[8] encamped under the command of Xerxes before the Acropolis, which was most accessible from this quarter. It seems not improbable, that this historical fact induced the Athenian poet and warrior Æschylus to place the besieging Amazons exactly in the same spot. The history of Athens appears to have thrown its shadow backward on Athenian mythology, not less than its mythology has projected its own over Athenian history. The conflicts of Amazons with Athenians described on the stage, painted by Micon[9] and other artists in frescoes, and sculptured with such profusion on the friezes of temples at Athens, were not, I think, thus treated merely on account of their own independent interest or beauty, but were intended to allude, with the indirect delicacy so characteristic of Athenian art, to Athenian struggles[10] with the Persians, to whom in costume, habit and extraction, as well as in their object and its result, the Amazons were conceived as bearing a near resemblance.

And if so, the reason is evident why, above all persons, Æschylus[11], to whom his share[12] in the battle of Marathon against the same Persians appeared more glorious than all his dramatic triumphs, has preferred the particular etymology by which he has explained the name of the Areopagus.

The decrees of the Roman Senate gained in authority by being passed in a consecrated building. And here it was an ingenious device of state policy to connect the council and court of the Areopagus with the worship of the Eumenides at Athens. The strong religious awe with which the latter were regarded, was thus extended to the former. It was consecrated by this union. The design of blending the interests and safety of the tribunal, with the awfulness of the temple, is seen in the position of both. Some wise well-wisher to the Areopagus placed the shrine of the Eumenides immediately at the foot of the Areopagus hill[13].

The exact position of this temple, if temple it may be called, is at the N.E. angle of the Areopagus, at its base. There is a wide long chasm there formed by split rocks, through which we enter a gloomy recess. Here is a fountain of very dark water. A female peasant, whom I find here with her pitcher, in the very adytum of the Eumenides, says that the source flows during the summer (τρέχει τὸ καλοκαῖρι.) She says that it is esteemed for its medicinal virtues: it is known by the name Karasou, which in Turkish signifies, as I am informed, black water.

That this is the *site* of the Temple of the Semnai it is superfluous to repeat[14] proofs. That this dark recess and fountain formed, with a few artificial additions, the very temple itself, is I think equally certain. The character of the temple is described by ancient authors with the same clearness as its position. To those descriptions the spot in which we are completely corresponds. Here is the chasm of the earth; this is the subterranean chamber; this the source of water[15], – which were the characteristics of the temple in question[16].

The place was well adapted to the solemn character of the deities to whom it was consecrated: the torches with which the Eumenides[17] were afterwards furnished as a poetic attribute, perhaps owed their origin to the darkness of this Athenian temple in which those goddesses were enshrined. Æschylus[18] imagined the procession which escorted the Eumenides to this their temple, as descending the rocky steps above described from the platform of the Areopagus, then winding round the eastern angle of that hill, and conducting them with the sound of music and glare of torches along this rocky ravine to this dark enclosure. In his time the contrast of the silence and gloom of this sacred place with the noise and splendour of the city, in the heart of which it was, must have been inexpressibly solemn. Now, the temple and its neighbourhood are both alike desolate and still.

CHAPTER XII

―――

.... *Caves*
O'ervaulted, lov'd by birds, the haunt of gods.[1]
Vid. Æschyl. *Eumen*. 22.

―――

AS affording instances of the simplicity by which the earlier monuments of Athens were distinguished, the consecrated grottoes, which have been excavated whether by nature or art in the rocky sides of the Acropolis are not to be neglected. The nearest of these to the Areopagus is the cave which was dedicated to Apollo and Pan. It is hollowed in the base of the Acropolis at its N.W. angle.

When and how the former of these two deities was established here, there is no record. His occupation of the grotto was probably of great antiquity. But Pan we know to have been placed in this distinguished part of Athens, in a residence so well adapted to his character and former life spent in the grottoes of Arcadia, in consequence of the services which he rendered to the Athenian army at Marathon. Here was his statue then enshrined. It was probably that which was dedicated by Miltiades, and for which Simonides[2] wrote the inscription. This cave measures about six yards in length, ten in height, and five in depth. There are niches cut in its rocky interior, for the reception of statues and votive tablets, which have now disappeared, and left their hollow sockets in the rock.

This cave is generally associated in ancient descriptions of Athens with another natural object to which it is contiguous. That object is the fountain called Clepsydra[3], so termed from the fact of its being supposed to *secrete* a part of its stream at a particular season of the year, which part was conveyed by a subterranean vein into the Athenian harbour of Phalerum[4].

The only access to this fountain is from the enclosed platform of the Acropolis above it. The approach to it is at the north of the northern wing of the Propylæa. Here we begin to descend a flight of forty-seven steps cut in the rock, but partially eased with slabs of marble. The descent is arched over with brick, and opens out into a small subterranean chapel, with niches cut in its sides. In the chapel is a well, surmounted with a peristomium of marble: below which is the water now at the distance of about thirty feet.

This fountain in ancient times was, as it is now, accessible from the citadel. This consideration will explain why, in the Lysistrata[5] of Aristophanes, the particular mode of defence is selected, which is there adopted by the besieged women in the Acropolis. The local objects suggested it. It was this fountain – the Clepsydra, which supplied the women with its water to extinguish the fire, and drench the persons of their veteran besiegers beneath the wall. The same fountain has since served to supply a Greek water-clock, and a Turkish mosque.

In modern times, this fountain has verified its name. The access to it from the Acropolis was utterly lost till very recently, for a considerable period. It was discovered in the year 1822, when both the steps and the fountain were enclosed in the fortified circuit of the Acropolis, by the erection of a new bastion projecting from the north wing of the Propylæa, and returning to abut upon the rock which adjoins the Propylæa to the east. This out-work was executed in the month of September of that year, by the Greek Chief Odysseus, when he was in possession of the fortress. He has commemorated the work, by the following inscription which appears on a marble slab in the external face of the bastion,

ODYSSEUS, GENERAL OF THE GREEKS RAISED FROM ITS FOUNDATIONS THIS BASTION OVER A SOURCE OF SPRING WATER, IN THE YEAR M.DCCC.XXII. AND MONTH OF SEPTEMBER.[6]

When as "General of the Greeks" he erected this bastion, and thus recorded its erection, little did he foresee his own melancholy end, which he was to meet in a few months, in the tower immediately behind it. There on the 17th of June, 1824, his body was seen suspended from a window: he having either destroyed himself, or having been murdered, after he had been confined there as a prisoner for several months.

The precise position of another grotto in the northern face of the Acropolis, the grotto namely of Agraulus, one of the three daughters of Cecrops, it is not so easy to ascertain. At the distance of sixty yards to the east of the cave of Pan, there is an excavation at the base of the rock of the Acropolis which is here very abrupt: and forty yards further to the east, there is another grotto near the summit of the rock, and immediately under the wall of the citadel. One of these two is certainly the cave of Agraulus. In the latter there are thirteen niches in the interior, which prove it to have been a consecrated spot. On ascending the rock of the Acropolis to reach it, which is not very steep, I should estimate its height above the base of that rock at about sixty yards.

The former cave I am unable to describe, as it is now blocked up by a wall. Its entrance is nine feet in breadth. This wall, which is of recent construction, though it obstructs our curiosity, is of some use as proving the existence of a subterraneous communication, which it is built to intercept, between this cave and the interior of the Acropolis. The obstructing wall itself is pierced with loopholes, in which the muskets of those within this subterraneous communication may be inserted. This communication is a strong argument in favour of those who believe this cave to be that of Agraulus.

The expression μυχώδεις μακραὶ[7] (*hollowed steep*) applied by Euripides to the cave of Agraulus, denoting both a secret cavity and a steep ascent, together with his indication of its proximity to the cave of Pan, correspond to this cave better than to any other.

The same conclusion arises from a consideration of a stratagem of Peisistratus[8]. He convened the Athenians in the Anaceium (the Temple of the Anakes or Dioscuri)[9] which was below the Agrauleium, to the north, with the view of disarming them. While he was addressing them there, they laid down their arms. The partisans of Peisistratus seize the arms thus laid down, and convey them to the Agrauleium. They were probably conveyed there, because of the communication between that place and the Acropolis, by means of which they might be readily taken to the armoury of Peisistratus in the citadel itself.

I would venture to suggest here a question, whether it was not by this same secret communication that the Persian besiegers, who mounted, as we know[10], by the sanctuary of Agraulus, first gained entrance to the Athenian Acropolis. Their attempt on the citadel in that particular spot, seems to imply the existence there of such a secret communication: for at the cave of Agraulus, the rock of the citadel itself being most precipitous, would have discouraged instead of suggesting such an attempt in that place.

If now a secret communication can be considered as proved between the Agrauleium and the Acropolis, the grotto which is now blocked up because it possesses such a communication, must be that which was once consecrated to Agraulus.

It seems to have been in consequence of the ascent effected by the Persians in this place, together with the tradition that Agraulus here precipitated herself from the rock of the Acropolis, devoting herself by that act as a sacrifice to save her country, that the sanctuary of Agraulus was chosen as the spot, in which the military oath was administered to the young soldiers of Athens[11], by which they bound themselves, in presence of the deity of the place, to defend their country until death[12].

CHAPTER XIII

---

*To hear the Tragic Song still Fancy seems
From the void Stage, and praises what it dreams.*[1]

Horat.

THE last monument of a similar character to which I shall now advert, is the Theatre of Athens[2]. It lay beneath the southern wall of the Acropolis, near its eastern extremity. It was there formed by the sloping rock, in which its seats were scooped, rising one above another. The curve of each seat was nearly a semicircle: and of the semicircles thus formed, the diameter increased with the ascent. Of these seats of rock[3] two only are now visible: they are the highest; the rest are concealed by the accumulation of soil, the removal of which would probably bring to light the whole shell of the Theatre.

Above these seats is a grotto, which was first converted into a temple by Thrasyllus, a successful Choregus, to commemorate the victory of his chorus, and more recently into a church. A large fragment of the architrave of this Temple of Thrasyllus, with a part of the inscription upon it, is now lying on the slope of the Theatre: it has been hewn into a drinking-trough. The Temple and the Church are both in ruins; and the decorated grotto has become once more a simple cave.

A little to the west of the cave is a large rectangular niche, in which no doubt a statue once stood: there are also some holes bored in the rock, as if for the insertion of horizontal beams, on which, in the more effeminate times of Athens, a velarium was perhaps extended. These are the only remains now visible of the Theatre itself.

The objects immediately connected with it are two columns which stand on the rocks above the Theatre and below the Cimonian or southern wall of the Acropolis. The triangular summits of the capitals of these columns once supported tripods dedicated to Bacchus by those who had gained the dramatic prize in the Theatre below by means of a chorus of which they had defrayed the expense. About the base of the more eastern of these two columns were inscribed the names of these victors: they are now in a mutilated state[4].

A little to the east of the cave above noticed are two other inscriptions[5] cut in the face of the rock. They are on our right as we ascend toward the two columns: the first is:

The oblation of Metrobius,[6]

and a little above it to the east, similarly engraved in the rock, is:

Aulus Pisonianus and Gripus dedicated this.[7]

If these inscriptions were placed here by successful Choregi under tripods dedicated by themselves, as seems most probable, they clearly prove, by the characters in which they are engraved, that the Athenian Theatre was used for dramatic exhibitions till a late period after the reduction of Athens by the Roman power.

The accurate[8] dimensions of the Theatre it is impossible now to ascertain. The projecting horns of its semicircle were constructed of a coarse pudding-stone. From the inner extremity of one of these horns to that of the other is about seventy-five yards. From this line to the highest seat, by the slope, is a hundred yards. There seems to have been an entrance for the spectators from the N.E. at an elevated point of this slope.

Dicæarchus is supposed to have described this theatre as the most magnificent existing in the world in his day. Such an assertion is thought to be confirmed by the authority[9] of Plato, who speaks of more than thirty thousand persons assembled in this place. If this were really ever the fact, the assertion imputed to Dicæarchus would certainly be true. No theatre in the world would then have vied with that of Athens in grandeur.

The evidence of this locality itself is so much at variance with those two assertions, that I am inclined to think that there is some misconception with respect to them both. As far as regards the passage of Dicæarchus, the expression of admiration which it contains, refers to the Athenian[10] Odeum, and not to the Theatre. And in that of Plato, it may well admit a question whether he ever intended to state, what he has induced others to believe, that an audience of thirty thousand persons[11] were ever contained in the Theatre of Athens at one and the same sitting.

But whatever its capacity might have been, the Theatre of Athens did not mainly depend on its dimensions for the attractions which it possessed. Here on this gentle slope, with the Parthenon and the Acropolis immediately above them, with the valley of the Ilissus not far beneath, at the beginning of spring, in a transparent atmosphere, beneath a clear sky, with a gentle breeze blowing on them from the sea, here the spectators sat to be charmed by the mixed enchantments[12] of nature and art, which the Athenian Theatre supplied, both in exquisite perfection.

The dramatic influence of this union, of this interweaving as it were of natural scenery with that of the theatre itself, deserves here a moment's consideration.

It is evident that it furnished the scenic poet with a greater range of subjects, and with greater freedom in treating them. To one of these Poets it gave free scope to his bold conceptions, and supplied objects for his imagination to deal with. It will be found that most of the metaphorical expressions of Æschylus are derived from objects which were *visible* to the audience while they listened to the recital of those expressions in the theatre. Seas and storms, building of ships and their navigation; feeding of flocks on the hills, hunting in the woods, fishing on the sea, walls and fortifications, the Stadium and its course; these are the usual, the simple and natural sources, from which Æschylus derived his copious streams of figurative diction. They were all either in the immediate field of view, or in near connection with that theatre where the language they enriched was uttered. They were almost the natural elements of which the poetical atmosphere of that theatre was composed: the dramatic poet breathed them as his native air.

Similarly, Sophocles (*Ajax* 596.) speaks with a local truth, when he says in the Theatre at Athens, of the islands of Salamis,

> O noble Salamis, Thou indeed
> Buoyed on the wave, dost happy dwell
> Conspicuous ever, in the eyes of men.
> While I &c.[13]

The peaked hills of Salamis stood in the western horizon, like a picture drawn to illustrate the poem with their visible beauty.

To Euripides again, this combination afforded the most favourable field for expressing the tenets of his own peculiar philosophy. While Æschylus exulted in the rich variety of natural objects before him, Euripides laboured to blend them into one: but unless the sky had been open, and the air free about him, he could never have here pronounced with the same energy as he did,

> Seest thou the abyss of sky that hangs above thee
> And clasps the Earth around in moist embrace?
> This to be Jove believe, This serve as God.[14]

His creed would have remained a dry theme of abstract speculation, and never become instinct with the life of poetic sensation.

To the dramatic Poets of Athens, not as inventors merely, but as addressing an audience for great moral and social purposes, the position of the theatre gave great advantages. To select one: being placed immediately under the Acropolis, being seated, if we may so say, on the very steps of that great natural Temple, for such to Athenians their Acropolis was, the audience were thus immediately connected with what was most sacred and beautiful in the Athenian city. They were themselves almost consecrated by such an union. Just above them was the Temple of Minerva, and the statue of the Jupiter of the Citadel[15]. They were sitting thus, as the Poet expressed it, under the wings of Gods. He might therefore well speak to them in this language from the stage,

> *Hail ye denizens, who sit*
> *Rang'd beneath the throne of Jove,*
> *To the dear Virgin-Goddess dear,*
> *By Time instructed to be wise.*
> *You who dwell beneath the wings*
> *Of Pallas, doth her Sire revere.*[16]

Æschyl. *Eumenid.* 953.

And while reminding them of these their sacred privileges, he might stimulate them by sensible appeals to prove by their acts that they did not themselves forget the favour of Heaven and their own consequent dignity.

To apply the same observation to another department of dramatic literature: it is evident that to the peculiar advantages arising from its position and character which the Theatre of Athens possessed, is to be ascribed, in a great degree, the successful daring of the Aristophanic plays. To cite instances: how, in the confinement of a modern theatre, could we imagine a Trygæus soaring above the sea in an aerial excursion[17]? There his journey would be reduced to a mere mechanical process of ropes and pulleys, and would be inexorably baffled by the resistance of the roof. But in the Athenian Theatre the sky itself was then visible, whither he was mounting, and in which he was placed by the simple machinery of the imagination of the spectators to which free play was given by the natural properties of the theatre itself. How again, if pent in by the limits of a modern theatre could the birds be imagined to build their aerial city[18]? How could the Clouds have come sailing on the stage from the heights of a neighbouring Parnes? How in such a position could the future Minister of Athens have surveyed from the stage, as he did[19], the natural map of his own future domains, the Agora, the harbours and the Pnyx, and all the tributary islands lying in a group around him?

These conceptions, and such as these, are characteristic of the genius of the Athenian drama: on a modern stage they would be forced and inadmissible: here, under an open sky, with the hills of Athens around him, and a part of the city beneath him, they would seem to the spectator to be in some sense the creations of the place, no less than of the poet himself.

This subject brings us back to what was before noticed as a peculiar characteristic of the Pnyx. Here we leave it; with one observation on these two buildings together, founded on their local character. Plato[20], in speaking of simultaneous expressions of feeling made by large masses of persons assembled in public places, as one of the most powerful instruments of education, thus describes the effect produced on an unformed mind by the voice of public acclamation in those places, to which effect the local properties of the places themselves much contributed. He is alluding particularly to the Theatre and the Pnyx.

When multitudes sit crowded together at Assemblies, Courts of Justice, or at Theatres, and with loud uproar condemn some things and praise others which are there said or done, doing both with extravagance, by bawling and tumultuous explosion: and when, in addition to this, the Rocks and the place in which they are, produce, by their echo, a redoubled din both of the praise and blame; in such a posture as this, what, think you, are the feelings, as the saying is, of our Young Man, or what private education deem you, will offer its resistance for him, so as not to be swept along by the deluge of such praise or blame, and dashed where these expressions may carry it?[21]

With which interrogation these remarks shall end.

CHAPTER XIV

―――

Let us ascend the Acropolis, that we may have a Panoramic view of the city.[1]

Lucian. *Piscator* xv.

―――

IN its best days the Acropolis of Athens had four distinct characters. It was at once the Fortress, the Sacred Enclosure[2], the Treasury, the Museum of Art[3] of the Athenian nation: thus a flat oblong rock, the greatest length of which was a thousand feet, and breadth half that distance, was made the most interesting spot of ground on the face of the heathen earth. From those four elements here blended together, the rock of the Acropolis at Athens might have claimed to be considered as the representation of the perfect Greek character, somewhat in the same manner as the Ehren Breitstein of Coblentz has been of the chivalrous and Christian.

The position of this rock has suggested some ingenious fancies. It was the heart of Athens, as Athens was the heart of Greece[4]: it was the centre of the imaginary spiral in which all that was great and beautiful in Greece was involved: again, from its sanctity, its beauty and its form, it was like a decorated Pedestal, or a massive Altar, one great Ἀνάθημα to the Gods. And thus the attainment of a place here in the citadel, was a sort of apotheosis for men and their works[5].

Eighteen hundred years ago Strabo almost lamented the multiplicity of objects claiming the notice of the topographer in Athens, and especially in the Acropolis. At this time were he to revive he would feel much relieved from his embarrassment. Descriptions of them have increased in number, while objects to be described have diminished. The Heliodori[6] and Polemons of modern times have been as active as their predecessors in the same field, and with less material to employ them. We need not therefore regret with the Greek geographer, that our subject is too wide for our limits. This remark is more particularly applicable to the decorated buildings of Athens. A great part of the old city might now be rebuilt from modern description.

We pass from the Theatre toward the S.W. angle of the citadel, in our way thither. At this angle stood the Temple of Venus Pandemus and Peitho[7]. This Temple, though no longer in existence, is noticed for the sake of a passage of Euripides, which seems still to require illustration. Euripides there tells his audience, that the Temple was erected by Phædra on this spot, which was near[8] the Theatre, and appealed to, no doubt, by Aphrodite, as she there recited the following lines, as commanding a view of Troezen, (which it does) where Hippolytus was residing.

> Close to the rock of Pallas, looking on
> This land a Temple she to Venus reared,
> Loving a foreign love: henceforth, she vow'd,
> Here Venus stood *Hippolytus to gain.*[9]

This latter clause is, I think, to be thus explained[10]. A temple on this same spot had been *before* dedicated to this same Deity, but by a different person and with a very different object. It was originally here dedicated to Venus by the husband of Phædra, Theseus, to commemorate his success in collecting the scattered inhabitants of Attica (πανδημὶ) under one federal head: this result he professed to have owed to the divine influence of Venus and Persuasion. The object of its dedication was now altered by Phædra. Venus was placed here no longer as having united in one state a domestic population: but in order that she might help to conciliate to Phædra the foreign object of her affection (ἔρως ἔκδημος): and therefore Phædra pronounced that the Goddess had been here enshrined for the future, (τὸ λοιπὸν) not to record a popular union, but for the sake of the absent Hippolytus. The erection of this temple by Phædra was therefore well mentioned by Euripides, as a proof of her infatuation. She had thus built for her own passion over the monument of her husband's policy; and had sacrificed the honour of her home and of her adopted nation to that of an individual stranger.

A little higher, on the right, is a spot connected with the history of the same heroic family. Ægeus is said by Pausanias to have watched from this place the return of his son's vessel from Crete. It is curious to observe how the oldest Athenian traditions cling to the Athenian Acropolis[11]; and while this rock itself is thus clad with a venerable ideal beauty, arising from the age and varied hues of these – if we may so call them, – its old mythological lichens clustering about its sides, – it is at the same time by their presence proved to have been, as we know from history it was, the cradle in which the infant population of Athens was nursed. This particular spot commands a wide prospect of the sea. From this rock Ægeus threw himself when he saw the black sail on his son's mast. There is a truth and beauty in the description of Catullus which can nowhere be more sensibly felt than on this spot,

> *Mounting the City's speculative crest,*
> *Spending on ceaseless tears his anxious eyes,*
> *When first the Sire the swollen sail espied,*
> *From the cliff's brow he headlong fell, believing*
> *His Theseus snatch'd away by ruthless Fate.*[12]

Catullus has been saved from an error, perhaps by his acquaintance with the scene, into which later writers have fallen. They, with few exceptions, make Ægeus throw[13] himself from the rock of the Acropolis into the sea, which is *three miles off.*

Here also stood the Temple of Victory, a little to the west of the southern wing of the Propylæa. The statue of Victory in this temple, was sculptured wingless. Such a representation of Victory was conformable to the more ancient, but not to the then[14] received method of exhibiting that Goddess. The difference in the modes by which Sparta and Athens respectively expressed the former feeling with respect to this deity, is characteristic of both. To secure the permanence of its favour the Spartans chained their Victory to her shrine: the Athenians relieved theirs of her wings[15].

This Temple of Victory brings Lysistrata and her opponents once more before us. These last mount toward the citadel by nearly the same path as we are now treading. They are come to what they well call the σιμὸν[16] of the Acropolis. No other word can so well express the character of the flat slope on its western side, the only accessible approach to the citadel. They are supposed to be arriving at this point. Hence their invocation for aid to Victory (δέσποινα Νίκη ξυγγενοῦ), before whose temple they stand. Again, the expressions by which their courage displays itself have a peculiar propriety, which a reference to the spot on which they are uttered, can alone explain. They declare their fixed determination never to yield to their female antagonists: they will, they say, extirpate all tyranny, they will wield the myrtle-braided sword, and take their stand here close to Aristogeiton, whose glorious deeds they intend to rival[17]. This boast is very appropriate; for the statue of Aristogeiton stood immediately beneath this very point. It was on the southern verge of the Agora, close to the ascent[18] to the Acropolis. It would not be difficult to multiply similar remarks illustrative of other passages in the same play. The Lysistrata of Aristophanes, in some of its scenes, is the best topographical guidebook to the Athenian Acropolis[19].

CHAPTER XV

Pause here, and scan the rich and antique Athens,
And mark the fane of Ceres on the left.[1]
                               Ennius Medea, p. 22. *Scriver.*

THERE is something of peculiar interest attached to that single door of St Peter's Church at Rome, which is opened by the hand of the Pope to admit into the church the crowds of the periodic Jubilee; and at all other times, remains shut. No one can look on that entrance without reflecting what a deep and strong tide of feeling has flowed through it. Here we stand now before the Propylæa of the Athenian Acropolis. Through that door in the centre of this building moved the periodic processions of the Panathenaic Jubilee. The marks of their chariot wheels are still visible on the stone floor of its entrance. In the narrow space between those two ruts in the pavement, the feet of the noblest Athenians, since the age of Pericles, have trod.

Here, above all places at Athens, the mind of the traveller enjoys an exquisite pleasure. It seems as if this portal had been spared in order that our imagination might send through it, as through a triumphal arch, all the glories of Athenian antiquity in visible parade. In our visions of that spectacle we would unroll the long Panathenaic frieze of Phidias, representing that spectacle, from its place on the marble walls of the cella of the Parthenon, in order that, endued with ideal life, it might move through this splendid avenue, as its originals did of old.

The erection of the Propylæa was commenced at the most brilliant period of Athenian history. The year itself, the archonship of Euthymenes, in which the enterprise was undertaken, seems to have been proverbial for its sumptuous conceptions[2]. The Propylæa were completed in five years. They were henceforth always appealed to as the proudest ornaments of the Athenian city.

The day in which it should be their lot to guide their festal Car in the sacred procession through this doorway into the citadel[3] was held out by fond mothers to their aspiring sons as one of the most glorious in their future career. Even national enemies paid homage to the magnificence of the fabric: for when in the Theban assembly Epaminondas intended to convey to his audience that they must struggle to transfer the glory of Athens to Thebes, he thus expressed that sentiment by a vivid image: "Oh men of Thebes, you must uproot the Propylæa of the Athenian Acropolis[4], and plant them in front of the Cadmean Citadel."

It was this particular point in the localities of Athens which was most admired by the Athenians themselves: nor is this surprising: let us conceive such a restitution of this fabric as its surviving fragments will suggest: let us imagine it restored to its pristine beauty, let it rise once more in the full dignity of its youthful stature, let all its architectural decorations be fresh and perfect, let their mouldings be again brilliant with their glowing tints of red and blue, let the coffers of its soffits be again spangled with stars, and the marble antæ be fringed over as they were once with their delicate embroidery of ivy leaf, let it be in such a lovely day as the present day of November – and then let the bronze valves of these five gates of the Propylæa be suddenly flung open, and all the splendours of the interior of the Acropolis burst at once upon the view,

> *But ye shall see! for the opening doors I hear of the Propylæa,*
> *Shout, shout aloud! at the view which appears of the old*
> *time-honour'd Athenæ,*
> *Wond'rous in sight, and famous in song, where the noble*
> *Demus abideth.*[5]

We return to what still exists there.

Of the building of the Parthenon I shall not venture to say much. Even were it possible, it would be needless to do so. The essay written by the architect Ictinus himself on his own fabric, were a manuscript of it now discovered, would probably add but little to our architectural knowledge of the Parthenon. In this respect material works constructed by laws and canons have an advantage over the more irregular productions of the intellect. The methodical organization of their structure gives them an element of permanence which the latter cannot have. For from the parts of the Parthenon still standing, from its fragments here scattered on the ground, from the tints with which its marble mouldings are still faintly veined, the architect by his inductive ingenuity will restore the Temple to all its original beauty of symmetry and colour. Even an inexpert observer will form an approximate conjecture as to its original form and character from the same data. The mæander which he just discerns winding beneath the cornice, the honey-suckle ornament sprouting below the pediment, the shattered plate-bande of a triglyph which he lights upon tinted with azure, and the guttae of the same hue, – thus looking like real rain-drops – the bronze nails under the triglyphs on the south side, by which festoons (ἔγκαρποι) were hung on days of festive solemnity; these, and many other vestiges of a similar kind, will furnish him with sufficient elements, to construct in his own mind a Parthenon of his own,

But how shall he describe
Thy Perfectness, when such Thy Ruins are![6]

Some of the sculptured parts however, as belonging to a different class of productions from the pictorial and architectural, will baffle all his processes of restoration. The attempt to *infer* the treatment and details of the altorilievo group which once occupied the eastern pediment from the fragments of it which remain, would be as futile an enterprise as that to reconstruct an Athenian Tragedy from a few broken lines. The group of the *western* pediment has been more fortunate. From the parts of it which remain, its subject – the contest of Minerva with Neptune for the dominion of Athens – and the manner in which that subject was treated have now, with a few reservations, been fully developed[7].

One of the vestiges in the fabric of the Parthenon, though of a very different and less obtrusive kind, possesses a peculiar interest. At Pompeii the impression of the ancient cyathus which is at this day visible on the marble slab of the shop there, is one of those incidents, – touching perhaps more sensibly because its touch is so slight – which makes the spectator feel toward the old inhabitants of that place as toward acquaintances who have just left him. This feeling, and more than this, arises naturally in the mind, when you look on the eastern front of the Parthenon, and there see beneath its metopes the visible impressions which have been left there by the round shields which were once attached to that part of its marble face. Beneath them are visible also the traces of the inscriptions which recorded the names of those by whom those shields in battle had been worn, and by whom they had been won. I will not pretend to the ingenuity which has recovered a whole sentence on the portico of the Maison Carrée at Nismes from the holes left by the bronze nails with which the letters of that sentence were attached to the temple, however much we should wish to be informed who, in the present case, the persons commemorated were.

We may, I believe, without any risk of being convicted of error, refer the dedication of these shields on the Parthenon to any Athenian favourite, whose memory we may wish particularly to honour. Still all their history is not involved in the same obscurity. We may, I think, venture to believe that these very shields, of which we now see the impressions, had caught the eye of Euripides, and that they suggested the expressions, by the mouth of his chorus, of a wish[8] for repose and tranquillity which in a long war that poet himself so deeply felt,

> *May my spear idle lie, and spiders spin*
> *Their webs about it! May I, oh may I, pass*
> *My hoary age in peace!* –
> *Then let me chant my melodies, and crown*

CHAP. XV.] ATHENS AND ATTICA 67

> *My grey hairs with a chaplet!*
> *And let me hang a Thracian target high*
> *Upon the peristyle of dread* Minerva's *fane!*⁹

The chorus itself which sang these lines as it danced in the orchestra beneath us probably pointed to these shields from the Theatre which is immediately below the eastern front of the Parthenon on which they were hung. The Parthenon was the only Temple of Minerva that possessed a peristyle.

I may here be permitted to notice one other expression of the same poet, which receives similar illustration from the remaining architectural members of this temple. Agave, in his Bacchæ[10], bearing the head of Pentheus, calls in her madness for Pentheus himself, in order, as she says

> *That on the triglyphs I may plant*
> *Here this grim Lion's head, my spoil to-day.*

The marble *lion-head*[11] antefixa, which still terminate the northern angles of the western pediments of the Parthenon, and which indeed are usual ornaments in other parts of such a building, indicate that Euripides has not neglected in the delineation of her character one of the most natural and pathetic elements of madness – namely, its partial saneness and sense of propriety.

With respect to the name of the Parthenon, it seems to have originated from two causes: first, for the sake of distinction, and next, as recording the peculiar grounds on which this temple was dedicated. The Minerva of this temple was to be distinguished from the Minerva Polias her immediate neighbour.

The title of Parthenos was assigned to the Minerva who occupied this temple, in order to designate her invincibility, an attribute which this temple emphatically declared. Hence the limited part of the Parthenon, in which part the statue of Minerva Parthenos, executed in gold and ivory by Phidias, was enshrined, was also itself more especially termed the Parthenon, as being the most intimate abode of her immediate presence. As such this adytum or lesser Parthenon is contrasted with the Hecatompedon[12], which is properly applied to the eastern division of the cella of the temple, and of which this lesser Parthenon is a part; just as the Hecatompedon is contrasted with the whole temple or Parthenon, of which it is a part likewise. Hence also, the opisthodomus or western division of the cella, in which division the treasure of the city was deposited, is described as being behind the goddess herself (ὀπίσω τῆς θεοῦ) because it was immediately behind her statue. There was, no doubt, design in this arrangement. For thus the Athenian goddess stood as a sentinel at the door of the Athenian Treasury. The external columns of the posticum were united by a bronze railing.

The question has been frequently discussed, without a satisfactory result, whether the Parthenon was *hypaethral*. This is an architectural point on which professional judges must decide. There seems to be no doubt that the *peristyle* was covered with a marble roof. It may be suggested as a conjecture, that the *cella* was not roofed in the same way, but only protected by an extended awning or velarium, worked with embroidery. This supposition is founded on the passage in the Ion of Euripides[13] which has been proved to allude to the structure of the Parthenon. In the building there erected, which is a copy of the Parthenon, we have this provision made for the roof,

> *He brought the hangings from the Temple's Store,*
> *And spread them over-head, a wond'rous Dome,*
> *In which were woven these embroideries.*

The site of the Parthenon is the highest point in Athens. It is also the centre of the Acropolis, as the Acropolis was of Athens. Looking northward from it, the city, and beyond it, the plain of Athens formed into a great peninsula by mountains lay before the view. The eye having been thus sated with the splendour of the objects in the city below it, might raise itself gradually from them, and passing northward over corn fields and vineyards, farms and villages, such as Colonus or Acharnae, might at last repose on some sequestered object on the distant hills, on the deep pass of Phyle, or the solitary towers of Deceleia. Then too there were appropriate living objects to enliven such a scene. There would be rural sights such as Aristophanes describes of husbandmen issuing out into the fields, with their iron implements of agriculture shining in the sun, at the conclusion of a long war[14]: perhaps a festal procession might just be losing itself in a distant grove. All this has now disappeared, and there is nothing of the kind in its place. Now from this point, here and there a solitary Albanian peasant is seen following his mule laden with wood along the road into the town; and the most cheerful sight in the plain before us, is that of the thick wood of olives still growing on the site of the Academy toward the left, – which looks now like a silver sea rippling in the autumnal breeze[15].

CHAPTER XVI

Triple Goddess[1]

Hor.

WE pass a little to the northward from the Temple of Minerva Parthenos to that of Minerva Polias.

For the sake of distinctness with respect to this important point of Athenian antiquities, let us here say a word generally on the most remarkable characteristics of the *three* different Minervas of the Athenian Acropolis[2].

The *first* which the spectator saw when he had entered the citadel from the Propylæa, was the colossal Minerva of bronze[3] standing erect, with helmet, spear and shield. This Minerva was a work of Phidias. From its position and attitude it was called the Minerva Promachus. The point of its spear, and the crest of its helmet, seen over the summit of the Parthenon, were visible to the sailor as he approached the Peiræus from Sunium.

This Minerva was emphatically termed "The Bronze, The Great Minerva." It was this statue, I believe, which was present to the mind of Euripides when he wrote[4]

> *Then there came forth, appearing like a Statue,*
> *Pallas; a spear she shook with crested helm.*

It was again this Minerva, the vision of whose gigantic form stalking before the walls of the citadel scared away Alaric when he came to sack the Acropolis[5].

The *second* Minerva was that of ivory and gold, the Minerva of the Parthenon: it was the work of the same sculptor; and a specimen of what was termed his *toreutic* as the other was of his plastic art.

The artist of the *third* Minerva was unknown or concealed; inquirers were informed that it had fallen down from heaven: it was neither of metal, nor of marble; but of olive wood. This was the Minerva Polias: the original Minerva of Athens; the Minerva who had contested the soil of Attica with Neptune, and had triumphed in the contest: the Minerva of the Acropolis, and of the temple now before us.

Inferior to the other two in value of material and beauty of execution, she was regarded with greater reverence. Hers was emphatically the *ancient*[6] statue: to the Minerva *Polias* it was, and not to the Minerva of the Parthenon, that the Panathenaic peplos – the embroidered fasti of Athenian glory – was periodically dedicated. For on this supposition alone can we account for the question (and the answer which it receives) which is put by Aristophanes into the mouth of the founder of the aerial city, in the description of which the principal objects of Athenian topography are ludicrously parodied:

EU. *What Deity shall we call*
 our Poliuchus? for whom weave our Peplos?
PEI. *And why should we discard Athena Polias?*[7]

This Peplos, again, was not a veil (παραπέτασμα) suspended before the statue in the temple: it was the drapery in which the statue itself was invested.

To this custom of draping the statue with the Peplos Euripides seems to allude[8].

Glad, though he hangs a fair robe on a rude

Statue, and with a peplus *tricks it out.*

The obscure epithet by which Æschylus describes an attitude of Minerva may, perhaps, be best explained by a reference to this treatment of this particular statue. There Orestes[9] is introduced by the poet as a suppliant in this very Temple of Minerva Polias; and clasping the knees of this same statue. He then invokes the goddess to come to his aid,

> *Whether on the Libyan plain*
> *She plants her foot outstretched or shrouded over,*
> *Fighting for friends...*

Some well-known Athenian statue of Minerva was probably here in the mind of Æschylus. The fact that the drapery of a statue should furnish it, as it does him, with a distinctive epithet, (κατηρεφὴς) seems to indicate that that drapery was a very characteristic attribute of the statue itself. Such an attribute the Peplos[10], in which the Minerva Polias was attired, eminently was. Hence I am inclined to think, that it is to the statue of Minerva Polias that the poet here alludes. The other two celebrated statues of Minerva were not then in existence.

The difference of these three statues of Minerva in the Acropolis is very curiously illustrated by a passage in the Knights of Aristophanes[11], which can only be understood by a reference to the peculiar attitude, position and character, as above specified, of each.

The two rival demagogues are there boasting to the Demos of the gratifications which they will respectively supply to the popular palate, gratifications which they owe to their influence with the three Minervas of the Acropolis;

CLEON
> *See! This fair barley-cake I bring you, I.*

SAUSAGE-SELLER
> *And I this loaf scoop'd out into* a spoon

By our own Goddess[12], *with her ivory hand.*

CLEON

Well, to be sure, she has a monstrous finger!

SAUSAGE-SELLER

*And I peas-porridge well-complexion'd, rich,
Pounded by Pallas the Pylæmachus*[13].

CLEON

*O Demus, clear it is our Goddess guards thee –
She wields a bowl above thee, filled with soup!
This morsel, Pallas, dread of armies, sends thee –*

SAUSAGE-SELLER

*To thee Jove's daughter, reeking from the broth
Presents boil'd meat, stomach and tripe and paunch.*

DEMOS

Sooth, she does well, not to forget the Peplus.[14]

This passage is the best commentary upon this remarkable feature in the religious antiquities of Athens, the worship of the Triple Minerva.

CHAPTER XVII

---

*She came to Marathon and broad-wayed Athens
And entered the well-built house of Erectheus.*[1]
Hom. *Odyss.* vii. 80.

Erectheus, whose shrine we saw at Athens.[2]
Cicer. *Nat. D.* iii. 19.

OF the Temple of Minerva Polias[3] now before us, a general idea may be formed by conceiving a cella, about ninety feet long, standing from east to west, intersected at its west end by an irregular transept; and at each of the three extremities thus formed, a portico. The southern portico was not, like the northern and eastern, supported by Ionic columns, but by Caryatides. The interior of the nave has been intersected by two marble partitions parallel to the east end; and was thus divided into three separate compartments or chambers, of which the eastern was the narrowest. The question hence arises, how these chambers were occupied, and to what deities were they respectively dedicated.

The arguments which may be used to determine this question are these. The sacred olive-tree which Minerva was said to have produced from the earth in her contest with Neptune for the soil of Attica, is known to have grown in the Erectheum, which is a general term applied to this temple. The same tree is placed by some writers in the Temple of Pandrosus. Now the Erectheum was a fabric with *two* chambers[4]: hence, one of these chambers was the Temple of Pandrosus. Again, the shrine peculiarly dedicated to Minerva Polias was attached[5] to the shrine of Pandrosus; hence the *other* of these chambers of the Erectheum was the shrine of Minerva Polias. Also, because the more western of these two chambers may be shewn[6] to be the Temple of Pandrosus, the eastern is that of Minerva Polias. Thus the same observation applies to this temple which was made with respect to the Parthenon. The whole building was called the Temple of Minerva Polias, generally: this eastern chamber bore the same name, particularly. The most western or third chamber, (if indeed there was originally a third chamber, and the wall by which it is now separated from the Pandroseium, be not of comparatively recent erection,) served, I conceive, only as a corridor[7] of communication between the northern and southern porticoes.

Another part of this fabric the object of which may be enquired, is the space enclosed by the beautiful Caryatid portico on the southern side. It may, I think, be inferred from the language of the Athenian inscription[8] found in the Acropolis, which exhibits the report of the architectural commissioners appointed in the year before Christ 409, to examine what was then defective in the Erectheum, or requisite for its completion, that this portico was the place in which Cecrops was believed to have been interred, and thence called the Cecropium[9].

It would require a much longer inscription than that just alluded to, to specify in minute detail what is now defective or dilapidated in this edifice. A general statement may suffice. Of the eastern hexastyle portico five columns are still standing: but the south wall of the cella is almost entirely destroyed. In the Caryatid portico one of the four marble beams of the roof has fallen; three only of the six Caryatides remain; there survive but two of the four *engaged* columns in the western wall: the north wall of the cella and three of the columns in the north hexastyle portico, with the roof over these last columns, are yet entire: the rest of the roof of this graceful portico has fallen. It fell during the siege of Athens, in 1827.

There were four objects of great interest, as connected with the early history of Athens, contained in this temple. In its eastern chamber was "the antient statue," above mentioned, of Minerva Polias; in the contiguous chamber of Pandrosus was the spring of seawater which, in the presence of Cecrops, Neptune had there fetched with his trident from the rock, to support his claim to the property of the Athenian soil: here also was the impression of the trident[10], the symbol of the god of the sea, stamped upon the rock; and lastly, here grew the sacred olive-tree[11] of Minerva, which she had produced from the earth, a pledge of peace and plenty by land, as the emblem of Neptune was of dominion by sea.

The olive of Minerva and the trident of Neptune were symbols of two rival powers. That they were understood as such is proved by a remarkable passage of Euripides[12], which is to be explained from the consideration that these two symbols were distinguished alike for their contrast and proximity. They were both contained in the same chamber of this temple.

In that passage Praxithea, the daughter of Cephisus and wife of Erectheus, thus confirms her intention, in obedience to the oracle, to devote her daughter to death in behalf of the glory and the religion of her country, which was then menaced by an invasion of Thracians under Eumolpus the reputed son of Neptune,

> Nay but, my husband, ne'er with my consent
> Shall man uproot our Country's Statutes old,
> Nor, for the OLIVE and the golden Gorgon,
> Eumolpus and his Thracian crew the TRIDENT
> Planted erect upon the City's base,
> Shall wreathe with crowns, and Pallas be forgotten.

These lines will appear still more descriptive when we consider that there stood a colossal statue[13] of *Eumolpus* in front of this same temple; that there was a statue also close to it of Erectheus, in whose reign this Thracian invasion took place; that Erectheus was said to have been killed by a stroke of the trident there mentioned, and of which the impression was shewn within the temple, and that he was believed to have been buried within this same temple; from which circumstance it derived its general name, Erectheum.

The Erectheum had not a religious merely, it had also a moral character. It served, as it were, to mediate between the two rival deities Athena and Poseidon, to reconcile them to each other, and to endear Athens to both. The Athenian hero Erectheus, the mortal Genius of the Temple, while associated here as her foster-child with Athena[14], bore also the title of Poseidon.

The olive tree of Minerva was preserved in this sacred edifice for a wise political purpose: it was designed that by its means a civil ordinance might be strengthened by a religious sanction. The olives of the Athenian soil were its most valuable produce. Their cultivation was therefore encouraged by express laws, which threatened the infliction of severe penalties on those who damaged them. This legal provision was confirmed by the powerful influence of a studiously inculcated belief that all the olives of Attica had been propagated from the Morian[15] olives of Colonus and the neighbouring Academy, which in their turn had all come from the single stock of the olive which grew in the central chamber of this temple now before us; and which stock itself had been originally produced from the soil of the Acropolis by the divine agency of the Athenian goddess herself. All the Athenian olives were thus conceived to be the offspring of one sacred parent: they were the offspring of the Will of Minerva; the sanctity of the parent served to protect its offspring. Of the parent's sanctity, proofs, even historical, were offered, and as willingly accepted by the Athenians. This original olive tree was burnt to the ground by the Persians when they took the Acropolis; its site was subsequently visited on the same day; the tree was then found to have shot forth fresh sprouts two cubits in height[16].

This olive has rendered much service to the poets of Athens. It enabled them to connect every part of Attica, in which the olive flourished, with the central splendours of the Acropolis. Every olive in Attica might be considered as but a branch of this sacred stem; and the branches and stem together might be regarded as one great tree of which the root grew in the consecrated Acropolis, while the arms shot themselves out over the hills and plains, covering the whole country with their shade.

To illustrate this assertion by an example: the chorus of Sophocles is singing at Colonus the praises of Attica[17]. In the treatment of such a subject some notice of the Athenian citadel was highly proper, and almost necessary. The olives of Colonus were descended from the twelve offsets of the Erecthean tree. By means of the connection which they thus afforded the chorus is brought from Colonus to the Acropolis[18]. They are brought to the shade of the sacred[19] tree which grew in this temple. Hence the allusion which they subsequently make in the same ode to the Athenian dominion of the sea, became easy and natural: for close to the sacred olive was seen the fountain which had been raised there by the deity of the sea[20]. It required therefore but a single step to pass from the praises of the olive to celebrate the empire of the ocean. The Athenian Acropolis was a sharer in both.

Before quitting the Acropolis, I copy the following ancient inscriptions, which are found here.

1. In the tower at the southern wing of the Propylæa is this poetical[21] fragment. It is inscribed on what was the base of an honorary statue,

THE ATHENIAN PEOPLE

ERECT THIS STATUE OF SOCRATES, THE SON OF SOCRATES, OF THORICUS.

> *The Sons of Athens, Socrates, from Thee*
> *Did learn the lessons of the Muse divine*
> *Hence this thy Meed of Wisdom: Prompt are We*
> *To render Grace for Grace, our loves for thine.*[22]

2. Inserted in the outside of the southern wall to the west of the Theatre is

> *The Cecropid Tribe gained the prize with*
> *a Chorus of Boys, of which* CTESIPPUS
> *the Son of* CHABRIAS *defrayed the expense.*[23]

This small fragment of a marble slab is a curious historical document. It informs us of a fact which cannot be learnt elsewhere. It communicates the result of one of the most important orations of Demosthenes. His oration against Leptines was composed in behalf of Ctesippus[24] the dissolute son of Chabrias, who is mentioned in the above inscription: its object was to secure to Ctesippus the immunity from public burdens, which he enjoyed in consequence of the exploits of his father and of which the law of Leptines threatened to deprive him. Of these public burdens the χορηγία was one of the most onerous. This marble presents us with a proof that Ctesippus performed the office of Choragus. Demosthenes therefore failed in his attempt.[25]

3. Near the descent to the source of the Clepsydra is inscribed on a pedestal:

The People erect a Statue to Gnæus Acerronius Proclus, Proconsul, on account of his good will and devotion to itself.[26]

This may be called a *palimpsest* inscription, for below the last line may be discerned the words nearly erased ΓΡΑΞΙΤΕΛΗΣ ΕΓΟΕΙ, proving that a statue sculptured by Praxiteles had been converted into a representation of a Roman Proconsul! To what degradation were Athenians sunk, when they also converted, as they did, the equestrian statues of the two Sons of Xenophon[27], which stood near this spot at the entrance of the citadel, into Patricians of Rome, and changed even Themistocles[28] and Miltiades into a Thracian and Italian conqueror.

Another statue by Praxiteles, which stood at the gate of Athens, shared the same fate as that which is recorded in the above inscription: other examples were no doubt common. Probably his portraits in marble, above all others, owed this their alienation to their excellence.

4. The following is on a pedestal, much defaced: it is the base of a statue erected by her relatives to an Athenian Virgin who had

performed an honourable office in the sacred processions, here in the Acropolis,

With Good Auspices; Apollonius of Aphidnæ, dedicates a Statue of his daughter Anthemia, having been a Canephoros; her uncle Ulpianus, and her mother Diphilone dedicate it with him. In the quinquennial priesthood of Hierocles of Phlya...[29]

5. On the inside of the gateway of the exterior gate of the Acropolis:

```
            I deliver to the
            Infernal Gods
            This Chapel to
            guard; To Pluto
   5        and to Demeter
            and Proserpine
            and the Furies, and to
            all the Infernal
            Gods: If any one
  10        shall deface this
            Chapel, or mutilate
            it, or remove any
            thing from it, either by
            himself or by any other, To
  15        That Man may not
            Land be passable, nor Sea
            navigable. He shall
            be extirpated utterly, he shall
            make trial of all evils, of Ague
  20        and Fever, and quartan
            Ague, and Leprosy:
            and as many other ills
            and sufferings as befall
            Man, may they befall
  25        that man who dareth to
            move aught from
            this Chapel[30].
```

CHAPTER XVIII

Every one, we see, adores the Temple of Theseus as well as the Parthenon.[1]
Plutarch *de Exsil.* 607, 8.

THE Church of St Mark at Venice and the Temple of Theseus at Athens have several points of comparison. They owe their origin to the operation of the same feelings. They are both at the same time Temples and Tombs. In both cases the venerated ashes interred within them came from a distant region. The relics of Theseus, real or supposed, were brought by Cimon[2] from the isle of Skyros to the Peiræus: those of St Mark to the quay of Venice from Alexandria. The latter were hailed on their arrival with the pageantry of a Venetian Carnival: the obsequies of Theseus were solemnized with a dramatic contest of Æschylus and Sophocles. The Hero and the Saint placed in their splendid mausoleums, each in his respective city, were revered as the peculiar guardians of those two Republics of the Sea.

Theseus did not enjoy alone the undivided honours of his own temple. He admitted Hercules, the friend and companion of his earthly toils, to a share in his posthumous glory. He even ceded to him, with the best spirit of Athenian delicacy, the most honourable place in that fabric. On the *eastern* façade of this temple all the ten metopes are occupied with the labours of Hercules[3], while only four, and those on the sides only, refer to the deeds of Theseus. The same disinterestedness is shewn in the selection of the subjects of the two friezes of the pronaos and posticum of the cella. Here, as before, Theseus has yielded to Hercules the most conspicuous spot at the very entrance of his own temple.

This association of Hercules with the Athenian hero has been well illustrated by reference to a parallel instance in a different department of art. What is done here by sculpture and architecture, Euripides has performed in poetry. He has blended together in the same spirit the deeds and glory of these two heroes and friends[4]. His Hercules Furens is a Temple of Theseus in verse.

It may be added, that the treatment of the same subject both in the temple and the tragedy was probably the result of the same state of national feeling between the two Grecian states, of which these two heroes were regarded as the respective representatives. The union of the Athenian Theseus with the Theban Hercules was doubtless thus *expressed*, at a time when Athens and Thebes were themselves united by a bond of national amity: and when the former state at least believed it to be expedient that this union should be permanent.

This temple therefore possesses an interest not only from the beauty of its structure, but as a consecration of heroic friendship, and an expression of political attachment.

To my companions and myself individually it has a personal interest which I cannot forbear recording here with a feeling of gratitude. We have now lodged near it, –almost beneath its shade, – for more than two months; during this time it has been our nearest neighbour.

Such is the integrity of its structure, and the distinctness of its details, that it requires no description beyond that which a few glances might supply. Its beauty defies all: its solid yet graceful form is indeed admirable; and the loveliness of its colouring is such, that, from the rich mellow hue which the marble has now assumed, it looks as if it had been quarried, not from the bed of a rocky mountain, but from the golden light of an Athenian sun-set.

CHAPTER XIX

---

*Here, men divide into a dozen hours
the journey of Phæton's luminous globe.*[1]
Anthol. T. ii. p. 263. *Jacobs.*

THERE are four other buildings which will be mentioned here, as completing our notices of the decorated edifices, belonging to the period of its independence, which still survive at Athens. These are the Tower of the Winds, the Choragic Monument of Lysicrates, the Temple of Jupiter Olympius, and the Panathenaic Stadium. They stand in the above order, and nearly in a line, drawn from the Temple of Theseus toward the south-east.

The Tower of the Winds, if we consider its object, will appear to have been well placed. It stands near the centre of the site of the new Agora, with the formation of which it was probably nearly contemporary. In form it is an octagon. Each of the eight sides faces the direction from which one of the eight winds blew, into which the Athenian compass was divided: and both the name and the ideal form of that Wind is sculptured on the side which faces its direction. It thus served to the Winds themselves as a marble mirror.

The names of the Winds being ascertained from these inscriptions, and the Winds themselves being there represented with their appropriate attributes, we are thus presented with an interesting picture of the influence of each wind on the climate of Attica. This octagonal tower is to the Athenian Winds what Spenser's Shepherd's Calendar is to the British months.

All the eight figures of the Winds are represented as winged and floating through the air in a position nearly horizontal. Only two, the two mildest, Libs and Notus, have the feet bare; none have any covering to the head. Beginning at the north[2] side, the observer sees the figure of Boreas, the wind to which that side corresponds, blowing a twisted cone, equipped in a thick and sleeved mantle, with folds blustering in the air, and high-laced buskins: as the spectator moves eastward, the wind on the next side of the octagon presents him with a plateau containing olives, being the productions to which its influence is favourable: the Eastwind exhibits to his view a profusion of flowers and fruits: the next wind Eurus, with stern and scowling aspect, his right arm muffled in his mantle, threatens him with a hurricane: the Southwind, Notus, is ready to deluge the ground from a swelling urceus which he holds in his bared arms, with a torrent of shower. The next wind, driving before him the form of a ship, promises a rapid voyage. Zephyrus floating softly along, showers into the air a lapful of flowers; while his inclement Neighbour bears a bronze vessel of charcoal in his hands, in order to dispel the cold, which he himself has caused.

The roof of the octagon was surmounted by a Triton turning on an axis: this was the vane. Nor did this tower serve alone as an index of the winds, and as a picture of their character; it was a chronometer also. On its eight sides, beneath the figures of the winds, are traced horary lines, which with the styles of the gnomons above them formed eight dials. This tower, placed in the public square, was the city-clock of Athens. By it the affairs of the inhabitants were regulated. The law-courts sat, and merchants transacted their business, from its dictation. If, too, we may trust the comic[3] descriptions of that class of individuals, we may imagine the ravenous parasite watching with ludicrous impatience the progress of the shadow cast by the sun over these lines on its marble face, in order,

When the shade on the dial has come to ten feet, to go to a sumptuous supper.[4]

Rome for many centuries possessed either no dials, or ill-constructed ones. But at Athens time, if not better spent, was at least measured with more diligence. For in addition to its external provisions, there was a water-clock in the inside of this tower, which served in cloudy weather as a substitute for the dial and the sun.

The line of similar fabrics, of which the small circular building of the most graceful Corinthian proportions, called the Choragic Monument of Lysicrates, is the only surviving relic, must have possessed great interest, both from their object and execution[5]. They were a series of temples forming a street. These temples were surmounted by finials which supported the Tripods gained by victorious Choragi in the neighbouring Theatre of Bacchus, and here dedicated by them to that deity, the patron of dramatic representations. Hence the line formed by these temples was called the Street of Tripods.

From the inscriptions engraved on the architraves of these temples, which recorded the names of the victorious parties, and the year in which the victory was gained, the dramatic chronicles, or didascaliæ were mainly compiled. Thus these small fabrics served the purposes at the same time of Fasti, Trophies and Temples. What a host of soul-stirring thoughts must have started up in the mind of a sensitive Athenian as he walked along this Street!

The Temple of Jupiter Olympius was one of the first conceived and the last executed of the sacred monuments of Athens. It seemed as if Athenian architects were not to be permitted to realize in architecture, any more than their philosophers were in philosophy, the idea which was due to the majesty of the king and father of the gods. The building of this temple went along with the course of the national existence of Athens: Athens ceased to be independent before the Temple of Jupiter was completed. It was reserved to a Roman emperor, Hadrian, to finish the work. This gigantic fabric stood therefore on its vast site, as a striking proof of the power of Rome exerted at a distance from Rome on the Athenian soil.

It is hardly possible to conceive where and how the enormous masses have disappeared of which this temple was built. Its remains are now reduced to a few columns which stand together at the southeast angle of the great platform which was once planted as it were by the long files of its pillars. To compare great things with small, they there look like the few remaining chessmen, which are driven into the corner of a nearly vacant chess-board, at the conclusion of a game.

CHAPTER XX

---

*And their excellence shines clearly
in the naked foot races and in the races
of armour with clanging shields.*[1]

Pindar. *Isth.* i. 30.

THE *Stadium* of Athens was the most remarkable monument on the south side of the Ilissus. On this side a sloping bank runs parallel to the river: and in this slope a semi-elliptical hollow, facing the north, has been scooped out of the soil, of somewhat more than six hundred[2] feet in length, and at right angles to the river. This was the Athenian Stadium. Its shelving margins were once eased with seats of white marble: it is now a long and grass-grown hollow retiring into the hill-side.

The concave extremity of the Stadium, which is its farthest point from the Ilissus, is somewhat of a higher level than that which is nearer to it. The racer started from the lower extremity, and having completed one course in a straight line (δρόμος, or στάδιον), turned round the point of curvature (καμπτὴρ) at the higher extremity, and thus descended in a line parallel to that of his ascent till he arrived[3] at the goal which was a point a little to the east of that from which he had started: thus he accomplished a double course (δίαυλος).

It was this inclination in the bed of the Stadium, which suggested the expressions of Plato[4] in a passage which has a peculiar reference to this spot. In comparing the transactions of life to those of the Stadium, he asks, whether the ultimate results of both have not some analogy also: *Do not those wily and unjust persons fare like runners in the Stadium, who run well indeed from its lower end, but not so from its upper extremity? At first they shoot forth impetuously, but at the end of the race they are smothered with ridicule; their ears flagging on their shoulder, and they themselves slinking off uncrowned.* The chaplets of victory of which he speaks, and the profusion of flowers which we know, from other sources[5], to have been showered on the heads of the successful competitors in the race, by the spectators in the seats above them, had probably been recently gathered for this purpose from the blooming banks of the neighbouring Ilissus.

It is observable, that the measure of time usually adopted in narratives on the Athenian stage is borrowed from the Stadium:

> *Now would a runner swift six hundred feet*
> *Have traversed on the course, and reached the goal.*[6]
>
> Eurip. *Med.* 1151.

is an expression used by a messenger to give the audience a distinct idea of the interval of time after which an event occurred: and for a similar purpose the audience is referred to the same standard of time in the recital of another dramatic intelligencer:

> *He flayed the hide more quickly than a runner*
> *Twice climbs the tall arch of his double course.*[7]
>
> Eurip. *Electr.* 825.

This practice is, I think, to be explained by the consideration of the fact, that the Stadium of Athens from which these illustrations[8] are derived, was nearly in the front of the spectators as they sat and listened to those narratives in the theatre. Being thus visible to the audience, the Stadium was properly appealed to by the dramatist, as a sort of theatrical chronometer. The number of courses which could be traversed by a swift runner in that Stadium during the occurrence of any given event, would thus give a clear idea of its duration. They would be like degrees of a visible dial[9] traversed by the shadow upon cast its face.

CHAPTER XXI

His mouth's a Conduit of twelve gushing Pipes
That pour a loud Ilissus down his throat.[1]
    Cratinus *apud* Suid. *s.v.* δωδεκάκρουνον.

WE return from the Stadium to the Ilissus. To-day (Jan. 3) the stream makes a fine cascade at the point to which Cratinus alludes. That point is a little to the south of Olympieium, and of the fountain of Callirhoe. The current of the river, or torrent rather, is there divided into two streams; the one nearer the left bank comes down over a stone bed cut and worn into a large and deep trough, the other division of the stream finds its way through the rock by subterranean artificial κροῦνοι or pipes bored through it, which suggested the description of Cratinus: seven of them are yet visible. Some Athenian women are now standing in the stream, and washing linen[2] under these pipes cut through the rock.

The fountain of Callirhoe is said to have been supplied by the Ilissus. The ducts by which its water was brought from the stream probably suggested its name ἐννεάκρουνος: it seems to have been on the outer side of the city-wall. This position is less surprising, when we remember the provisions of the Amphictyonic oath, which obliged all the contracting parties never to prohibit a confederate city from the use of its Mountains either in peace or war.

The banks of the Ilissus have received no favourable notices from the poets of Athens[3], while its rival stream, the Cephisus, which has no better claims on the ground of magnitude or beauty, has been honoured by much harmonious and enthusiastic praise. Ilissus was too near the city, and connected with too many associations of civic life, to be a favourite with poets. There was no retirement here such as the Muses loved. They found the quiet, which they sought here in vain, in the groves of the Academy, on the banks of the Cephisus, where

> *Harmonia fair, as Poets dream,*
> *Did the nine holy Muses bear,*
> *And Venus, from Cephisus' limpid stream,*
> *Breathes o'er the vales ambrosial gales*
> *Of soft and scented air.*[4]

The poetical disabilities of the Ilissus were not, however, absolute and unqualified. They were not without their compensation: their cause was even in some respects advantageous to it. To poets writing *at a distance* from Athens, its proximity to the walls, which alienated from it the minds of *Athenian* poets, conveyed no unpleasing idea, but was a recommendation, on the contrary, as connecting it immediately with that city. Ilissus was by them promoted to a distinguished place in the poetical map. To them, from Apollonius Rhodius down to Milton[5], the Ilissus, and not the Cephisus, was the appropriate River of Athens.

Plato dwelt in the Academy, and therefore near the Cephisus; but he has honoured the Ilissus with a place in one of his most beautiful landscapes. The banks of this stream, a little above the fountain before noticed, derive their principal interest from their having been chosen by him as the scene of the dialogue of Phædrus with Socrates. However bare and treeless they now may be – and indeed they are entirely so – the leaves of the plantain which the genius of Plato has planted on their side still seem to cast their shadow over its stream, and the agnus castus which then flowered in its bed has been endued by him with a perennial freshness.

Connected with this same spot, and with the same dialogue of Plato, is a pleasing incident of more recent times. The philosophic Fronto, in a letter[6] which was lately discovered in an Italian library, addressed to his pupil Marcus Aurelius, the future emperor of Rome, at that time studying at Athens, comments on the subject and language of the above-mentioned Platonic dialogue in a strain of observation which does equal credit to its author as a philosopher and a man. He concludes his letter by inviting his young scholar to join him in a walk, out of the city of Athens, and toward the same spot as had been visited by Phædrus and Socrates; not for the sake of enjoying the shade of the plantain, or the fragrance of the agnus castus, which the genius of Plato has planted there, but in order to search for a small and more neglected flower – the heliotrope – which he describes as growing in that spot, and from the properties of which he has drawn an emblematic moral.

The invitation is thus expressed in the edition which A. Mai has given of those letters from the MS. in the Ambrosian library: which words, unintelligible as they there may stand, may, by reference to the localities of the spot, and the dialogue of Plato in question, thus be presented in a more intelligible form; *You seem anxious to see the flower I mention, and I know where it is, and will point it out to you: Come, let us go together in quest of it, outside the city-wall, to the Ilissus.*[7]

This district[8] near the Ilissus was called Agra; another name which it bore was Helicon, a name derived from its sinuous slopes ἕλικερ. It resembled in this respect, both in its name and the cause of it, the illustrious mountain of Attica, Mount Pent-elicus.

CHAPTER XXII

Where shall I find the Pnyx, where the Cerameicus, the Agora, the Tribunals, the fair Acropolis, the Temple of the Furies?[1]
Alciphr. Epist. Menand. p. 346. *Meineke.*

IN looking at the bare site of the Athenian city, with a view to observe the prominent physical features of Athenian topography, the following objects present themselves. The central rock of the Acropolis, declining westward toward the Areopagus: the bed of rocky soil re-appearing in the cliff of the Areopagus: the Areopagus shelving downward, at its western edge, and after a narrow dip converging to meet a range of rock coming towards it from the south-east. On this latter range was the Pnyx and Museum. The angular valley which was formed by this convergence, being thus fenced by hills, except at the south-east, where it is bounded by the Ilissus, offered an advantageous site for the future city of which the rock of the Acropolis[2] was the citadel.

In this valley accordingly, as we find, together with that rock, stood the most ancient part of the Athenian city. Here were its oldest temples. Here, in a word, was Athens, and to this part was its splendour restricted, until the age of Themistocles.

In that age existed a public monument, which still remains. This is the Pnyx. Its site will assist us in illustrating and confirming the positions which we have assigned to other buildings necessarily connected with it.

It is evident that the site of the Pnyx would have been so selected that it should be of easy access to the people who were to assemble there. It would therefore be placed near the Agora. Accordingly we find that the Agora was in the valley immediately beneath it. Again, the political connection subsisting between the two assemblies, that of the Senate and that of the People, and the transmission of legislative enactments from the senate of Five Hundred to the Popular Assembly, would seem to furnish a presumption that the Senate-house would be placed in the neighbourhood of the Pnyx. For a similar reason we should infer, that as the existing laws were frequently appealed to by the orators in the Pnyx, the depository of those laws would be of easy access from that place. The facts are so[3]. Both the senate-house (Βουλευτήριον) and that depository (the Μητρῷον), as can be shewn from Pausanias, were placed in the valley of the Agora below the Pnyx. The council of the Areopagus was called the "Higher Senate" (ἡ ἄνω βουλή). Hence we should infer that the *lower* senate met at no great distance from it. Accordingly, the Senate-house was at the foot of the Areopagus hill. Again, the Prytanes, as presiding in the Pnyx, and as members of the senate, would have their official residence near to both. Their residence (the Θόλος) was so. It was close to the senate-house. The altar of the *Twelve Gods* was the *milliarium aureum*[4], from which the roads of Attica were measured. It would therefore stand in some central spot, as did its counterpart at Rome: and in fact, the altar in question stood in the Athenian Agora, probably in its centre. A little to the east of the Tholus stood the statues of the Ten Heroes (the Ἐπώνυμοι) who gave names to the ten Athenian tribes. To these statues the programmes of laws were attached for public inspection, before they were discussed in the assembly. The situation of these statues illustrates that practice. They stood[5] in the Agora, in the centre of the political quarter of Athens. Mars, at the southern foot of his own hill, occupied a temple between the statues of those Ten Heroes on the west, and those of Harmodius and Aristogeiton on the east: and thus we are brought to the western foot of the Acropolis, at which point, as has been before noticed, these two statues stood.

We return to the Metroum, and proceed westward from that point. Near this temple to the Mother of the Gods was that of the Father-Deity of the Athenians – of Apollo Patrous. It was on the north-east of the Metroum. To the north-west of the same building was the spot chosen by Plato[6] for the scene of Euthyphro's dialogue with Socrates: the subject of which was in unison with the character of that place. It was the porch in which sat the archon who took cognizance of *religious* suits, and from him was called the Stoa Basileios[7]. Parallel and contiguous to it was another porch, much frequented by the same philosopher, Socrates: this was the Stoa of Jupiter Eleutherios. Not far to the north-west of this stoa, as Pausanias[8] informs us, was the western wall of the city, and a city-gate in the wall: a little to the east of which, and therefore *within* the city, were two buildings, one the Temple of Ceres, the other called the Pompeium.

What the name of this particular gate was, has been a subject of much controversy. It is of importance to determine that question, as this was the precise gate at which Pausanias commences his description of Athens, (not that he consequently must be supposed to have entered the city by that gate); and could it therefore be identified with some gate the position of which is known, it would serve to determine with more accuracy the site of those objects which Pausanias subsequently describes[9]. The following considerations may assist in this enquiry.

Near the gate in question, as has been said, stood a building called the Pompeium. The Pompeium[10] now, as its name indicates, served as a depository for the objects employed in the sacred πομπαὶ or processions, namely, in the Panathenaic procession, and in that to Eleusis. Such a building must necessarily, have stood in a spot by which those processions passed. Now, it is well known that the Panathenaic procession commenced its progress at a little distance outside the walls, and then entered Athens, moving eastward: the Eleusinian, on the other hand, started within the city, and having issued from it, advanced westward to Eleusis. It is also known that these two processions – the former in its entrance to the city, the latter in its exit from it – both passed through one and the same gate[11]. That gate was the Dipylum. But they also passed the Pompeium: and the Pompeium is described as near a gate of the city. Hence that particular gate which stood near the Pompeium can be no other than that through which these processions passed. It was therefore the Dipylum. And Pausanias therefore, I conceive, begins his description of Athens from the Dipylum gate, which it was very probable he should do, for this was the most distinguished of all the avenues to the city of Athens.

The Dipylum led to Eleusis; it led also to Colonus, and it was sometimes used as an entrance by persons coming from the Peiræus[12]. The position to be assigned to it must satisfy these three conditions: it has also been shown to be near the Pompeium. The Pompeium was near the Stoa of Zeus Eleutherios, which stood on the western verge of the Agora; and the Agora was a circular area lying in the hollow between the Areopagus and the Pnyx. From these premises I should infer that the Dipylum stood in the hollow to the north of the hill on which the Pnyx stands. Hence it might be said to stand in the *mouth of the city*[13], as it is described to be.

The Dipylum was the gate which served as the communication from the Inner Cerameicus to that which was outside the city. The statues of Harmodius and Aristogeiton which stood at the western foot of the citadel, were also contained in the wide range of the Cerameicus: hence therefore all the buildings which we have noticed in this chapter, since they lie between these two limits, that is, between the Dipylum on the north-west, and these two statues on the east, were comprised within the Inner Cerameicus[14].

The site occupied by the Agora coincided with a part of that district which was in later times called the Inner Cerameicus: it extended indeed to the same point eastward, for the same two statues which stood in the Cerameicus are often mentioned as existing in the Agora: but in a westerly[15] direction it did not reach to above half the distance to which the Cerameicus extended. The Agora seems to have been bounded on the north-west by the narrow passage which lies between the Areopagus and the western range of rocky elevations. In this passage was probably the gate of the Agora.

Of the public buildings, antecedent to the age of Pericles, there were but few on the northern side of the Areopagus. The Leocorium[16] was one of the most ancient. It stood to the north of the Agora, on the way to the Temple of Theseus. That temple is a remarkable point in this quarter of the city. It was one of the earliest buildings, of any public importance, erected in this district. The elevation of its site no doubt recommended it for a temple; and its tumular form might have strengthened its claim, when that temple was to be also a tomb.

It may be observed also that Cimon, who discovered at Skyros[17] the remains of Theseus, and conveyed them thence to Athens, was then enjoying the greatest popularity at Athens. Perhaps therefore a reference to that quarter of the city, with which Cimon was connected[18], might have influenced the choice of that particular site on which the temple now stands. Cimon possessed a place of domestic burial near that part of Athens which was called Melite. It may, I think, be shown that that quarter was called Melite in which the Temple of Theseus now stands[19].

A part of the city, which adjoined Melite, and which in consequence was sometimes confounded[20] with it, was termed Colonus. Colonus was bounded by the northern extremity of the Agora: whence it was sometimes distinguished by the title Agoræus, in order to contrast it with the more celebrated suburban Colonus which Sophocles has immortalized, and which was a mile to the north-west of the city and near the Academy. In the *urban* Colonus stood the Temple of Hephæstus[21]. The name and site of this temple lead us to infer that it was the goal proposed to the racers who ran with the lighted torches, having started from the outer Cerameicus and running through the Dipylum into the city.

Assuming the position of Melite to be accurately fixed, we are enabled to determine some other positions of importance in Athenian topography. The district called Cœle lay between Melite and the city-wall: and in the wall itself was the gate[22] called the Melitensian, as leading into Melite. This gate must have been on the north-west of the city, a little to the north-east of the site assigned above to Dipylum. Here then we may imagine to have been the Cemetery[23] in which the family of Cimon reposed, here the Olympian coursers of Cimon were buried, and here then Cimon himself, and his own relatives Miltiades and Thucydides, were interred. This Cemetery was in the outer Cerameicus, the most beautiful suburb, and the most honourable burial-place of Athens.

The positions which we have thus attempted to fix, are illustrated and confirmed by incidental testimony in ancient writers. Cephalus, in the Parmenides[24] of Plato, in his way from the Agora to the outer Cerameicus where Parmenides was lodging, calls upon Antipho to request him to introduce him to Parmenides. Now Antipho lived in Melite, that is, in the quarter between the Agora and the outer Cerameicus. The visit therefore to Antipho it was very natural for him to make, if Melite stood where we have placed it, and very unnatural for Plato to imagine, if Melite did not.

In a speech written by Demosthenes[25], a plaintiff in a case of assault detailed the following circumstances. He was taking his walk in the evening, together with a friend, in the Agora; he meets the defendant near the Leocorium, which was at the northern verge of the Agora: the defendant passes northward, in his way toward Melite: the plaintiff pursues his walk: he takes a turn to a temple[26] at the southern end of the Agora, and is returning back towards the Leocorium: he is there met and attacked by the defendant, who is attended by a party of friends whom he brings with him from Melite, where they had been drinking together. This incident tallies exactly with the results of our previous enquiry.

Adjoining Melite on the east was the quarter called Collyttus. As the limits of Colonus sometimes trenched upon Melite on the south, so on the east were they sometimes invaded by Collyttus. It was necessary to obviate this confusion between these two last by a distinct land-mark[27], which was erected on the line of their mutual contact. Melite was probably jealous of such a confusion; for the least respectable quarter in the whole of Athens was Collyttus. Hence it seems that Demosthenes, when he speaks of Æschines as acting with very limited success, in a tragic character, intends to add to the bitterness of his sarcasm by specifying also that the representation took place in Collyttus. Hence too the district of Collyttus was probably assigned by Lucian to Timon the Athenian man-hater, as an appropriate place for his extraction. Connected with Collyttus on the east was the quarter called Diomeia. Their relation was expressed by the legend, that Diomus was son of Collyttus.[28] Here were the Diomeian gates, which led into the Cynosarges and the Lyceum[29]. This is our limit on the east.

Not far to the east of the Theseum a building of considerable interest is supposed to have stood, the Stoa which from the frescoes with which it was adorned was called Pœcile. The Pœcile has been identified with an ancient building which still exists in the position above specified. This opinion does not seem to me to be well founded. The architecture of this building is of a style posterior to the date of the Pœcile. And on the walls of this building is an inscription which appears from its position to be coeval with the building itself; but which, as its language and the character of the letters clearly evince, must have been engraved a century and a half at least after the battle of Marathon; soon after which the Pœcile was built.

The part of this inscription which is still legible is as follows:

> *Nor Cyclopean hand with labour strong*
> *This pile did raise, nor Amphionian song.*[30]

I should conjecture from this distich that the building on which it appears had been the school of some sophist rather than the Stoic Pœcile.

In fact, the Pœcile really stood at the northern entrance of the Agora. A building decorated with the splendid representations of

Athenian heroism, as the Pœcile was, would naturally be placed in the most illustrious part of the city. Æschines too, speaking on the bema of the Pnyx, refers his hearers to the Pœcile for the memorials of their ancestral glory; and he adds, that they have only to descend in imagination into the Agora[31] to visit them there. Hence too, as standing in the most splendid quarter of Athens, the Pœcile was chosen as the spot in which the Spartan shields taken at Pylos[32] should be suspended as trophies.

I should place the Pœcile at the northern entrance of the Agora[33]; for it stood near the Temple of Hephæstus, which was in the urban Colonus: and also near the Mercury Agoræus[34], who guarded the entrance of the Agora.

Thus have we now surveyed the principal objects of Athenian topography. From the scattered notices of antiquity of which we are cognizant, and from the labours of others in the same field, we have attempted to fit together, as harmoniously as we are able, the separate pieces of the dislocated map. How much of labour, and perhaps of error, we might have been spared, had we been present but for a single minute at the Macedonian entertainment, at which the Athenian orator Demades, – *when ambassador at Philip's court, and when Philip asked him what and what sort of place Athens was, drew a map of it on the table where they were sitting.*[35] But still how much of pleasure too, arising from this enquiry, should we then have lost also!

CHAPTER XXIII

I have heard this description of the Panathenaic festival: they tell me that a Peplus, more lovely than a picture, was hung from the ship wafted by its swelling bosom; that the ship sailed along, not drawn by animals, but gliding secretly on machinery passing over the ground; that it got under weigh at the Cerameicus with crowded sail, and made for the Eleusinium; that it doubled this point and passed the Pelasgicum, and then hove to, at the Pythium, where it is now moored.[1]

Philostrat. Vit. Herod. Soph. 11.

WE will make an application of these observations on the topography of Athens, by endeavouring to trace the route of the Panathenaic procession. The principal feature in that procession was the Panathenaic peplos, which was carried to the Acropolis as a periodic offering to Minerva Polias: and with which her statue, in her temple there, was subsequently invested.

The peplos, at the commencement of its course, was hoisted aloft[2] with cables, like a ship's sail, on a horizontal bar attached to the summit of a vertical mast: in this position the peplos moved above the heads of the crowd, with its variegated tissue of battles, its pictures of chariots and horses, gods and giants, floating in the air above them.

Such was the principal feature of this procession in the best days of Athens. In later times[3], when a fantastic ingenuity sought to display itself, even in religious solemnities, it attracted the wonder rather than the veneration of the spectator, by its bold and complex machinery. Then the peplos assumed the character of a real sail; the nautical genius of Athens displayed itself in this its most gorgeous national pageant: the props of the peplos performed the functions[4] of a yard-arm and a mast: its cables were converted into rigging: and the whole equipage was planted on a stately ship, which sailed on secret wheels, wafted along by the gale filling the bosom of its embroidered sail.

The magnificent ship-like car, with all its splendid accoutrements, in which Santa Rosalia now makes her annual solemn procession through the gates and streets of the maritime city of Palermo, presents no doubt a striking resemblance to that which once sailed through the city of Athens at the Panathenaic festival. The correspondence in other respects – as the season of the year chosen for their celebration, and in the diversions by which they were enlivened - between the Athenian and Sicilian solemnity, is also worthy of notice[5].

The particular route which was chosen for the progress of the Panathenaic Procession through the Athenian City, was dictated no doubt by the characteristic suggestions of Athenian taste. To pass through the most splendid streets of Athens, to spread itself abroad in the noblest squares, to visit the most august temples, to display a new and pompous spectacle to the theatre, and to pause at last in the highest and proudest spot in the whole city – in a word, after its festal voyage, to anchor in the Acropolis, – was a duty which this procession owed both to itself and them. The route therefore which it followed, may serve us as a tacit guide to conduct us through the city of Athens in the most advantageous way.

Let us take our station with it at its commencement, at the north-west of the city, a little outside the walls, and at the point where Hippias[6] was engaged in marshalling this same procession, when his brother Hipparchus fell near the Leocorium in the inner Cerameicus: we then follow it into the city by the Dipylum: it passes along an avenue formed by the two parallel arcades[7], which have been described above as leading to the Agora, and traverses the circle of the Agora[8] between the Areopagus and the Pnyx: it enters the valley of Limnæ lying on the south of the Acropolis, it passes beneath the theatre, and at length reaches the Eleusinium[9]: this is the point of curvature in its course. It now tends westward, coasting[10] the northern rocks of the Acropolis. It ascends the Acropolis itself by the western entrance through the marble portals of the Propylæa. Here the procession halts. The Peplos is carried to its destination in the Temple of Minerva Polias.

There is, I believe, a direct allusion to this movement and destination of the Peplos, in the minute description by Euripides of the progress and dedication to Minerva of the wooden horse in the Acropolis of Troy. (Troad. 517.)

> *Standing upon the rocky Citadel*
> *Of Troy, the City shouted, and a flood*
> *Of Men rushed onward to the Gate:*
> *What Virgin then went forth not from her Cell?*
> *What Old Man idly sate?*
> *By twisted Cables tow'd, as sailors moor*
> *Some sable Vessel, at the marble shore*
> *Of Pallas' holy Fane at length it anchor'd stood.*[11]

The course of the peplos through the streets of Athens to the *rock* of the *Acropolis*, the joy with which it was welcomed at the *Propylæa*, the ardour with which it was drawn along in its course, to its final resting-place in the marble shrine of Pallas, are well represented to our imagination in this poetical picture.

But the naval car does not remain here: it descends again into the city toward a temple which stood, as may be shown[12], not far from the western roots of the Acropolis, on the south side of the Areopagus, in the Agora. In this temple the vessel was laid up to be exhibited in after-times as an object of admiration to travellers, when it had ceased to perform its festal voyages – as the ducal Barge of Venice, the Bucentoro, in which the Doge solemnized the annual marriage of the sea, is now preserved for the same purpose in the Venetian Arsenal.

CHAPTER XXIV

The outstretch'd arms of the Thesean Way.[1]
Propert. III. 20. 24.

MUCH has been said with respect to the number and direction of the Long Walls which stretched from the city of Athens to the sea. For my own part, I do not perceive how we can avoid the conclusion that at the time of the Peloponnesian War – for of later times we do not here speak – there were *three* distinct lines of fortification reaching from the walls of the Athenian city to the sea-shore.

Of these the *two exterior,* namely, that extending to the harbour of Phalerum on the south, and that to the harbour of the Peiræus on the north, were the first[2] erected. As long as they stood alone, without a third, they bore the name of '*The* Long Walls:' but subsequently[3], when, at the instigation of Pericles, and under the direction of Callicrates, a third was erected lying longitudinally between them, and connecting the southern point of the Peiræus with the city, then this third wall, together with the northern, seem to have appropriated that title. These two[4] then became peculiarly the *Long* Walls, Τὰ μακρὰ τείχη; for they were the two *longest*; and they were naturally connected as a pair, abutting as they both did on the Peiræus: they were strictly the legs of the *Peiræus,* Πειραικὰ σκέλη[5]; for the other wall ended at *Phalerum.*

Hence it is that the middle wall, and not, as might perhaps have been anticipated, the *Phaleric* one, was termed the *southern* wall, (τὸ νότιον τεῖχος); not because it was the most southern of them all, for that it was not, but because it was the more southern of the *two* Peiraic walls: for it was considered with respect to the other Peiraic wall alone, which was termed the northern wall[6], (τὸ βόρειον τεῖχος). Hence these Peiraic walls are called the legs, σκέλη, as being *two*, and *two only*: hence we hear of '*either* of the two Long Walls,' τῶν μακρῶν τὸ ἑκάτερον, for the same reason.

In all these cases an abstraction, as it were, is made of the Phaleric, or most southern[7] and shortest wall of the three: but when the *middle* wall is considered, as it very rarely is, with reference not to the northern Peiraic wall alone, but to the Phaleric wall also – as, for instance, whence its erection of this middle wall after that of the other two is mentioned – then it is very properly no longer termed the *southern wall*, τὸ νότιον τεῖχος, but it is then called the *intermediate* wall, τὸ διὰ μέσου τεῖχος[8], as lying along between the other two. The reason why, in ordinary cases, the Phaleric wall was neglected in this assignation of names, seems to have been the insignificance of the Phaleric harbour, compared with that of the Peiræus.

By these considerations, all the difficulties which have been occasioned by the varieties of designation by which the Long Walls are characterized, may, I think, be satisfactorily removed.

The execution of the middle or most recent wall, commenced by Pericles, seems to have been very dilatory, as was often the case with the construction of public works at Athens. The comic poet Cratinus[9], remarking on the tardiness of its progress, said that it was then extending itself to the sea by means of long words and prolix sentences, while in act and deed it did not stir an inch:

> ... *for Pericles, an age since,*
> *In word extends it, though in deed he really does not touch it.*

And I cannot but suspect that there is an indirect allusion to some architectural work at Athens, only just executed, in the very minute and copious detail of the processes of masonry adopted by the birds in the construction of *The Long Walls* of their own City, which was but a picture of Athens suspended in the air[10]. If so, the middle wall would not have been completed long before B.C. 414, when that play was acted[11].

CHAPTER XXV

House of the Nymphs.[1]

Virgil.

Dec. 27.

THIS evening we spent some time in a grotto on Mount Hymettus. It is about twelve miles from Athens, on the way to Sunium, and near the village of Bári, the ancient Anagyrus.

It is a natural subterranean cave, entered by a descent of a few stone steps, from which access the interior is dimly lighted: it is vaulted with fretted stone, and the rocky roof is gracefully hung with stalactites.

There are some ancient inscriptions engraven on the rock near the entrance. From one of these we learn that the grotto was sacred to the nymphs. Another similar inscription admits the sylvan Pan, and the rural Graces, to a share in the same residence. The pastoral Apollo is likewise united with them in another expression of the same kind.

The Attic shepherd to whose labour the cave was indebted for its simple furniture, is also mentioned in other inscriptions here. His figure too, dressed in the short shepherd's tunic (βαίτα), and with a hammer and chisel in his hands, with which he is chipping the side of the cave, is rudely sculptured on its rocky wall.

To any one who comes here from the magnificent fabrics of Athenian worship now lying in ruins in the city of Athens, this simple grotto – a natural temple on a solitary mountain dedicated to natural deities – will be an object of much interest. Here are no ruins. Time has exerted no power here. The integrity of the grotto has not been impaired by lapse of years. When left alone in the faint light of this cavern, and while looking on these inscriptions which declare the former sanctity of the place, and on the basins scooped in the rock from which the sacred libations were made, and the limpid well in the cave's recess from which water was supplied for those libations to the rural deities – with no other objects about you to disturb the impression which these produce – you might fancy some shepherd of this part of Attica had just left the spot, and that he would return before evening from his neighbouring sheep-fold on Hymettus, with an offering to Pan from his flock there, or with the spoils of his mountain-chase, or with the first flowers which at this season of the year have just peeped forth in his rural garden[2]. If we may pursue the conception further, he might be imagined to come here with his pipe and crook in his hand, and then to pour forth his feelings in a simple strain, such as the following, which from the objects it notices would have here been very appropriate:

> *Grot of the Nymphs, where from the rocky brow*
> *Refreshing streams of liquid crystal flow,*
> *Thou echoing Crypt, where pine-crown'd Pan resides,*
> *Pacing within the vaulted valley's sides;*
> *Hail, and reward Sosander's rural toil,*
> *His chase assist, who gives you of his spoil.*[3]

The inscriptions which are seen engraved on the sides of the grotto, still deserve[4] some further notice. The cave is of a horse-shoe form, of which the concave part is the most distant from the entrance. On entering the right-hand arm of this curve, the spectator will perceive the following words on his right hand[5]: they are cut on the planed face of the rock there: the letters are arranged in *rank and file,* στοιχηδόν.

Archedemus of Pheræ, the Nympholept, completed this grotto, by the suggestion of the Nymphs.

It will be observed, that though in this inscription the long *ē* is introduced, the long *ō* is not: and that, since the conclusion forms an iambic verse, the last word must be read (not ἐξηργάσατο, but) ἐξηργάξατο, as the vestiges of the inscription themselves suggest; a dialectic license[6], which is to be accounted for by the Thessalian origin of Archedemus, in whose honour this inscription was engraved.

The inconsistency in the orthography of the first syllable of the word Pheræ, the native place of Archedemus, which is observed on comparing this inscription with another in older characters, near the exit of the grotto, where he is described as ὁ Φεραῖος, is to be attributed, not to the difference of date in the two inscriptions – for, on this principle, νυμφόν would not have here been written, as it is, for νυμφῶν – but to another cause. I believe the commencement of the inscription is intended to be poetry, and not prose, as well as the end: and, it being so intended, the form Φηραῖος was employed, and not the other, in order to satisfy the conditions of the verse. The sentence then may be thus exhibited as a distich[7].

Archedemus of Pheræ, in a nympholepsy,
By counsel of the Nymphs this cave did execute.

On the left hand at the entrance is the word **ΧΑΡΙΤΟ** (that is, χαρίτων, *dedicated to the Graces*, and not χάριτος) similarly inscribed; and a stone basin beneath it to supply water for libations to the Graces.

Proceeding to the interior, we meet on the right side with another inscription, of which the sense is less intelligible, as the rock in which it is cut is more corroded by time.

ΤΑΝΤΕΛ
ΣΟΚΥΥ—
ΚΑΙΤΟ
ΘΟΝΙ

Having turned to the left round the corner into the other arm of the cave, we see on the left side a horizontal ledge chiselled in the rock, in which two basins, now filled with clear water, are excavated. Here, as in the Nymphæum of Homer,

Are basins hewn and amphoras of stone.[8]

On a perpendicular margin beneath these two basins, two words are inscribed, one under each;

ΑΠΟΛΛΩΝΟΣ ⁞ ΕΡΣΟ

the former of which words enjoins that libations should here be made to Apollo, the pastoral or Nomian Apollo, who was here an appropriate deity. Perhaps too his connexion with Pheræ, the native place of Archedemus the adorner of this grotto, gave him a stronger claim to a place here. It was in the plains of Pheræ that Apollo exercised his pastoral functions: he there fed the flocks of Admetus the Pheræan King,

With menial fare contented, though a God.[9]

The name of the second deity is not of so common occurrence. Still the characters are so distinct, and the etymology of the word so significant, that they overcome the doubts naturally arising from the rarity of the word. The second basin was, then, I believe, the property of Ersus (ΕΡΣΟΥ). He appears to have been venerated here, as the beneficent power[10] to whose influence – shed like dew (ἔρση) upon the earth, – all rural produce in its infant state, the tender blade, the opening blossom, and the young firstling, were alike indebted for their preservation and increase.

The mention of this deity furnishes us, I think, with a clue for the interpretation of the former inscription, which from its corroded state seemed too mutilated to warrant such an attempt.

In the first inscription then of all, the word τἄντρον occurs: it seems to prepare the mind for an abbreviation occurring, as it appears, in this mutilated inscription, which would hardly otherwise have been admissible. The first four letters in this subsequent inscription are, I think, an abridgement[11] of τἄντρον: and as it borrows this word from the first, so may the name of Ersus be supplied from the last. This mutilated inscription may, on these grounds, be restored as follows:

This Cave belongs to Ersus and the subterranean Deities.[12]

The deities of the earth (θεοὶ χθόνιοι) might very fitly be honoured in this subterranean crypt, by the peasant who lived on the earth's produce, and was reminded by the poet of agriculture to invoke their blessing on his labours,

And pray to Jove Terrene, and pure Demeter:[13]

and whom another poet might have supplied with language to be addressed to them, and to their associate Pan, in this grotto:

To goat-legg'd Pan, to Bacchus, and the shrine
Of Ceres the Terrene, this gift I bear;
Oh! grant me fleeces white, and mellow wine,
And corn-fields waving with the loaded ear.[14]

The name of Pan is twice carved in rude letters ΠΑΝΟΣ on the rock near the exit of the cave.

From the images and votive offerings, it appears to be consecrated to some Nymphs[15], is a notice which Plato has left us of another spot, and which might well have been applied to this grotto: and what is more, it might have been applied to it by Plato himself from his own acquaintance with the place.

In his early youth, Plato, as we are told by one of his biographers[16], was carried by his parents up the slopes of Mount Hymettus, and conducted by them to a spot which was dedicated TO PAN, THE NYMPHS AND THE PASTORAL APOLLO; and offerings were there made by them in his behalf to the tutelary deities of the place.

We may, I think, be allowed to indulge the conjecture, that the grotto in which we now are, situated on Mount Hymettus, and dedicated, as these inscriptions carved on its rocky sides evince, to PAN, APOLLO and THE NYMPHS, was itself witness of that scene, and that we are now looking on the same objects which arrested the eye and perhaps inspired a feeling of devotion in the mind of the youthful Plato.

CHAPTER XXVI

O Ferryman, Cities die as well as Men.[1]

Lucian. *Contempl.*

Lágrona[2] near Sunium, Dec. 28.

THE desolate state of this country is almost indescribable. Of the numerous Athenian towns and villages which once covered its soil hardly any vestiges remain. It is almost a wilderness. We have not met five persons on the road during a two days' journey on our way from Athens hither. We see occasionally a few shepherds on the hills at a distance tending their sheep, but at the first sight of our party they scamper away for fear; as if they were sheep, and we wolves. To gain any information from them as to the localities of the country is utterly impossible.

The natural aspect of this country is as dreary, as its actual condition is desolate. It is bare and dry: there are no fountains or rivulets to refresh it: its surface is broken up into small groups of low rocky hills, on which there is scarcely any vegetation but stunted brushwood. Towards Sunium we meet with pine-trees, in the thin foliage of which the winter's evening wind sighs with a melancholy tone.

In this scene of loneliness the traveller is more impressed by the appearance of the few traces which he meets with of the ancient population, with which this country was formerly thronged. The route along which we are riding was the high road from Athens to

Laureium. By it the silver ore, which had been dug from the Laureian mines there by the labour of several thousand slaves, was carried to the city, and thence issued to circulate through the whole civilized world. The stony road over which we are passing is deeply worn by the tracks of the wheels which then went along it, groaning with their precious freight. In some places, for a considerable distance, the wheels have worked deep grooves in the rock. The road is now a mere mule-path.

This route seems to me to coincide with what was called in ancient times the Sphettian way; the direction of which is an important subject in Attic topography[3]. The Sphettian way was so called as communicating from Athens with the borough of Sphettus. Now Sphettus, in the mythological language of Attica, was *brother*[4] of Anaphlystus. Sphettus, therefore – for such seems the meaning of the fable – was most probably near to Anaphlystus. The site of Anaphlystus is known: its name and site correspond to that of the modern Anáphyso, which is on the western coast of Attica, five miles to the north of Sunium. Again, Sphettus[5] and Anaphlystus were both *sons* of Trœzen. Anaphlystus we know to have stood on one of the points of Attica nearest to the Trœzenian shore. Sphettus, the brother of Anaphlystus, and son of Trœzen, satisfied doubtless the claims of both relations, by occupying a similar and contiguous position to that of Anaphlystus, and facing Trœzen. Hence we conclude, that the Sphettian way is identical with our present route.

Sophocles, in a fragment of the lost drama of his Ægeus, gives a detailed account of the division of the Attic territory among the four sons of Pandion, in which he informs us that the *southern* district, that is, the district between Athens and Sunium, fell to the share of Pallas[6].

> ....*The district to the south*
> *The sturdy Pallas, fosterer of giants,*
> *Holds as his share*...

Now it is observable, that in the narrative which is preserved by another author[7] of the invasion of Athens by this same Pallas, it is particularly specified that the route by which he marched from his own residence to Athens was the *Sphettian* way. This incident confirms our previous conclusion.

We pass the night at Lágrona[8], in a metóchi (μετόχιον), or out-building, belonging to a Greek convent. It consists of an open court with sheds round it: it is now quite deserted, and its walls falling into ruins. All its doors have been torn off from their hinges. There are no other signs of life near it beside some owls hooting in the night from the trees about us.

CHAPTER XXVII

The Goddess, the Guardian of high citadels herself, made for them a flying chariot.[1]
Catull. LXIV. v. 8.

THE Temple of Sunium is about five miles to the south of Lágrona. Standing above the shore on a high rocky peninsula, its white columns are visible at a great distance from the sea. There is something very appropriate in the choice of this position for a Temple dedicated to the tutelary goddess of the Athenian soil. Minerva thus appeared to stand in the vestibule of Attica. The same feeling which placed her statue at the gate of the citadel of Athens erected her temple here. In the former situation, however, as the nearer and more vital of the two, she was the Champion (Πρόμαχος) of Athens: while standing in the more distant, and therefore taking a wider survey, she was the (Πρόνοια[2]) Providence of the whole country.

By means of her temple on this promontory her protection was felt, and her power asserted, in the extreme limit of the land. By means of her presence here, extended to this point from her residence in the Acropolis at Athens, Sunium was connected with Athens; it became, in common language, a promontory not of Attica, but of Athens, Σούνιον ἄκρον Ἀθηνῶν[3].

A little to the north-east of the peninsula on which the temple stands is a conical hill: here are extensive vestiges of an ancient building: it seems probable that they are remains of a temple, most likely of that dedicated to Neptune, the Σουνιάρατος (Aristoph. Eq. 558).

The peninsular form of this promontory gave it great advantages as a military post. Its nearness to the mines of Laureium conduced to its prosperity, which passed into a proverb:

> *For many men to-day do quake like slaves,*
> *Who will to-morrow strut like Sunians.*[4]

It was the principal fortress of this district, and a place of much importance while Athens remained independent[5]. When that city ceased to be so, Sunium sunk speedily into decay; so much so, that we have Cicero[6] proposing, as a critical question to his correspondent Atticus, whether Sunium had not now arrived at that state of desertion to require before its name in Latin the prefix of a preposition, – which was the nigrum theta of a deceased town. Some modern traveller, in a spirit of less refined sympathy for its former greatness, has daubed in uncial letters on the shaft of one of the columns of its temple the words, "Homage des Siècles présents aux Siècles passés. 1818."

It was a distance of sixty stadia from Anaphlystus on the western to Thoricus on the eastern shore; and Sunium is nearly at the same distance of sixty stadia from each of them. Thus these three towns stood at the three angles of an equilateral triangle. We now pass along the eastern shore towards Thoricos, now Thericó. The hills are scattered over with juniper-bushes. The ground which we tread is strewed with rusty heaps of scoria from the silver ore[7] which once enriched the soil. The silver-source of these mines, which was once the treasury of the land, is now dried up. On our left is a hill called Scori, so named from these heaps of scoriæ with which it is covered. Here the shafts which have been sunk for working the ore are visible, from which the name[8] of this country is derived. These strewn heaps of scoria are a fit emblem of the country itself on which they lie. What with the smelting which it has endured from war, famine, oppression, and pillage by its successive masters, Goths, Greeks,

Spaniards, Venetians, and Turks, it has hardly a thin vein of its ancient ore left.

The view of the ancient Theatre at Thoricus affords an agreeable relief to the dismal dreariness of this district. It is a vestige, one of the few which remain, of the pleasures which an Attic village enjoyed in the cheerful seasons of the year. The agreeable landscape which has remained to us of an ancient Italian[9] audience collected on the sloping sides of a rural theatre, might have been supplied with a Greek counterpart here. The mimicry of the village Dionysia[10] which Aristophanes exhibited in his Acharnians, was doubtless a frequent reality in this place. Here also we are reminded of the scene which Virgil[11] has sketched from the antique life of the Attic peasantry:

> *The ancient Games are ushered on the stage,*
> *And in Cross-ways and Towns the Attic swains*
> *Strive for the scenic prize, and cheer'd with wine,*
> *Leap mid the swoll'n smeard shins on meadows green...*

a scene which, no doubt, has often enlivened with mirth and laughter the now void and silent sides of this hollow theatre[12].

A theatre was an appropriate feature at Thoricus, for it was in the port of this place that Dionysus, the deity of the Athenian drama, first landed in Attica.

The outline of this theatre is not of a semicircular form; it is of an irregular curve, nearly resembling the fourth of an ellipse; the longer axis commencing with the stage, and the seats beginning from the lesser axis, and running, in tiers rising above each other, concentrically with the curve. They faced the south. The curved outline of the κοῖλον of the theatre formed part of the town-wall: this irregular form was perhaps adopted, as more defensible than any other.

In the wall near the theatre is an old postern, surmounted by a pointed arch formed in approaching horizontal courses, in the same manner as the arches in the galleries at Tiryns. We trace the walls of the Acropolis stretching for a considerable extent over two rugged hills, which rise to the north-east of the theatre. The style and massiveness of this postern, and of these walls, afford clear evidence of the great antiquity and local importance of Thoricus.

The harbour of Thoricus, now Porto Mandri, lies on the south side of the citadel. It has the reputation of being an excellent place of refuge, both in a northerly and southerly gale: it is a semi-circular bay, half a league in breadth, from north to south: its anchorage is completely sheltered by the long island of Macri, the ancient Helena, which was well described as

> *Stretch'd* as a *rampart by the shore, an isle,*
> *Which shall henceforth the name of Helen bear.*[13]

There is one great defect here, as in this district generally, the scarcity of fresh water.

Thoricus was principally remarkable, in early Athenian history, as the residence of Cephalus. He died here, and, as it seems, while in the prime of life; for Aurora was said to have carried him off from the shores of Attica to dwell with the Gods. Thoricus became famous as the place from which that Athenian hero was removed to a heavenly climate: and with the name of Thoricus was probably associated, in the Athenian mind, the idea of such an Elysian translation[14].

A migration of this character was the lot of Œdipus at Colonus[15]. Its description by Sophocles may derive some light from this the *Elysian* character of Thoricus. Œdipus is there represented as standing on the brink of another world. He has reached the brazen threshold, and the rugged descent which is to lead him to it. Near him stands registered the solemn compact which Theseus made with Peirithous, when they took together the same journey on which Œdipus is going alone. There is a marble tomb at the entrance. All these objects are in character with the place as leading to another state of existence; and their relation to that state is easily perceived. And may it not be suggested that, on the principle which I have just supposed, namely, the connection of Thoricus, derived from the story of Cephalus, its prince, with the idea of an Elysian migration, the obscure relation of the θορίκιος πέτρος, Thorician Stone, which Sophocles next introduces into the same scene, may now be perceived also[16]?

CHAPTER XXVIII

―――

...and you Iphigenia, in the holy meadows of Brauron must serve this goddess as her temple warden.[1]

Eur. *Iph*. T. 1462.

―――

LEAVING this morning the hut in which we had lodged at Thoricó, we enter a glen between Mount Koróra on the right and Mount Tibári on the left. The country becomes more cheerful as we approach the village of Keratiá. Heaps of scoriæ still occur near the road-side: a peasant who accompanies us calls them by their ancient name, (σκωρία).

These heaps suggest the meaning of the title of a lost comedy by Antiphanes[2], which was inscribed Θορίκιοι, ἢ διορύττων. I conceive that the Thoricians were satirized in that play, as guilty of unfair dealing, by *piercing through from*[3] their own into their neighbours' shafts in working their mines for the ore, of which the scoria is now visible near their own village.

We leave a hamlet on the left called Metropísi: it lies at the south-east foot of Mount Paní. The Πανεῖον or grotto of Pan, from which this mountain derives its name, is about half an hour to the west of Keratiá. It contains no ancient remains of interest. Keratiá is about six miles to the north-west of Thoricó.

This village is prettily situated among vineyards. After our lonely journey, the sight of a group of cottages ranged among trees is a very pleasing object. Besides this, there is an appearance of greater comfort and security in this village of Keratiá than we have seen for a long time. There are flocks feeding at liberty in the open fields, under the sides of the hills: and there is no apparent alarm of the military robbers who now infest the other parts of Attica. The women of the village are neatly dressed: the population is Albanian.

There is a church at Keratiá dedicated to S. Demetrius. Cased in its walls I find a large fragment of carved stone, with the following metrical inscription, in very ancient characters:

ΜΟΙ ΘΑΝΟΣΕΣ ΕΙΜΙ
ΕΜΑ ΜΥΔΙ : ΝΕΣ

This is an epitaph: by which the monument simply records, speaking in its own person, the name of a woman, whose tomb it is, and the malady of which she died. The fracture of the marble hides from us the last particular: but it may be conjectured, from the above vestiges of the word which remain on the monument, that the malady was a pestilence, λοιμός; perhaps even, – to judge from the characters of the inscription, which seem to be nearly cotemporary with that event – that it was the same epidemic which made such havoc at Athens at the commencement of the Peloponnesian War.

Hence we may represent the epitaph in an Iambic verse in this form,

Here rests Myrina, who died of plague. [4]

After passing through the plain of Keratiá and bearing to the right, we enter a picturesque glade overhung with pines; its sides are furrowed by torrents, and indented with clefts and grottoes. This glen runs in an easterly direction toward the sea. On its north side is Merónda, and south of Merónda[5] another spot called Malizé; east of Malizé is Kourúgni, which is a rocky peninsular promontory on the south-east of Port Raphté, which was the harbour of the ancient Prasiæ. From Merónda there is a chain of hills stretching westward, and at last, intersecting the chain of Hymettus: of these hills the most remarkable is that which is called, from its peculiar form, Strongúle (Στρογγύλη). North of it is the plain of Marcópoulo. On Kourúgni we are told that there are ruins of antiquity: near the western side of this harbour of Prasiæ rises Mount Maleventi; on its north-west extremity is Mount Trivla, on which is a small chapel of S. Nicolas; on the northern brink is Mount Peraté (Περατῆ), under which stands a church of S. Spyridhon.

The western branch still bears the name of Prasá, which leaves no doubt, together with other proofs, that its site is identical with that of the ancient Prasiæ, and that the ancient fragments which are still visible on the north-west shore of the bay, are vestiges of that city. From the ancient pier, which is now washed by the sea, sacred processions once embarked on their voyage to Delos.

The harbour is an excellent one, both from its size and depth: it is the best on the eastern coast of Attica. Its entrance is rather more than a mile in breadth; in the centre of the entrance is the rocky islet on which stands the marble statue, from the attitude of which the port derives its present name. The statue is a mile from the central point of the shore of the harbour.

We enter the church dedicated to S. Nicolas on the beach of Porto Rapthé. It is now nearly filled with βαλανίδια, or acorns of the *quercus ægilops*, which grows here in abundance. In the harbour lies a vessel which has just arrived from the island of Ceos (Zia), which will carry these acorns to Constantinople, to be used as a mordant for dyeing black. The vessel is freighted with barley (κριθάρι), which it exchanges for this commodity.

It is an hour's walk from Prasiæ to Brauron: we pass some ruins on our way thither, which are those of the ancient Steiria.

Here the country is of a very pleasing character. A little before arriving at Braóna (a name derived from Brauron) we cross a picturesque hill fringed with wood, beneath which runs a pretty stream, probably the Erasinus. It is edged with a line of white poplars.

Beneath them, by the side of the stream, is a garden of fruit and vegetables – which is a rare sight in this country. To our left is a grey square tower on a hill. The landscape is softened by the quiet light of the evening, which is now coming on. Iphigenia, the daughter of Agamemnon, was brought here, as the legend related[6], from the gloomy regions of the Taurica Chersonesus, and placed as a priestess of Diana's temple in this cheerful valley, where she was said to have lived and died; and where her supposed tomb was shown in after ages.

In a little more than an hour from Braóna[7], we reach Marcópoulo, a village on the south-west; and here we spend the night. Our lodging is an Albanian cottage. The family consists of the mistress of the house and her two sons, who have now with them some visitors from the village. As we approach the doorway they are going to sit down to their supper, when they invite us to enter. In a few minutes the members of the family have taken their seats on the clay-floor round a low round table, on which is a large bowl of gurgouti, or porridge, to which each guest helps himself by dipping his bread into the bowl. The mistress of the house pours out the wine, and hands it to the guests, who acknowledge the attention by complimentary speeches, to herself and family, in the same spirit and character as Minerva does in the Odyssey to Nestor and his son, on a similar occasion.

When supper is over, the youngest son, who is about twelve years old, rises and turns his face to the wall of the cottage and towards a sacred picture hanging upon it: he then takes off his red scull-cap, and standing before the picture, begins to repeat some prayers in Greek, which he follows by the recital of the Creed, and concludes with frequent repetitions of Κύριε ἐλέησον. These are the vespers of an Albanian cottage. They then retire to rest.

The youth who here conducted the devotions of the family, on our visiting with him a church in his own village, and when one of the party was proceeding from the nave of the church to enter into the chancel, or ἅγιον βῆμα, deterred him from so doing by warning him that it was a hallowed place, and that those alone who were ministers of the church might enter there[8].

The character of the Albanian peasantry is of a more serious and pensive cast than that of the other inhabitants of Greece: perhaps this incident may be taken as an illustration of this: for I have not observed the same feeling, which was here expressed, prevail in any class of the *Greek* villages. It was observed to me by a well-educated Greek – and the observation is generally just – that the character of the Albanian population bears the same relation to the Greek in modern times, which that of the Dorian race did formerly to the Ionic.

I should not here omit, what I afterwards learnt, that our young Albanian guide had already himself attained to some dignity in the church, for whose honour he was zealous; there too, as well as in his own cottage, he performs a ministerial duty. He is there an Anagnóstes.

The elder brother of this boy is a youth of sixteen. He has just been married. His bride is now staying in the village of Lópes, which is near. She is said to be very beautiful: the expression by which they describe to us her beauty, is remarkable. "Yes, he is married," say they, "and his wife is so lovely a person, that you would take her picture."[9] It is an expression which could not have been suggested by the rude lineaments or colouring of the modern paintings of this country. It has probably remained in the language from the deep-felt influence of ancient art.

Marcópoulo is situated near the central point of that district of Attica which still retains its ancient name of "Mesogæa", or "Interior." Whether one of the 174 demi[10] or boroughs, which once peopled the soil of Attica, stood on its site, cannot now be determined from any vestiges on the spot. It appears however to have served as the central point of resort to one of the 360 clans (γένη)[11] into which the 12 curiæ (φρατρίαι) or whole free population of Attica, were divided. This fact I infer from the following inscription, which I copy here at Marcópoulo.

Epameinon, the Son of Ameinias, made this motion: Since certain individuals continue to act and speak against the Eikadenses at variance with their oath, and with the imprecation which Eikadeus uttered, to the detriment of the common property of the Eikadenses, from which property the Eikadenses offer their sacrifices to the Gods, and since they abet indictments against the Eikadenses, and have given evidence falsely in the Court, to the detriment of the Corporation of the Eikadenses; (that it be decreed) to elect three individuals forthwith, from the Eikadenses, to co-operate with Polyxenus, who has impeached this evidence of perjury, in order that the false witnesses may be brought to punishment; and to eulogize Polyxenus, the Son of Diodorus, for his probity with respect to the Corporation of the Eikadenses, and because he brought an action of perjury against the witnesses; and that the magistrates of the Office of Information should inscribe this decree on a marble slab, and erect it in the Temple of the Parnessian Apollo.[12]

CHAPTER XXIX

...the ground's too muddy.[1]

Aristoph. *Pac.* 1148.

Dec. 30.

MARCOPOULO is six hours, or about twenty miles, from Athens. The showery season has now set in, and our ride is accompanied by violent and incessant rain. The road lies along a shrubby plain; it leaves the path to Brauron, and a village called Hieráka, on the right; passes between two villages, Kókla and Lópesa; the latter being on the left. In a church at this point is a sepulchral bas-relief, inscribed with the name ΑΡΤΙΜΑΣ. There are vestiges here of an ancient village. The name of the hamlet on the right suggests that it may have been the site of the borough called Kykala.[2]

At a distance of three miles further, and eight from Marcópoulo, we leave to the right the villages of Kangiá and Leontári. The latter, no doubt, derives its name from the colossal lion, or λεοντάρι, of white marble, which lies here near the road, by the Church of S. Nicolas. This was perhaps a trophy to commemorate a victory; for which purpose the statue of a lion was often employed. The peasants look on this huge figure with a feeling of awe, which thus expresses itself in the mouth of a countryman, who informs us that – *The monster has a den on the mountains*,[3] pointing to the heights of Hymettus, from which he descends to hunt his prey in the plains beneath it.

The whole of this district, to judge from the remains of ancient buildings which occur here, was very thickly peopled. The Mesogæa was one of the most fertile parts of Attica[4]. Hence its dense population.

At an hour and a half from Kangiá is seen a tower on a hill, which is near the village of Krabáta: from which a road converges toward that we are now treading, (which probably coincides with the old Steirian road[5]), and falls into it at a point called, from that circumstance, the Cross, (σταυρό). Here we find a Turkish guard stationed, for the purpose of protecting the peasants who are coming from their villages to the Athenian market; for this is the market-day at Athens. We now turn to the left, and approach Athens by the same way as we first entered it.

CHAPTER XXX

We turn aside
To trace the footsteps left by ancient Time.[1]

Æsch. Suppl. 533

Jan. 7.

I walk to-day from Athens in a north-easterly direction towards Mount Pentelicus. All the villages among which I pass have suffered from the depredations committed upon them by the soldiers of the Greek chief, Captain Vassos: most of them are deserted.

My route lies through the plain of Athens, and extends as far as Cephissiá, the pleasant village which Herodes Atticus chose for the place of his summer-retreat. It is about nine miles to the north-east of Athens. A fountain of transparent water, and groups of shady trees which charmed the repose of the wealthy and munificent philosopher, still remain here. It retains also its ancient name. Cephissiá was the demus of Menander.

At Cephissiá is a grotto, dedicated to the Moirai or Fates, to which the female peasants resort, to learn thence their future destiny, or, as they express it, in order to behold their own Moira.

> At the peak'd Olympus height,
> And at Æther's triple crown;
> Where prophetic sprits hie,
> Hither, airy, gentle Sprite,

Come, I pri'thee, hither down;
Come, O come to me![2]

is one of the fanciful airs which they sing to evoke the spirit on their entrance. It is said, that if a loose fragment should happen to fall from the vault of the grotto, the Moira is believed to be propitious to their prayer.

In our way to Cephissiá a village is visible, which is on the road from Athens to Mount Pentelicus. It is called Garitó: it may correspond with the country of Epicurus, the ancient town of Gargettus, which was certainly in this neighbourhood[3].

A similarity of name is one of the principal clues by which we are now to be guided in detecting an ancient Demus lurking in a modern village. Such resemblances are not rare. The names of the modern villages in this portion of Attica present many interesting reminiscences of their early character and usages. In our return from Cephissiá to Athens we pass the village of Marousi. Marousi preserves in its name a record of the Amarusian Artemis: for an ancient inscription which is inserted in the wall of a church[4] ten minutes to the west of Marousi, informs us that it served to define the limits of the sacred precinct (τέμενος) attached to a temple of that goddess. Again, Pausanias[5] tells us, that the tutelary deity of the village of Athmonum was the Amarusian Artemis. Hence we infer that the Athmonian Demus stood on a site near the modern village of Marousi. The vineyards (ἀμπέλια) which we cross in our way westward perhaps belong to that borough. They suggest an appropriate record of the Athmonian hero of the Aristophanic[6] comedy, the Peace, who there describes himself as Trygæus,

Of Athmonum, a clever Vine-dresser.[7]

It would appear that the Amarusian Artemis was connected with another Artemis, who bore the title of Kolænis. The jeu-d'esprit in the Birds of the same Poet, in which this last Artemis is mentioned[8], seems to intimate that the word ἀκαλανθὶς had then some connection with Κολαινίς. Now, not far from Marousi stands the modern village of Kalandra. The word Καλάνδρα in modern Greek has the same signification with the word ἀκαλανθὶς in ancient. It is in fact the same word. Hence, if we may take it for granted, that the Artemis Colænis was not far from Marousi, and that the modern name of Καλάνδρα is a vestige of the identical ancient ἀκαλανθὶς, attached to the same spot, we are furnished with a local illustration of the expression in Aristophanes, which lends in its turn a support to confirm the positions indicated above.

The title of another Athenian deity survives in the modern appellation of a village which lies between Marousi and Cephissiá. This deity is Hercules. Plato[9] bequeathed, by will, to his son Adeimaiitus a farm which he possessed in this neighbourhood. It lay between these two villages. He describes it in his will as adjacent to the road running to Cephissiá, on the north, and reaching on the south to the Temple of Hercules, or Heracleium, which appertained to the borough of Hephæstia. I have no doubt that the name of this very temple is still surviving in that of a village which we pass to-day in our way between Marousi and Cephissiá, – namely, the village of Haraklí ('Αρακλεῖ).

A little to the south-west of Haraklí is the village of Chalcomatádes (χαλκωματάδες). In the present language of Attica this term has a peculiar meaning, which is here to be noticed. It is a noun substantive plural, and means 'The Workers in brass'. Connected, in ancient times, with the demus of Hephæstia, were the three contiguous demi, which bore in their names the evidence of their near relation to the metalworking Hephæstus. These were the Εὐπυρίδαι, Δαιδαλίδαι, Αἰθαλίδαι[10].

I think that the village of Chalcomatádes preserves still, in its name, the indication of a similar connection with the same deity. Their functions are similar to his: his festival, the χαλκεῖα, was connected with them by name: and his temple has been above shewn to have stood near the site on which the village of Chalcomatádes now stands.

Not far also from this spot was, I believe, the site of one of the most celebrated objects in the ancient topography of Attica. This was the Temple of Pallas of Pallene. Pallene was in a direct line from Marathon to Athens. At Pallene, the sons of Peisistratus[11], marching from Marathon, were met by and repulsed the Alemæonids; at Pallene, they were themselves, on another occasion[12], repulsed by the popular party. Pallene was also, I conceive, on the road by which an invader would come to Athens over the northern passes of Mount Parnes. For, in the popular fable, the body of the Argive Eurystheus[13] was buried at Pallene, in order that it might ward off an Argive invasion from that quarter. Hence it would not be far from Acharnæ: and thus the expression put into the mouth of the Acharnians issuing from Acharnæ,[14] would be very natural and appropriate.

This word was sometimes written Pellene[15]: from this form the temple would be called Πελληνικόν. Perhaps a record of it is still preserved in the name of the modern village of Pellikó[16], which is ten minutes to the east of Marousi, and not far from the site of Hephæstia.

There is an additional reason which confirms me in this supposition, that Pallene was either at or adjacent to this place. I infer that Pallene was near the demus of Hephæstia, from the following circumstance. On the birth of the Athenian king, Ericthonius, Pallas is said[17] to have brought in the air the mountain of Lycabettus from Pallene, and to have dropped it where it now lies, a little to the northeast of Athens, as a bulwark to the Acropolis. The explanation to be given to this legend seems to be this. Pallas comes from Pallene, her own demus: she comes on the occasion of the birth of Ericthonius: now Ericthonius was, according to some traditions, the son of Pallas by Hephæstus. If, therefore, Pallene be near Hephæstia, where I suppose it to have been, Pallas will then come, with her natal gift, from the two demi of the two parents[18]; from the demus of Hephæstus, as well as from her own. Her coming, and from that place, and on that special occasion,– the birth of Ericthonius, – would be rendered more appropriate by that particular circumstance of their proximity.

Another incident confirms me in this conjecture. There was a Corporation[19] of Parasiti attached to the Heracleium, or Temple of Hercules, which stood at Hephæstia. The archives of this Corporation were preserved in the Temple at Pallene. This fact seems to imply a contiguity of these two Temples.

On the whole, the reflection which arises from the result of this investigation is deeply interesting. In accosting any of the villagers whom we may meet in our walk this morning – in speaking with one, for instance, who is now busily employed in gathering his olives from the trees by the way-side, and in making enquiries of him concerning these five neighbouring villages, Marousi, Kalandra, Haraklí, Chalcomatádes, and Pellikó, we have been employing in our intercourse with him the names which have grown out directly from the worship of four pagan deities celebrated among these woods and gardens more than two thousand years ago.

After returning to Athens, I visit the two white knolls which rise from the plain a mile[20] to the north-west of Athens, and gave their name to the demus which stood there – 'the white Kolonus', (ἀργῆτα Κολωνόν[21]). In our way we leave the olive-grove of the Academy[22] on our left. It is still called by the same name as in the time of Plato.

On the two hills of Colonus are two churches. That on the northern hill is dedicated to S. Æmilian, the southern is sacred to the Panagia Eleousa. They are both on the sites of ancient buildings, probably of temples. A little to the west of this point is a chapel of S. Nicolas[23].

What may be the character ascribed to S. Æmilian in the modern Greek hagiographies (or συναξάρια), I am not able to say. But Eleousa is, I am informed, there represented as a saint of much mildness and clemency. This, her name – ἐλεουσα, or 'the merciful', – would import. She is regarded as εὐμενής. As such she has with much propriety succeeded to the Εὐμενίδες of old, who formerly occupied the same spot. S. Nicolas, it is well known, corresponds to the Poseidon of the ancient Greek religion. With these three modern temples in its limits,

> The place entire is holy: here resides
> Awful Poseidon, here the Fire-bearer,
> Here Goddesses, the race of Earth and Darkness[24] –

may still, in some measure, be said of Colonus.

The modern walls of the Athenian city (πύργοι μὲν οἳ πόλιν στέγουσιν), are distinctly visible from this place: so is the site of the Temple of the Furies at the base of the Areopagus, with both which objects the demus of Kolonus is connected in the Œdipus at Colonus of Sophocles. An opinion has been expressed above on some of the circumstances connected with the death of Œdipus, as treated by Sophocles. At Kolonus, the question naturally suggests itself, whether we are to fix here the last scene of the life of Œdipus. Are we to imagine Œdipus as meeting his death at Colonus? I think we are not. Sophocles does not, I think, place the scene of his death here. Yet it is not easy to discover where he does place it, if it is not to be at Colonus.

This ambiguity probably arises from the conflicting traditions which prevailed at Athens on this point. The tomb of Œdipus was shewn to Pausanias[25] in the city of Athens itself, at the foot of the Areopagus, in the precincts of the temple of the Eumenides there. And this was an appropriate position for the body of Œdipus to occupy. For the body was to serve as a defence against an invasion. Being placed at the Areopagus[26], it defended the Acropolis of Athens in the quarter where it was most exposed to the assaults of an invader, namely, on the west.

Still there was strong authority in favour of those who placed the scene of his death and sepulture at Colonus. Sophocles, a native of Colonus, would naturally be tempted to acquiesce in this belief.

Thus he was embarrassed by the claims of a double obligation. The expedient by which he has contrived to satisfy these conflicting demands, and to convert the difficulty itself into a source of poetical beauty, is well worthy of notice.

A few scenes before the close of the play he leaves Œdipus alone. Œdipus, without a guide, goes forth, about to die. But whither he is going the audience are not told. Still, a slight local intimation directs their minds to the site of the Areopagus at Athens. His daughters fetch him some clear water from a spring: the site of this spring is specified: it is at the Temple of Demeter Euchloos[27]; and that temple stood on the ascent at the south-west angle of the Acropolis at Athens. Thus are the minds of the hearers induced, by a gentle suggestion, to suppose Œdipus in the immediate neighbourhood of that spot.

The mention of the compact of Peirithous and Theseus more remotely, of the broken chasm of steep rock, more nearly – for such was the character of the Furies' Temple at Athens – would confirm them in this supposition. Thus did Sophocles endeavour to satisfy the popular belief of those who clung to the opinion, that the body of Œdipus lay interred in that sacred site.

Yet was not the poet faithless to his own native village. Colonus, and the Temple of the Furies there, might still be regarded (and indeed they have been so regarded, and on the direct authority of Sophocles[28],) as the depositories of the same venerable trust. In vain does Antigone conjure Theseus to inform her where the body of her father lies. That is a secret which cannot be divulged. But when her father was seen for the last time by the spectators, he was still lingering at Colonus. The impression therefore might still remain on their minds that he is yet there. No explicit contradiction of the fact is given. He may yet be at Colonus.

Thus was Sophocles involved in an embarrassment arising from the very conditions of the subject which he had chosen; thus has he extricated himself from that embarrassment; and thus has he improved the difficulty itself into a source of mysterious beauty – a beauty singularly appropriate to the dark and awful character of the story which he was handling.

CHAPTER XXXI

Yes, – and it lies beneath a lovely sky.[1]
Incert. *Comic. ap Dio. Chrys.* 1. p. 197.

Athens, Feb. 1.

DIOGENES[2], when he had been exiled from Sinope, migrated into the south of Greece, where he used to spend his summers at Corinth, and his winters at Athens. Corinth he preferred during the warmer season of the year, as standing upon two seas, and ventilated by a double breeze. Corinth also was refreshed by the cool shadows which were flung over it by its broad and lofty citadel, the Acrocorinthus.

But Athens was recommended as a winter-residence by other advantages: it was not overhung by mountains; it was gently fanned by soft and pure airs; it was not subject to be deluged by violent rain; and its dry and light[3] soil speedily absorbed the showers which fell. Diogenes in this respect imitated, as he was wont to say, the habits of the great King of Persia, who moved into Assyria from Media, for the winter months. Athens was the Susa of Diogenes – his Ecbatana was Corinth.

Our own experience would lead us to admire the wisdom of this choice. We returned yesterday to Athens from an excursion to Delphi, having passed through Thebes, Platæa, Leuctra, Haliartus, Lebadeia, and Ambryssus, in our way thither; and through Daulis, Chæroneia, Orchomenus, Lebadeia, Coroneia, Thebes, Delium, and so over the river Asopus, and the passes of Mount Parnes, on our return. The overflowings of the Asopus in the plain of Platæa were then covered with ice, as they were at the time of the siege of that city described by Thucydides. On our way back, the cold was excessively severe: it was, in a word, one of Hesiod's Bœotian winters. On Mount Parnassus we were detained by a snow-storm. The snow was drifting with incessant violence as we passed the Triodos, where Œdipus encountered his father, in our way to the city of Daulis. The hill on which the citadel of Daulis stands was covered with a deep snow: the cold was too severe to allow a transcript to be made even of a few lines of some ancient inscriptions which are found in a ruined church on its summit. We entered Thebes in a snow-storm. It did not abate for several days, and confined us at Thebes in a room with no window – there was not then a pane of glass in the whole of Thebes – for exactly a week. The same cause prevented us from pursuing the ordinary and shortest route from Thebes, that by the pass of Phyle. That passage was completely blocked up by snow. We were therefore compelled to follow the long and circuitous route over the high and open plain on the north of the Asopus, which brought us out on the sea-coast a little to the south of the Euripus.

Thence we followed the shore southward, passing by Delium, and crossing the Asopus, which was then swollen to a formidable stream; and then mounting the acclivities of Mount Parnes. Here however the snow befriended us. For in passing over these heights, at a distance of a few miles to the north-east of Deceleia, our party was waylaid and attacked by two detachments of a large armed troop of the military bandits who at present infest and pillage this province. We owed our escape from that detention by these persons in their mountain-haunts – by which other travellers have suffered, for the sake of a ransom on their release – to the singular inclemency of the season, which rendered their access to these their abodes difficult, and their residence in them impossible.

After an experience of such continued rigorous weather during this excursion, we were much surprised to hear, on our arrival at Athens, that the cold had not been severe in this place; that in the plain of Athens scarcely any snow had fallen, and that none had remained upon the ground. The climate therefore of Attica still may retain the character, which it enjoyed formerly, for this peculiar excellence. And we are therefore far from acceding to the opinion expressed by one of the persons in the following dialogue, which deplores the degenerate state of this lovely and once fortunate country.

> A. *Fairest of all, O Athens! Queen of Cities!*
> B. *Nay, but, my friend, she is no longer Queen.*
> A. *How fair to me thy arsenals appear!*
> B. *Thanks to Lysander, and the Hellespont,*
> *To thee alone –* A. *Peiræus too how fair!*
> B. *You see it then with all its former walls?*
> A. *What land can boast such stately groves as thou!*
> B. *Of yore – which now, for grief she oft has shorn.*
> A. *Yes, and she lies beneath a lovely sky!*
> B. *How, – when she pines with hunger and disease,*
> *And more here perish by the noisome air*
> *Than by the Foeman's sword?*[4]

Nor is there at present any exaggeration to be found in the agreeable picture[5] which was drawn in its better days of the particular features which distinguish the city of Athens from every other in Greece:-

Of the natural properties of Attica, the air possesses superior excellence, as its ports do likewise; besides this, the position of the Acropolis itself, and the loveliness of its circumambient atmosphere, are admirable; for while the atmosphere of all Attica has this character, that especially which hangs over the citadel is the fairest and most pure, so that you might recognize that spot at a distance by the crown of light which encircles it.[6]

CHAPTER XXXII

Hail, Agora of Athens.[1]

Aristoph.

THE Bazaar or Market at Athens is a long street, which is now the only one there of any importance. It has no foot-pavement; there is a gutter in the centre, down which, in this wintry weather, the water runs in copious torrents. The houses are generally patched together with planks and plaster. Looking up the street, you command a view of the commodities with which this Athenian market is now supplied. Barrels of black caviar, small pocket-looking-glasses in red pasteboard cases, onions, tobacco piled up in brown heaps, black olives, figs strung together upon a rush, rices, pipes with amber mouthpieces and brown clay bowls, rich stuffs, and silver-chased pistols, dirks, belts, and embroidered waistcoats, – these are the varied objects which a rapid glance of this street presents to the spectator.

The objects which are not to be found here, as well as those which are, ought not to be neglected in this description. Here there are no books, no lamps, no windows, no carriages, no newspapers, no post-office. The letters which arrived here a few days since from Napoli, after having been publicly cried in the streets, if they were not claimed by the parties to whom they were addressed, were committed to the flames.

Such is the present state of Athens, as far as its streets speak of its condition. This city is still in the hands of the Turks. All the other continental towns of Greece south of Thermopylæ are independent of Turkey. Strange it is that of all the towns of southern

Greece, a distinction of this nature should have been reserved for Athens!

Such however is the case. The Muezzin still mounts the scaffold in the bazaar here to call the Mussulman to prayer at the stated hours; a few Turks still doze in the archways of the Acropolis, or recline while smoking their pipes, and leaning with their backs against the rusty cannon which are planted on the battlements of its walls; the Athenian peasant, as he drives his laden mule from Hymettus through the eastern gate of the town, still flings his small bundle of thyme and brushwood, from the load which he brings on his mule's back, as a tribute to the Mussulman toll-gatherer, who sits at that entrance of the town; and a few days ago the cannon of the Acropolis fired the signal of the conclusion of the Turkish Ramazam – the last which will ever be celebrated in Athens.

Such alterations will probably have occurred within a few years in the general aspect of things in this place, that this description of its appearance at this time will then be perhaps considered as a chapter taken from the fabulous history of Athens, and its condition in a short period be as far removed from its present, as from its ancient state under the old Cecropian monarchs, and at that obscure epoch, when its soil was trodden by the feet of the roving Pelasgi.

CHAPTER XXXIII

In all things, typically Athenian.[1]

Aristoph.

THE arrival of the new King of Greece, which took place at Napoli on the 30th of January, has produced much excitement at Athens. The Athenians propose to send a deputation from Athens to Napoli, to welcome their new monarch to Greece. But who are the particular individuals to be selected as delegates on this embassy, is a question which is now frequently put, and answered in many different ways. Had an embassy been decreed yesterday in the Pnyx, to meet Philip of Macedon at Thermopylæ, there could not be more agitation at Athens than there is now.

For the purpose of settling this question, meetings and counter-meetings have been held by the rival factions into which the political society of Athens is divided: a fray has just occurred in the marketplace, which was attended by bloodshed. The two principal combatants have been since reconciled to one another by the mediation of the Bishop of Athens, who ratifies this work of reconciliation by a religious ceremony provided expressly for such occasions in the Greek Ritual. The existence of such an office[2] in the Greek Liturgy, is a curious evidence of the irritability of the Greek character, which the national religion now, as of old, steps in to mitigate. *I, at the instance of my friends, was reconciled to these persons in the Acropolis, in the presence of witnesses, who reconciled us to each other at the Temple of Minerva there,* – expressions used by an ancient Athenian orator[3] on a similar occasion, might now be used, *mutatis mutandis*, by the political rivals of Athens, of whom we have just spoken.

No better evidence can be given of the miserable jealousies which distract the political parties of modern Athens, than the expressions used by the same Bishop at the conclusion of a public harangue[4] which he delivered a few days ago, (on the 14th of February,) standing at the south side of the low hill on which the Temple of Theseus is placed, on the occasion of the first public dispatch being received at Athens from the new King.

The harangue itself, the occasion of its delivery, the place from which it was delivered, the character of the audience assembled around the speaker, – a Christian Bishop of Athens, – were in themselves objects of no ordinary interest. The Bishop was escorted to the spot with all the civil and ecclesiastical pomp which still survives in this almost exhausted city. He spoke in the open air, although the largest church of Athens, once the Temple of Theseus and now dedicated to St George, was close at hand to admit the audience under its roof, and though it was a winter's day on which he delivered his oration. But, as we noticed before, public life at Athens was and is naturally *hypæthral*.

Some of his audience were standing on the rising ground near him, others sat on the steps of the Temple.

What a change has been wrought in this city, since the supposed relics of Theseus, the old Athenian king, were welcomed by the people of Athens with the sound of poetry and music to this very spot! and how little changed is the Temple, which once witnessed that scene, and now witnesses the present demonstrations of welcome to the New Monarch of Greece! Were this Temple endued with sense how must it marvel at these vicissitudes – how, having beheld that ancient pageant, must it wonder at the ceremony of to-day; how must it be astonished to hear a Bishop of Athens pronouncing that three Powers, England, France, and Russia, countries whose existence it never dreamt of before, have sent hither a King, from a strange and distant land, to be proclaimed to the Athenian people on that self-same spot, which was formerly believed to contain beneath its soil the venerable ashes of Theseus!

CHAPTER XXXIV

It was dangerous to travel by the road leading from the Morea to Athens, since no part of it was clear from the outrages of robbers.[1]

Plut. *Thes. c.* vi.

Oct. 19.

THIS description of the state of the Isthmus of Corinth in the days of Theseus, gives a very correct picture of what it is now. For several months the entrance into the Peloponnesus from Continental Greece has been rendered impassable for travellers, by the violence of the military bandits who now infest the pass. The advice which was then given to Theseus by his mother Æthra is as prudent now as it was then, and for the same reasons. In performing the journey[2] in the reversed direction, we adopt the counsel which she then offered, and avoid the route by land, to choose the passage by sea.

On setting out this morning from the gate of Athens in our way to the Peiræus, we were cautioned by our guides to delay our steps till we had formed a strong party – καλὴν συντροφίαν – to go with us. But a few days ago, two Greeks coming from the Peiræus in the evening were plundered and severely wounded on this road. Such is now the miserable state of this country. If any one requires to learn by a practical lesson what are the results which political disorganization will produce on his own personal freedom and convenience, he has only to spend a week in Greece. To a person who is content to remain stationary in one spot, the embarrassments resulting from this disastrous condition are not trivial; but to one who comes here for the purpose of exploring different districts, the difficulties which it involves cannot be enumerated.

It is no exaggeration to say that he cannot now calculate his future movements by land in any direction whatever, with any confidence, for the space of two days together. It would be regarded here as an act of incredible rashness for a traveller to venture on a ride from Athens to Acharnæ. In the village of Menídi[3] near Acharnæ resides the Greek Captain, Vassos. His soldiers, if they deserve the name, procure for themselves an indemnity for the pay of which they are defrauded, by appropriating to themselves without mercy whatever falls in their way.

By this system of depredation the whole of the province is reduced to beggary. Many of its villages are deserted; their population has quitted them, either to take refuge in the mountains, or to swell the numbers of these depredators, first, as the best means of self-defence, and then, by their own aggressions, to inflict on others the same evils which they themselves have suffered, but which their experience has not taught them to pity, but to transfer.

Another incident of a similar nature may be mentioned to shew that even the immediate neighbourhood of Athens itself is now in such a state, that unattended and leisurely excursions into its environs are difficult and dangerous. The delineation of a chart of Athens and its suburbs was lately commenced by two architects resident here. They were desirous of completing it as expeditiously as possible. Instead, however, of being accomplished, their task has just been abandoned, on account of the insecurity with which they found that, even within sight of the walls of Athens, their researches were attended[4].

CHAPTER XXXV

To Salamis![1]

Solon.

Peiræus, Oct. 19.

ALCIPHRON[2], in one of those imaginary letters which he has written for illustrious correspondents, while addressing himself, in the name of Menander, to Glycera, informs her that he has just declined a pressing invitation to the Court of Alexandria, which he had received from King Ptolemy. The reasons which induced him to do so he details to Glycera, who is supposed to be at Athens, while the poet is writing from the Peiræus.

Nothing, he says, in Ægypt would console him for the loss of those objects which by going thither he would leave behind him at Athens. He derives an argument for his reluctance to leave home from the spot itself where he is writing. There were before his eyes local objects of powerful interest, which he loved to contemplate – scenes of beauty and glory such as no other country could equal, ποῦ γὰρ ἐν Αἰγύπτῳ, – For where in Ægypt, he asks, shall I see such objects as I see here; where else shall I behold *the Eleusinian Mysteries, the neighbouring Salamis…the island of Psyttaleia…in a word, the whole of Greece concentrated in Athens?*[3]

This passage of Alciphron suggests itself for notice here, partly as exhibiting to our view the same objects as meet the eye of the spectator on the shores of the Peiræus, and also as throwing some light on the circumstances of the battle of Salamis, which took place in sight of these shores.

But before it can be assumed to illustrate the circumstances of that event, the passage in question requires some illustration itself. The word ΣTHNA, which occurs there, is corrupt: several emendations have been proposed for it[4], but they are not very successful ones. The true reading is τὰ ΣTENA. The place in which this battle was fought, which crushed the Persian power, could not be more properly or more emphatically designated than by this simple name, *The Straits*.

They were called, by excellence, *the* Straits, as the noblest scene of Athenian valour; and it was to their peculiar *straitness* that the Athenians were indebted for an opportunity of displaying that valour against a hostile force which was there embarrassed by its own magnitude[5].

Hence it was that when the Athenians expressed their grateful acknowledgements to Themistocles, through whose ingenuity and courage the splendid result of the battle of Salamis was realised; they did so on the ground, that he alone...*was the main instrument of the naval conflict's taking place in* THE STRAITS; *a circumstance which clearly saved the cause of Greece*[6].

We pass the night in a small boat in the bay, having spent the afternoon on the shore in exploring the ruins of the town of Salamis, which are seen at Ampelákia, the modern village on the western side of the Strait.

The southern outlet of the Strait is faced by the small island of Psyttaleia. It was on account of this its position that this island was chosen as the post of a detachment of the noblest and bravest of the Persians, who were commanded to intercept the flight of the Greeks from their station in the bay. Here, when instead of pursuing, they were themselves pursued by their antagonists, the principal carnage of the Persians took place.

Psyttaleia is a low and barren islet. Its present name is Lipsokoutáli. This is, I think, a corruption of the older name, which, in the mouth of a Greek, would be pronounced Psyttália. The attempt to give the word some meaning in the modern language[7] produced the present modification of the old name.

It was the spectacle of the slaughter made by the Greeks here which struck the mind of the Persian monarch[8] with so much horror, that he sprung from the silver-footed throne on which he was sitting on the hill-side upon the main-land, sighing deeply at the same time, and tearing his garments in an agony of despair.

A little to the east of this hill is a harbour on the main-land, which retires with a deep inland recess: from this harbour a small Greek vessel is now seen issuing, which is rendered more conspicuous by the dark-red colour of its sails, which are strongly contrasted with the gloominess of the shady creek. This is the only object which is now moving on the Bay of Salamis.

CHAPTER XXXVI

O Mistress Muse,
Come to this much-visited
Dorian island of Ægina. [1]
                             Pindar. Nem. iii. 1.

AT eight o'clock this morning we arrive in the harbour of Ægina. The modern coincides with the ancient port: it is at the north-west angle of the island.

In shape Ægina is an irregular triangle, the north side of which is nearly parallel to the equator; and its other two sides are inclined to the northern at an angle of about 45°. The three most remarkable objects of the island stand at these three angles. At the western, is the site of the ancient port and city. The eastern angle is distinguished by the remains which it possesses of the temple which has obtained such celebrity in Europe, by means of the Æginetan Marbles, which once were attached to its pediments, and are now in the Museum at Munich: and near the southern corner of the island there rises a magnificent conical mountain, which, from its grandeur, its form, and its historical recollections, is the most remarkable among the natural features of Ægina.

Ægina was the eyesore[2] of the Peiræus: its position in the direct line from the emporium of Corinth, to the rich islands of the Archipelago, and thence to the Asiatic ports, furnished it with commercial advantages superior to those of Athens itself. Even its barrenness was of service. It drove the inhabitants of Ægina from tilling their meagre and rocky fields, to plough the ocean as a more fertile soil than that of their own island; and their Doric extraction gave them, on the ground of consanguinity, a claim to the mercantile favour and protection of many thriving marts, where the Athenian trader, for the opposite reason, did not gain so ready an admittance, or so advantageous a reception.

Remains of the maritime power of Ægina may be traced in the harbour where we now are. From its size and beauty it once[3] attracted the admiration of its Athenian neighbours and enemies. The entrance to it is through a narrow opening between the two moles (χῆλαι), which project from the shore, and then converge toward this opening. They terminated in two towers, by which the opening was flanked and protected. That on the left side has been succeeded by a small modern chapel, dedicated to S. Nicolas, the modern Neptune of Greece. There are foundations near the shore of docks and basins, stretching for about a hundred and eighty yards to the north of this harbour and connected with it. Toward the northern extremity of these substructions is the *scala*, or wharf, which leads to the modern Lazaretto: beyond the Lazaretto, in the same direction, are the remains of an ancient Temple. Its foundations are of considerable extent. Of the rest of the building there now only survives a broken shaft of a marble column.

Various dates have been assigned to the erection of this temple. To determine this question, a circumstance otherwise trivial is worthy of notice. The temple has been employed by the modern Æginetans as a quarry, from which they have excavated materials for the construction of buildings, public and private, in the town, to which, unhappily for its own sake, it is immediately contiguous.

In hewing out the masses of the ancient fabric, several blocks of it were found to be inscribed with letters of red chalk, which were still distinctly legible. These blocks were drawn from the lowest foundation of the building; the characters, therefore, which are inscribed upon them, are coeval with the building itself. The following are specimens of these characters, which, from their form, may serve as authentic data for determining the time of the erection of the temple itself. The two names which they exhibit, Prothymius and Euphamides, belonged perhaps to two builders employed in the construction of the fabric.

ΓΡΟΘΥΜΙΟS

ΕΥΦΑΜΙΔΗS

From a comparison of the characters in these inscriptions, with others of which the date is known, it is evident that the foundation of this temple is not of an earlier date than the Peloponnesian War.

Following the coast in the same direction, we find a tumulus on the shore, probably the same which Pausanias[4] saw there, and which he believed to be the work of Telamon, who landed in the neighbouring port, and raised this monument to Phocus. Near it was the Theatre and Stadium, of which no vestiges remain.

Oct. 21.

The beautiful ruin of the Æginetan Temple, at the north-east corner of the island, has been the theme of the general admiration of Greek travellers. It stands on a gentle elevation near the sea, commanding a view of the Athenian coast, and of the Acropolis at Athens, and beyond them of the waving line traced by the mountain ranges of Pentelicus and Hymettus. Its site is sequestered and lonely. The ground is diversified by grey rocks overhung by tufted pines, and clusters of low shrubs, among which goats are feeding, some of them placing their fore feet on the   boughs of the shrubs, and cropping the leaves with their bearded mouths. It is such a scene as this which proves that the religion of Greece knew how to avail itself of two things most conducive to a solemn and devotional effect, namely, Silence and Solitude.

There was perhaps another reason why a site at the distance of eight miles from the city of Ægina was preferred to one in its immediate neighbourhood for the position of this temple.

It is probable that this building did not owe its origin to the exertions of the Æginetans themselves. It has, indeed, by many topographers, been considered as identical with the temple of Jupiter Panhellenius, and even as the same fabric which Æacus, the king of Ægina, erected to that deity.

But not merely does the position of this temple, standing not on a mountain, as that temple did, but on a gentle hill, as well as the character of its architecture, clearly indicate that it is not the Temple of Jupiter Panhellenius;[5] but there is also another and distant site, which can be clearly proved to coincide with that of the Panhellenium.

To whom then was this Temple dedicated? In order to answer this question, let us represent to our minds a picture of the temple in its original state. Let us imagine the groups of sculpture which once stood against the azure ground of its two pediments. They had no doubt an immediate reference to the object of that worship which was paid in the temple itself. In both these groups one figure, that of Minerva, is more prominent than the rest. I should therefore argue that the temple was dedicated to that goddess, and the following circumstance leads to the same conclusion:

In our return to the town of Ægina from the temple, we pass a small Greek church, at the distance of a quarter of an hour to the west of the temple. The spot is called Bilikáda; the church is dedicated to S. Athanasius. The door of the church is surmounted by a large marble slab, inscribed

[HOPOΣ]
TEMENOΣ
ΑΘΕΝΑΙΑΣ

that is, *The limit of the sacred precinct of Minerva*[6]; an inscription which probably once defined the boundary of the consecrated enclosure around this very temple.

That it was dedicated to the Goddess of Athens not by Æginetans, but by the Athenians when in possession of Ægina, may be inferred from the site which it occupies, removed to a distance from the town of Ægina, and looking directly upon Athens. It may be inferred also from the language of the inscription itself; there, it will be observed, the name of the goddess is expressed not in the Doric dialect of Ægina, but, on the contrary, according to the Attic form.

Oct. 22.

We visit to-day the site of the Panhellenium[7]. It was placed on the summit of the conical mountain at the southern angle of the island, which has been noticed as so prominent a feature in the scenery of Ægina. This hill is now called τὸ ὄρος, *The mountain*. The name is derived from the ancient language of Greece; it denotes at the same time that the object which bears it, is the highest mountain in Ægina.

This mountain was an object of great interest to the ancient inhabitants of the island. On its summit Æacus the king of Ægina was believed to have prayed to Jupiter in the name of the whole Hellenic[8] nation for a supply of rain, which was then greatly needed, and which was sent by Jupiter in compliance with his prayer.

I believe the summit of this mountain, called ὄρος, to be the site of the Temple of the Panhellenian Jove (which derived its name from the circumstance above mentioned), upon the following grounds.

The Panhellenium is placed by Pausanias on a mountain (ὄρος): there is no elevation in Ægina which deserves such a title but the present, which bears the express name by which he characterises the site.

The Panhellenian Mountain served, as we know, for a meteorological beacon. If its conical apex was capped with cloud, then rain was expected[9]. This notion prevails still. In this respect the crest of the Æginetan Oros is now to the Ægean mariner what the heights of Roseberry and Belvoir[10] are to the landsmen of Yorkshire and Leicestershire.

The legend of Æacus is doubtless to be connected with this observation. This mountain supplied the first prognostic of the coming shower. Hence Æacus wisely selected this spot as the scene of his supplication to Jove, knowing as he did that the mountain would probably give the first intimation by its clouded summit of the wished-for rain. He perhaps chose for his prayers a moment when such indications were visible. The shower however which followed them was considered by the Hellenic strangers, who were collected in the plain below him, not as a consequence of these intimations, but of his prayers. Thus a coincidence was converted into a cause; and Æacus the King of Ægina became the Son of Jove.

There is another argument to establish the identity of the summit of Oros with the site of the Temple of the Panhellenian Jove.

It is well known to have been the practice of some early Christian Churches to modify the objects of heathen adoration, rather than to destroy them. The stream of Paganism was thus taught to glide into a Christian channel with a soft and easy current. On this principle, when Pagan temples became Christian churches, and deities and heroes were transformed into saints and martyrs, there was generally some analogy, which regulated the transforming process, between the character transformed and that with which it was invested after the transformation. The truth of this assertion may be established on the evidence of numerous examples[11] of this particular process.

From the fact of its common operation I would argue the identity of Oros and the Panhellenium.

The Panhellenian Mount was consecrated in the pagan creed of Ægina by the tradition that Æacus had prayed on its summit, and obtained a shower from heaven in answer to his prayer. The mountain now called Oros has on its vertex a small chapel; its foundations are constructed of huge blocks in a style of very ancient masonry. This chapel is dedicated to the Prophet Elias. A more appropriate successor than Elias could not have been devised in the room of Æacus, to occupy the consecrated fabric standing on this hill.

For while the Pagan might assert, *that Æacus having sacrificed and prayed to Panhellenian Jove caused the rain to fall upon Greece*[12], the Christian assured him, from a much graver authority[13], *that Elias prayed, and the heavens gave rain, and the earth brought forth her fruit.* The foundations therefore which I have just noticed of the small Chapel of Elias, are, I believe, the vestiges of the ancient Temple of Panhellenian Jove.

On the western side of this mountain at its roots are some considerable remains of antiquity. They are probably the vestiges of the peribolus and Temple of Aphaea, the Dictynna[14] of Ægina which Pausanias saw in his way from the city of Ægina to the Panhellenian Mount. A church now stands upon the site of the temple. It is dedicated to Ai Asomatos. An old column was formerly cased in the walls of this church, and now lies on the western side of the building. Engraved upon this column, in the direction of its length, is the following inscription:

```
HOSTOΔΑΛΑΛΜΑΝΕΘΕΚΕ
ΦΙΛΟSTΡΑΤΟS : ΕSTONVMAVTOI
ΠΑΤΡΙ ΔΕ ΤΟΙ ΤΕΝΟ ΔΑΜΟ
ΦΟΟΝ ΟΝVΜΑ
```

that is, in an elegiac distich,

> *Philostratus, who rear'd this votive Stone,*
> *Himself is called; His Sire, Demophoön.*[15]

This inscription affords, I believe, the earliest specimen of the occurrence of Æolo-Doric forms, in a monument of this nature, with the single exception of the Elean inscription.

On returning towards the modern city, we pass a site on the western coast of the island called Marathóna. Here, in the church of S. Michael, is a marble slab, which proves that the temple of Apollo, which Pausanias notices in his description of Ægina, was not far from this spot.

HOPOΣ
TEMENOΣ
ΔΠΟΛΛΩΝΟΣ
ΠΟΣΕΙΔΩΝΟΣ

Boundary of the sacred precinct of Apollo and Neptune.

The temple of Neptune, to which it was contiguous, probably obtained its site here, from its connection with the harbour, now called Pertica, which is about a mile to the north of this spot.

Near this place is a small chapel. Its interior is very gloomy, the light being derived from the door only, (as was usually the case in the old Greek temples,) and from one small lamp which burns dimly near the Sacred Picture by which the chapel is hallowed and adorned. To this picture two hands of tin are attached, evidently intended to be engaged in the act of prayer. Religious worship may still it seems be performed by proxy in Greece, as it was in pagan times.

There is a road of recent construction from the port of Pertica to the town of Ægina: the distance is about three miles. On our arrival there in the evening we find the streets and quay in a state of confusion. A large detachment of *irregular* troops had quartered themselves here, where they are said to have made themselves compensation for the retrenchment of their pay, from the resources of the Greek mint, which is worked at Ægina, as formerly in the age of Pheidon. They have, no doubt, taken care to pay themselves in drachmas of sterling Æginetan weight. A company of Greek *regulars* (τακτικοὶ) has just arrived here, with the view of dislodging the others, who are determined not to retreat. It is supposed, without much appearance of probability – for the regulars are entirely without pay as well as their opponents – that a fray will take place between them: and with a view to prevent a disturbance, an order has been issued that all the inhabitants should immediately retire to their homes.

We embark the next morning for Nauplia.

APPENDIX

I have much satisfaction in being able to communicate to the reader the following details with respect to the recent discoveries made at Athens, and the present condition of that capital, from a letter written by Charles Holte Bracebridge, Esq. which reached me after the preceding sheets had gone to the press.

MY DEAR SIR,

MY answer to your inquiries as to the newly-discovered objects of interest at Athens, will not, I fear, give any high idea of the exertions which have been made, or the success which has rewarded them. Here, indeed, these discoveries are hailed with delight, not only for their own importance, but as the first fruits of a rich harvest; – here, too, where the difficulty of digging down even to the surface of the earth is seen, and the small sums which can be appropriated to research, known, every allowance is made. Nor do we expect, after so many eras of pillage as Athens has passed through, to come at once upon such treasures as have been raised from the remains of a Roman bath or an imperial villa. Yet the antiquities of Athens now under investigation have their great and peculiar interest – they belong to an earlier epoch – and are parts of one great whole. The excavations in the Acropolis, conducted by Dr Ross, have been carried to a depth of twenty or twenty-five feet below the surface of the soil, on the south side of the Parthenon. Venetian casemates and Turkish subterranean galleries have been pierced through, and the foundations of the great temple laid bare on one side, and the Pelasgic walls on the other. It is intended to reduce the ground generally to its original level round the temple, and in this process to move the earth ten or fifteen feet deep. Not only have the vast masses brought for erecting the Parthenon (but unused on account of defects) been found strewn about, but the *workshop* of the Parthenon has been found, that is, drums of columns of Pentelic marble lying in huge masses of chippings of marble, and fragments left by the hammer and the chisel; nay more, some blocks have been discovered which belonged to the old Hecatompedon, and a number of bronze, pottery, and marble fragments, together with *burnt wood*, at a level below the above-named marble chippings, which can be attributed *only* to an era of distinction preceding the erection of the unrivalled fane we now see, namely, the Persian invasion. A very spirited horse's head, in a style intermediate between that of the Egina and Parthenon reliefs, and the relievo of a fish, appear to be undeniable remains of the older temple; and a vast variety of beautiful bronze-work vases, helmets, utensils, little figures, handles of vases, attest the advanced state of the arts at that remote period. I was particularly struck with a bronze Minerva, about ten inches high, finished with all the minute taste of the best specimens from Pompeii. A large collection of terracotta fragments, lamps, vases, and architectural ornaments, was also found at the sub-Parthenon depth, if I may so express it. Among these is a patera of the lightest and finest material, with exquisite figures in dark brown. But the most interesting perhaps of these remains are the painted figures and heads, (some of which retain their colours, and represent the Greek costumes of this day,) and especially the fragments of columns, triglyphs, and capitals, which still retain their original colours, blue, red, and the brightest ultra-marine. The capital in the Theseum, and many vestiges about the Erectheum, show that the temples were in part coloured, but no proof has been given, before the discovery of these primitive Attic remains, that bright and highly contrasted colours were used generally on marble edifices. On the edge of a fragment of a vase, taken from the lowest pit, I remarked in very ancient characters the word ΑΘΕΝΑΙΑΣ. Six pieces of the frieze, three of which are well preserved, are now only seen about the Parthenon: two of them seem to be the work of inferior artists, but one (the subject of which is two priests and an assistant leading two bulls to sacrifice) is a relief equal to any of those of which the Parthenon has been plundered. One only of the metopes, a most spirited piece, is to be found, except the much injured ones still in their places.

The great discovery of the day is the long lost temple of the Wingless Victory, seen by Wheler, and subsequently blown up and enclosed in a Turkish bastion. It is not of the Doric order, as that traveller asserts, but of beautiful Ionic, the columns about fifteen feet high, and fluted: four columns stand on the front, and four on the back; the sides of the cella being in line with the external columns. The whole is of Pentelic marble, and finely finished: the position is exactly that specified by Pausanias, on the S.W. angle of the Acropolis, on the right as you ascend to the Propylæa, turning the S.W. wing of which this exquisite little temple fronts. Parts of all the columns of the Victory have been found, several entire with their capitals, and these, with the walls of the cella, and most of the entablatures have been replaced, and will have a grand effect as soon as the scaffolding is removed. The reliefs of its frieze are very bold and spirited, and tolerably preserved: the subjects are supposed to be the Athenian victory over the Amazons, and that over the Persians at Marathon. Nearly the whole frieze has been found, except the two pieces in the British Museum. Two very fine pieces of relief, about three feet high, have been found near the Victory Temple: they do not appear to have belonged to it – the subject is a bull led by three winged victories.

The Erectheum has not yet been opened, nor has the base of the great statue of Minerva been sought for; but between these points the passage and steps cut in the rock has been laid open, which led from the Acropolis to the city through the grotto of Aglauros, through which subterranean passage the canephoræ bore the sacred baskets from Minerva Polias to the gardens of Venus.

Within a very few weeks two sarcophagi have been discovered near the modern mint, which have excited much interest. They are not of the first style of art, but yet possess bold and elaborate relief; the one wreaths and lions' heads – the other, two lions drinking from a vase, and a Bacchanal of dancing infants. A skeleton was found in the former, which is thought to belong to the early Christian æra. A third sarcophagus found in the same neighbourhood contains three objects of great interest; a sistrum, an incense-box, and a vase, all of silver. The vase is about ten inches high, and resembles a cream-jug of the last century; the box is octagonal, and about four inches diameter. The owner of these objects has very naturally been named a priest of Isis, and consequently but a modern among the ancients.

The mint above mentioned (which, after all, is not to be a mint, but a bank, it is said), with the royal stables, a hospital, and a barrack, are the only public buildings of consequence yet erected; but the new palace, the foundation-stone of which was laid by the King of Bavaria two months since, is the object of first attention among the modern improvements. No less than three sites had been previously fixed on, much to the dismay of successive speculators in land; this last, however, seems by general assent allowed to be the best; and the actual building of the palace has placed the minds of landed proprietors and street-projectors at ease on the subject. The spot chosen is just without the old Bobonistra Gate, where the inscription to Hadrian remains, in a line between Lycabettus and the Parthenon, and on an eminence overlooking the town, the Hymettian chain, and the gulf. The front of the building, which is to be adorned by a portico, faces the Acropolis, that is, is about S.S.W. Gardens and a square are to connect the palace with the town. The plan, which embraces two quadrangles, is handsome and commodious, without being extravagant. Nor are the Athenians the less pleased with it because it is to be executed at the King's private expence. The King of Bavaria is said to have contributed munificently; to him, indeed, and to his talented architect, Professor Gartner, the whole honour of the palace belongs. Many large houses have been erected within the last year, and buildings are going on with such spirit that the price of ground in good situations far exceeds the sum which could have been calculated on: £300 was lately given for about half an acre, and an adjoining piece has just been sold at the rate of £1200 or £1300 an acre. This is at a distance from the commercial streets, where enormous prices are obtained for the square yard of frontage-ground. Three great streets have been some time since opened – the Adrian, Athena, and Æölus street – all of which now assume a regular appearance; and though the dilatory system of some parties, and want of zeal and funds to overcome difficulties, has as yet prevented the opening of many of the minor communications, yet an attentive observer remarks the huge masses of grey walls and rubbish disappear by little and little, crooked encumbered lanes become straight, and wherever two or three good houses are built, walls are thrown back, and a street of twenty feet wide appears. The style of building is rather modern German than any thing else: neither the picturesque (and in this climate agreeable) Turkish house nor the Italian colonnade is seen; happily the English red brick is also absent. The solidity of the walls of rough limestone, which are carried only two stories high, compensates in some measure for the rough manner in which they are finished. Many of the common houses are built after the Constantinople fashion – an upper story of wood-work filled up by dried bricks on a basement of broad stone walls. On the whole, considering the necessary want of funds, taste, good practical architects, and workmen who have any knowledge at all, the appearance of the new buildings is highly creditable. I should have mentioned before, that the walls of the old town were pulled down last spring, which gives the place a much better appearance. The town is now spread out in a fan-shape to the north of the Acropolis, and its diameters may be a mile and a mile and half: the population probably does not yet exceed 15,000. One peculiarity of Athens is the number of its churches, which are said to exceed 300; with few exceptions they are in ruins. Such a fine opportunity for making open and planted squares will, I trust, not be lost, when the dispute between the municipality and the government as to the right of property of these churches shall have been settled. The supply of water brought into the town by the ancient aqueducts is abundant and excellent. When the town advances, no doubt many useful and beautiful Mountains will vie with those of Rome or Naples. At present the Turkish fountains only are used; and as the Hymettian and Pentelican quarries of marble have not yet been re-opened, it may be as well that no attempt should be made at present to adorn the Grecian city in this respect. In connection with modern Athens I must not omit Piræus, where several large houses are built: some good streets, flanked by low but respectable dwellings, have already been completed. A large custom-house has been built, and a quay and lazaretto are in immediate contemplation, the population may be about 1,500. The trade cannot be said to flourish at the Piræus, yet it has become a bustling place. Besides the small coasting vessels which crowd the harbour, four or five brigs and as many schooners are generally at anchor in the ancient Aphrodisian port. Four or five men-of-war frequently lie in the Piræus together, nor is any great difficulty found in such heavy frigates as the American Constitution or the British Portland in passing the narrow entrance where the Lions, now at Venice, crowned the pier-heads. The vestiges, considered those of the Salaminian trophy and sarcophagus of Themistocles, still give interest to the outer point, and on the next (inwards) the remains of the famous Admiral Miaulis are laid. A most interesting ceremony took place on the occasion of his obsequies, and a national monument is to be erected over the remains of this modern Themistocles.

The little dock-yard at Poros, is in a promising state: eight or ten small vessels and gun-boats are in commission, and form excellent *guardacostas*. A change of ministers has lately taken place, and all the offices are not yet disposed of: most of the *employés* are Greeks, and there is every reason to hope that a public system of business will be adopted, which may prevent intrigues and overcome jealousies which much injure this country. Nor will, I conceive, the decrees, which have been, from their non-efficiency, the ridicule of every one, be persisted in. The great difficulty is to obtain here practical results rapidly; while some diplomats write "rapports" and orders; the Greeks talk and promise; both seem equally averse from *doing*. Of all the difficulties with which the Government have to contend, that of not having obtained a moral influence from the high principle and worthy intentions of its "personnel," is what strikes an Englishman most. The courts of justice are, it is said, well filled by Greeks, who are learning to act on the code of Maurer, and the trial by jury is conducted with regularity and efficiency, and is becoming popular.

Though the capital is of course infested by the low and vicious population of many nations, which is never wanting in such towns in the country, peace and security may be said to reign; the peasantry enjoy their possessions in quietness, and have been gradually improving their condition; the want of capital among proprietors has been a great cheek to this. Nevertheless, one enters no village where either fresh land has not been brought into cultivation, or vineyards planted. When the National Bank, which is to be put in action by an English Company in two months, has supplied capital on landed security, agriculture must advance rapidly; but it is much to be wished that the judgment and experience of foreigners were called in to assist, and the richer productions aimed at. I have seen most of the richer parts of Greece, and have been lately over the lovely and fertile island of Eubœa, where nature seems to have united the forests, snows, and waters of Switzerland, to the richness and variety of Greece. From the inquiries I have made, and the experience of some most intelligent resident gentlemen, Greek and foreign, I am convinced that a well-educated Englishman may lay out his capital there, to greater advantage than in Canada or Australia; he may live on his estate, and make ten per cent. on it immediately, and if he buys with judgement, will have every prospect of very shortly doubling that amount of interest. An English farmer will prefer places where his language is spoken, but for an educated young man, who can learn Greek, and feels some interest in the beauty, history, and climate of Greece, as well as the intelligent society of the capital, (which is within easy reach from any part of that island) who is willing to attend to the details of land-management, and can feel enjoyment from extent of domain, I must say, that such a one emigrating, with a capital not less than £1500 or £2000 has every prospect of a happy and useful life here, and with (as it seems to me) fewer sacrifices than he would have to make in Canada. Notwithstanding all delays in her path, I can only see for Greece success in the future. However great the difficulties of her government, and the inferiority of her situation, compared with European states, yet we cannot forget how rapid and how great has been her rise, not only from slavery, but a war of destruction, and then we shall more fairly judge of her powers for happiness. The paltry rebellion, near Missolonghi, which never boasted of more than

300 men, has been put down by the light troops sent there, and the robbers on the Turkish frontier have received some severe cheeks and well-deserved punishment for the blackmail they collected in the winter.

We have just bought the ground for the Protestant chapel, but in consequence of the delay in the business we shall now defer till autumn the erection of the building. By then I trust we shall have completed our subscription, and be enabled to demand the government-money. The Protestant cemetery on the Ilissus has lately been completed and planted with cypresses. You will have ere this received Pittachi's book by Mrs Hill, who is gone alone to America on the business of the Mission. Mr Hill* is well, and desires to be remembered to you; his schools are flourishing.

Believe me, my dear Sir,

Very truly yours,

C. H. BRACEBRIDGE

Athens, *April* 25, 1836.

* The author of this volume cannot allow the names of Mr and Mrs Hill to appear on this page without at the same time recording his obligations to them. It was to their kindness at Athens in 1833, at a time and in a place which offered little prospect of such good offices, that he was indebted for the alleviation of an illness which was the consequence of his journey into Bœotia and Phocis, during a winter of remarkable severity.

ENDNOTES

Chapter I

[1] A Chalcide Aulidem trajicit, inde Oropum Atticæ ventum est; ubi pro Deo vates antiquus colitur; Athenas inde plenas quidem et ipsas vetustate famæ, multa tamen visenda habentes, Arcem, Portus, Muros Peiræeum urbi jungentes, navalia magnorum Imperatorum, Simulacra Deorum hominumque.

[2] Works and Days, v. 649.

[3] Εὔριπος is in the mouth of a modern Greek pronounced ῎Evrĭpos; from Evripos comes ῎Egripos; from Egripos, 'N῎Egripon, (in the accusative case, as from Ἀβαρῖνος comes Navarino, the στὸ or εἰς τὸ being suppressed), and from Negripon, by aid of its bridge, we arrive at the modern name of Eubœa, Negro-*ponte*. This prefix of the article with the preposition (*i.e.* εἰς τὸ, &c.) deserves notice, as the cause of topographical difficulties. In the Greek Synecdemus of Hierocles (p. 646) we have a list of Ægean islands. There the mention of Eubœa is soon followed by that of other islands, Δῆλος, ΣΚΥΡΟΣ, ΤΑΛΑΜΕΝΕ. On which Wesseling observes, "Ταλαμένη ex Σαλαμὶς νῦσος orta videtur." Such is his conjecture. But the corrupt word is probably nothing else than ΣΤΑ ΛΙΜΕΝΙ, (*i.e.* ἐς τὰ λιμένια, *The harbours*), or Staliméni, which is the modern name of *Lemnos*. Then the combination of the islands in Hierocles becomes a very appropriate one: it is precisely the same, and in the same order, as that in Euripides (Troad. 89):

– Δήλιοί τε χοιράδες
Σκῦρός τε Λῆμνός τε......

– *The Delian cliffs,*
Scyros and Lemnos.

[4] The bridge over the Euripus was built by the Bœotians B.C. 410. (Diod. Sic. xiii. 47). If Plutarch be right in doubting the genuineness of the passage ascribed to Hesiod above, that passage is at least older than this date.

[5] Now corrupted to Cavo d'oro, (the golden cape).

[6] ὅτ' ἐς Αὐλίδα νῆες 'Αχαιῶν ἠγερέθοντο, &c. (Iliad ii. 303).

[7] Eurip. Iphig. Aul. 120:

— Αὐλιν ἀκλύταν
τὰν κολπώδν πτέρυγ' Εὐβοίας.

— *where Aulis spreads her waveless bay,*
The unruffled pinion of the Euboic shore.

[8] Strabo, p. 403. C. In his route from Oropus to Chalcis: After Delium, he says, is the great harbour which they call the *Deep* harbour. Λιμὴν μέγας, ὃν καλοῦσι βαθὺν λιμένα. εἶθ' ἡ Αὐλις, πετρῶδες χωρίον, λιμὴν δ' ἐστι πεντήκοντα πλοίοις, ὥστε εἰκὸς τὸν ναύσταθμον τῶν Ἑλλήνον ἐν τῷ μεγάλω ὑπάρξαι λιμένι.

[9] Pausan. ix. 19. 8. ἄνθρωποι ἐν Αὐλίδι οἰκοῦσιν οὐ πολλοὶ γῦς δέ εἰσιν οὗτοι κεραμεῖς. There are few inhabitants in Aulis, and these are potters.

[10] Αὐλις is derived from αὐλὸς (canalis), of which it is a feminine form, and is the same word as the Latin *Vallis*.

[11] Liv. xlv. 27.

[12] Delium could not have stood at Dramise: for Delium was only five miles from Tanagra (Liv. xxxv. 51), and ten stadia from Delium placed the Athenians *just on the Oropian frontier*, (μάλιστα ἐν τοῖς μεθορίοις τῦς 'Ωρωπίας. Thuc. iv. 91.) Hence in Strabo's assertion, Δήλιον Αὐλίδος διέχον σταδίους τριάκοντα, *Delium distant from Aulis thirty stadia*, for the number λ' (*i.e.* ρ') 30, should probably be substituted ρ' or 100.

[13] Thuc. iv. 92. τὸν Βοιωτίαν (οἱ Ἀθηναῖον) ἐκ τῦς ὁμόρου ἐλθόντες,τεῖχος (ἐν Δηλίῳ) ἐνοικοδομησάμενοι, μέλλουσι φθείρειν. *The Athenians, having marched from the border-land, and erected for themselves a fortress at Delium, intend to ravage Bæotia.*

[14] B.C. 424.

[15] δέκα σταδίους. Thuc. iv. 90.

[16] λόφος. Thuc. iv. 96.

[17] ῥύακες. Thuc. iv. 96.

[18] Plutarch de Socrat. Dæmon. 581. 32. Πυριλάμπης ὁ Ἀντιφῶντος ἁλοὺς ἐν τῇ διώξει περὶ Δήλιον, ὡς ἤκουσε τῶν ἐπὶ τας σπονδας ἀφικομένων Ἀθηναίον ὅτι Σωκράτης μετὰ Ἀλκιβιάδου καὶ Λάχητος ἐπὶ ΡΗΤΙΣ ΤΗΣ καταβὰς ἀπονενοστήκοι, πολλὰ μὲν τοῦτον ἀνεκαλέσατο, πολλὰ δὲ φίλων τινὰς, οἷς συνέβη

μετ' αὐτοῦ παρὰ τὴν Πάρνηθα φεύγουσιν ἀποθανεῖν. Müller (Orchomenos, p. 491) for the corrupt words ΡΗΤΙΣ ΤΗΣ proposes ΡΕΙΤΟΥΣ (ῥειτοὶ are ῥωγμοὶ. Hesych. in v., and identical with the ῥύακες described as existing here by Thucydides). Plutarch probably wrote ΡΕΙΤΟΙΣ ΤΙΣΙ. The confusion arose from the modern pronunciation in which the sounds of ῥητίστης and ῥειτοῖς τις are identical.

[19] Alcibiades and Laches. Plat. Sympos. 231. A. and with Xenophon. Strabo. 403. C.

Chapter II

[1] Ἐντεῦθεν (ἐξ Ὠρωποῦ) εἰς Τανάγραν στάδια ρλ'. ὁδὸς δὶ ἐλαιοφύτου καὶ συνδένδρου χώρας, παντὸς καθαρεύουσα τοῦ ἀπὸ κλωπῶν φόβου.

[2] *Route from Oropus to Tanagra:*

	H.	MIN.
viii.		10. Oropus.
		35. Cross Asopus. Sycamino. Road is along left bank of Asopus.
		43. Follow a path to r.
		46. Ascend. Pines.
ix.		19. Descend into a small plain. The Asopus is seen turning l. through a fine woody chasm. Platans.
		35. Ascend. View of plain. Road and River turns r. Βαλανίδα trees.
		7. Vestiges. Mount Kakó Shállesi and Parnes behind it l. Pass along plain between low hills.
x.		14. Pyrgo of Staniáti 20 min. r.
		20. Bridge over Asopus 2 min. l. Well 5 min. l. Church 7 min. l.
		25. Cross stream Larí running into Asopus from r.
xi.		10. Tanagra.

[3] Literally 'a clean road,' an expression used as ὁδὸς καθαρεύουσα in Dicæarchus.

[4] See an example in Zoega Bassirilievi. T. ii. p. 239.

[5] Candida dividuâ colla tegente comâ. OVID.

[6] Γραῖμα in romaic is derived from γραίνω (*i.e.* ἐκραίνω) to moisten or bathe, and has thus a similar signification to Τέναγος, a *marsh*, with which Τανάγρα is probably connected, being placed

       – ἔνθα πεδίον Ἀσωπός ῥοαῖς
       ἄρδει.
                 Æschyl. Pers. 791.

[7] Pausan. ii. 20.

[8] Γεφυραῖοι.

⁹ Paus. ii. 20. ὄρος Κηρύκιον ἔνθα Ἑρμῆν τεχθῆναι λέγουσι.

¹⁰ Strabo, 410. Β. Νυνὶ Θεσπιαὶ μόνη συνέστηκε τῶν Βοιωτικῶν πόλεων καὶ Τανάγρα.

¹¹ Pausan. ix. 22. 3. Κόριννα......γυναικῶν τότε δὴ καλλίστη τὸ εἶδος, εἴ τι δὴ εἰκόνι δεῖ τεκμαίρεσθαι......ἣ μόνη δὴ ἐν Τανάγρᾳ ᾄσματα ἐποίησε.

¹²   Ταναγρίδεσσι λευκοπέπλοις·
    μέγα δ' ἐμὴ γέγαθε πόλις
    λιγουροκωτίλης ἐνοπῆς·

where these three Glyconics are preceded by a fourth,
    καλὰ γεροια εἰσομένα.
Which should perhaps be written
    καλὰ γὰρ οἶδ' ἀεισομένα
(*i.e I know that I shall sing pleasing strains.*) To white-stol'd, &c.
    Ταναγρίδεσσι λευκοπέπλοις

¹³ 'Ελατί is the present name of Mount Cithæron, derived from the silver-firs (ἔλαται) which grow there. Hence Euripides very properly places Pentheus on an ἐλάτι, whence he observes the Bacchæ on Mount Cithæron. (Eur. Bacch. 750. 1070. 1090).

¹⁴ Strabo. 405, c. ἔστι τῆς τετρακωμίας τῆς περὶ Τανάγραν, Ελεῶνος, Ἅρματος, Μυκαλησσοῦ, φηρῶν.

¹⁵ Pausan. ix. 22. 3. Ταναγραῖοι νομίσαι τὰ ἐς τοὺς Θεοὺς μάλιστα (qu. μάλλιστα, i.e. κάλλιστα) δοκοῦσιν Ἑλλήνων. χωρὶς μὲν γὰρ αἱ οἰκίαι σφισιν, δὲ τὰ οἱέρὰ ὑπὲρ αὐτὰς ἐν καθαρῷ τε ἐστὶ καὶ ἐκτὸς ἀνθρώπων.

¹⁶ This inscription has been already very accurately copied by Colonel Leake, and published by him in the Museum Criticum, ii. 570, whence it is reprinted in Rose Inscript. Gr. Vet. p. 308; Boeck. Corp. Ins. n. 1582; and Welcker Inscr. Syllog. p. 203. It is therefore not inserted here. The only variations supplied by my transcript are, line 1. ΑΝΕΘΕΚΕ. 5. ΣΤΕΦΑΝΩ (cf. Dissen. Pindar. Pyth. ii. 6). 9. ΔΙΟΥΣΚΟΠΙΔΑΝ.

Chapter III

¹ Οὗτοι δ' εἰσὶν συοβοιωτοὶ κρουπεζοφόρων γένος ἀνδρῶν

² Aristoph. Acharn. 851.

³ Acharn. 868.

⁴ αὐλησεῦντι δὲ οἱ δύο ποιμένες, εἷς μέν 'Αχαρνεύς.   Theocrit. vii. 7.

⁵ They are principally sepulchral.

(1)	(2)	(3)
ΖΩΣΙΜΗ	ΒΟΥΛΑΡΧΗ	ΖΩΣΙΝΙΚΟΣ
ΑΝΤΙΟΧΟΥ	ΑΡΙΣΤΑΡΧΟΥ	ΚΑΛΟΞΕΝΟΥ

In the church of S. George on a marble sun-dial is:

ΙΑΣΟΝ ΙΑΣΟΝΟΣ
ΑΖΗΝΙΕΥΣ ΑΝΕΘΗΚΕ

⁶ Aulus Gellius, vii. 14.

⁷ 'Απόστολα πλοῖα (see Plato Epist. vii). The ἀπόστολοι were superintended by officers called 'Αποστολεῖς.   Harpocrat in v.

⁸ Hence I would propose to reconcile the discrepancies in the estimate of the distance from Oropus to Tanagra noticed above, p. 7, see below, p. 14.

⁹ Thuc. iii. 91. He speaks of *sailing* to, and *anchoring at*, Oropus: ἐκ τῆς Μήλου ἔπλευσαν εἰς 'Ωρωπὸν τῦσ πέραν γῆς, εὐθὺς δὲ σχόντες –viii.95. ἐκ τοῦ 'Ωρωποῦ ἀπήγαγε τὰς ναῦς. Pausanias, i. 34, places it on the coast.

¹⁰ B.C. 402, by the Bœotians. Diodor. xiv. 17.

¹¹ Diczearchus, p. 12. ἡ πόλις 'Ωρωπίον ΟΙΚΙΑ Θηβῶν ἐστιν, μεταβολέων ἐργασία,...τελωνοῦσι πάντα τὰ μέλλοντα πρὸς αὐτοὺς εἰσάγεσθαι· τραχεῖς ἐν ταῖς ὁμιλίαις. On comparing this character with the *very similar* one which Dicæarchus gives to the Thebans (p. 15), whom the Oropians strove to imitate (p. 12), I suspect he wrote, instead of the unintelligible ΟΙΚΙΑ, ἡ πόλις τῶν 'Ωρωπίον CKIA Θηβῶν ἐστιν, *The city of Oropus is the fac-simile of Thebes* (σκιὰ Θηβῶν). Of the confusion between αἰκίν and σκιὰ, in this sense of σκιὰ, see Bentley Phalaris, p. 137, on λόγος ἔργου σκιά. In Andocides (p. 112. Bekker) for ὑπὸ τὴν σκιὰν, the best MS. has ὑπὸ τὴν οἰκίαν.

Chapter IV

¹ Πᾷ μοι ταὶ ΔΑΦΝΑΙ

² iii. p. 235. Chap. xxxiv. Nous partimes d'Athènes dans les premiers jours du mois Munychion. Nous arrivâmes le soir même à Orope, par un chemin assez rude, mais ombragé en quelques endroits *de bois de lauriers*.

³ Dicæarch., p. 11, thus rendered by all the editors. εἰς 'Ωρωπὸν διὰ ΔΑΦΝΙΔΩΝ καὶ τοῦ 'Αμφιαράου Διὸς ἱεροῦ ὁδὸς ἐλευθέρῳ βαδίζοντι σχεδὸν ἡμέρας πρόσαντα.

⁴ See Colonel Leake's very valuable Memoir on the Demi of Attica, p. 201 (in Transactions of Royal Soc. of Lit. Vol. i.). The inscriptions are now in the British Museum, Nos. 368, 378.

⁵ Where games were celebrated in his honour. In Philemon Lexicon Technolog. p. 42. (ed. Burney) πολλοὶ ἄγονται ἀγῶνες· ἐν Λεβαδεία τὰ καλούμενα Ἐρώτεια, βασίλεια, καὶ Τροφώνεια, ἐν δὲ Ὠρωπῷ τὰ Ἀμφίκαια– the last word should be written Ἀμφιαρᾶια. See Schol. Pind. Ol. vii., 154.

⁶ Kruse also (Hellas. ii. p. 283) speaks of this country as being "einer Gegend, wo der weisse lehmichte Boden, den schon *Diecæarch.* bemerkte, *Lorbeerbäume* auf der Hohen ernährte."

⁷ Herodot. ix. 73. λέγουσι τοὺς Δεκελέας κατηγήσασθαι ἐπὶ τὰς Ἀφίδνας.

⁸ Thuc. vii. 28. ἐκ τοῦ Ὠρωποῦ κατὰ γῆς διὰ τῆς Δεκελείας.

⁹ In the passage of Herodotus, for ΑΦΙΔΝΑΣ, the Sancroft MS. has exactly the same error, ΑΦΝΙΔΑΣ. This word has been singularly fruitful in this confusion. In Demosth. 238. 17. for Ἀφίδναν Bekker's MSS. S.Q.O. u have Ἀφνίδα, and F.Y. p. v. give Ἄφνιδα: again in Plutarch Thes. c. 32. and in Harpocrat. v. Θυργωνίδαι was written for Ἀφιδναῖος before the edition of Valesius.

¹⁰ Thuc. vii. 19, cf. vii. 18. 27. vi. 93.

¹¹ Cp. Müller's Dorians, i. p. 172.

¹² Plutarch. Sympos. i. qu. x. Whence the peculiar propriety of the reference to their examples in the speech of Miltiades before the battle of Marathon to the General Callimachus, who was an *Aphidnæan.*   Herod. vi. 109.

¹³ Hesych. in. v. Περρίδαι.

¹⁴ Steph. Byz. v. Τιτακίδαι Cp. Herod. ix. 73, where Helen is *discovered* at Aphnidnæ to the Tyndaridæ by Decelus (f. δείκω) of Deceleia, and Aphidnæ is betrayed to them by *Titacus* the indigenous monarch (τίταξ, βασιλεὺς Hesych.) of the Titacidæ. The modern village of *Tatoi* may preserve in its name a vestige of this demus.

¹⁵ There may indeed be some verbal connexion between Mount Barnaba and Parnes (Πάρνηθα accus.) on the one hand, and Tirlos or Trilos and on the other.

¹⁶ Plato. Critia. iii. c. πολλὴν ἐν τοῖς ὄρεσιν ὕλην εἶχεν.

¹⁷ The dimensions are: Tower 24 ft. square: greatest height about 30ft. The door at bottom 5 ft. 3 in.: at top 4 ft. 2 in. Windows 2 ft. broad at top. The lintel of the door 8 ft. in length.

Chapter V

¹ Ἐν ταῖς οἰκίαις ἦσαν αἶγες, ὄϊες, βόες, ὄρνιθες καὶ τὰ ἔκγονα αὐτῶν. τὰ δὲ κτήνη πάντα χιλῷ ἔνδον ἐτρέφετο· ἦσαν δὲ καὶ πυροὶ καὶ κριθαὶ ἐν τοῖς κρατῆρσι — ταύτην μὲν οὖν τὴν νύκτα διασκηνήσαντες οὕτως ἐκοιμήθημεν.

² πάπλωμα, i.e πέπλωμα serving for the same uses as the ancient στρώματα.

³ The supplementary or conjectural portion in this and following inscriptions, is distinguished from the rest by square brackets.

[ΨΗΦΙΣΜΑ ΤΗΣ]
ΒΟΥΛΗΣ
ΚΑΙ ΤΟΥ ΔΗΜ[ΟΥ ΤΩΝ]
[ΡΑΜΝΟ]ΥΣΙΩΝ ΗΡΩΔΗΣ ΒΙΒΟΥ[Λ]
[ΛΙΟΝ] ΠΟΛΥΔΕΥΚΙΩΝΑ ΙΠΠ[ΕΑ ΑΝΕΘΗΚΕΝ]
[ΕΚ ΤΩΝ ΙΔ]ΙΨΝ Ο ΘΡΕΨΑΣ ΚΑΙ ΦΙ[Λ]
ΗΣΑΣ ΩΣ ΥΙΟΝ ΤΗ ΝΕΜΕ
[ΣΕΙ]Η ΜΕΤ ΑΥΤΟΥ Ε[Θ]ΥΕΝ ΕΥ[ΜΕ]
ΝΗ ΚΔΙ ΑΙΜΝΗΣΤΟΝ ΤΟΝ
[ΕΑΥΤΟΥ ΤΡΟ]ΦΙΜΟΝ

That is, adopting the proposed additions,

ψήφισμα τῆς
βουλῆς
καὶ τοῦ Δήμου τῶν
Ραμνουσίων· Ἡρώδης Βιβούλ–
λιον Πολυδευκίωνα ἱππέα ἀνέθηκεν
ἐκ τῶν ἰδίων, ὁ θρέψας καὶ φιλ–
ήσας ὡς υἱόν, τῇ Νεμε–
σει, ᾗ μετ' αὐτοῦ ἔθυεν, εὐ–
μενῆ καὶ ἀίμνηστον τὸυ
ἑαυτοῦ τρόφιμον...

Compare Boeck Corp. Ins. n. 995. Of this Polydeuces the τρόφιμος of Herodes, see Philostrat. Vit. Sophist. ii. 1. 10, Πολυδεύκην καὶ Μέμνονα ἴσα γνησίοις ἐπένθησε τροφίμους ὄντας; and an inscription found as Cephissià near another villa of Herodes, (Marm. Oxon. lx); and that copied by Fourmont, Boeck Inscr. n. 992, of Vibullius. See the observation of Boeck n. 995.

⁴ The singular story of the Parian origin and Persian transport of the marble block from which the statue of Nemesis was made, rests on the single authority of Pausanias (i. 33. 2). It has therefore been suspected. Did the error arise from the circumstance that Paros was not the native country indeed of the statue, but was the supposed sculptor, Agoracritus? Tzetz. Chil. vii. 930.

Φειδίας ἀγαλματώσας κάλλιστα Φειδιακῇ τῇ τέχνῃ
τὸ ἐν Ραμνοῦντι ἄγαλμα Νεμέσεώς Διός τε
ἐκεῖνο ἀνατίθησιν ἐπιγραφὴν χαράξας
'Αγορακρίτου ἄγαλμα τοῦτό ἐστιν Παρίου.

⁵ Kruse Hellas. Attica. cap. vi. p. 278. Compare Unedited Antiquities of Attica, published by the Society of Dilettanti, p. 42.

⁶   ΝΕΜΕΣΕΙ
        ΣΩΣΤΡΑΤΟΣ
        ΑΝΕΘΗΚΕΝ.

That on the *left* is inscribed thus,

        ΘΕΜΙΔΙ
        ΣΩΣΤΡΑΤΟΣ
        ΑΝΕΘΗΚΕΝ.

⁷ Demosthen. 197. 21 εὑρήσετε τὸν βασιλέα τὴν πόλιν διὰ Λακεδαιμονίων ἀσθενῆ ποιήσαντα.

⁸ ἐν γὰρ ὄρει ῥαμνοί τε καὶ ἀσπάλαθοι κομόωντι. From ῥαμνόεις,–οῦς. Compare the remark of Schol. Aristoph. Plut. 586 on the similar botanical names of the Attic Demi Μυρρινοῦς, Ἀγνοῦς, &, to which may be added Φηγοῦς, Ἀχραδοῦς, Ἀναγυροῦς, and Ἐλαιοῦς. The modern name of Rhamnus is Ὀβριὸ–Καστρο, for Ἐβραῖο–Κάστρο, Jews-Castle. (See Koray. Ataka, i. p. 55. λέγουν Ὀβριὸς ἀντὶ τοῦ Ἑβραῖος, as ὀχθρὸς for ἐχθρὸς, ὄξω for ἔξω). The term Ἐβραῖο seems to be applied to persons or things in a wandering or desolate state. Ὀβριὸ νῆσι is a *desert* island east of Corinth: so ὀβριὸ ποτάμι. In the same way the term Γύφτο–Κάστρο (or, Gypsy-Castle) is now applied in Greece to a ruined and uninhabited fortress.

Chapter VI

¹ Πάντες Μιλτιάδη, τὰ σ' ἀρήϊα ἔργα ἴσασιν
 Πέρσαι· καὶ Μαραθὼν σῆς ἀρετῆς τέμενος.

² Callimach. ap. Suid. v. Μαραθών. Callimachus called it ἐννότιον Μαραθῶνα... οὔτεστὶ δίυγρον... Schol Plat. p. 140. Μαραθών τραχὺς δυσίππαστος, ἔχων ἐν ἐν ἑαυτῷ πηλοὺς, τενάγη, λίμνας. (Some of these scholia evince a personal acquaintance with Attic topography: see p. 105 on διὰ μέσου τεῖχος.) Herod. vi. 102 seems to speak in rather too unqualified terms, when he calls Marathon ἐπιτηδεώτατον χωρίον τῆς Ἀττικῆς ἐνιππεῦσαι. It is singular that he does, not mention the *marshes* of Marathon.

³ Pausan. I. 32. 7. λίμνη ἕλδης...τοῖς βαρβάροις τὸν φόμον τὸν πολὺν ἐπὶ οὕτῳ συμβῦναι λέγουσι.

⁴ Pausan. I. 15.

⁵ ἀλλ' ὅμως ἀπεωσάμεσθα, ξὺν θεοῖς, πρὸς ἑσπέρα.   Aristoph. Vesp. 1080.

⁶ From its size and copiousness considered as a prodigy by the neighbouring inhabitants, and therefore called Δρακονερὰ. Δράκο is in Romaic a common expression for any marvellous object.

⁷ Strabo viii. P. 377. Hercules was the hero of Marathon. The fountain was thus the daughter of the plain: and the mythological story of Macaria probably means nothing more than that this flowing stream rendered a similar service in battle to the Heracleidæ, which the marshes did subsequently to the Athenians in the engagement with the Persians.

⁸ Hence Aristoph. Lys. 1032. ἐμπὶς Τρικορυσία.

⁹ The term Κόρυθος is preserved in the Latin Corythus, (the old name of Cortona): it is merely another form of Κόρινθος, which city Cortona resembles in its lofty peaked acropolis.

¹⁰ Schol. Soph. Œd. Col. 1047. Elmsl.

¹¹ Which is the mountain of Παραίλεως: ὄρος ἐν τῷ Μαραθῶνι? (Hesych.)

¹² From ἅλς, as βέλη from ἔλη &.. βρεξίσι is from βρέχω.

¹³ Pausan. I. 32. ῥεῖ ποταμὸς ἐκ τῦς λίμνης, τὰ μὲν πρὸς αὐτῇ τῇ λίμνῃ ὕδωρ βοσκήμασιν ἐπιτήδειον παρεχόμενος, κατὰ δὲ τὴν ἐκβολὴν ἐς τὰ πέλαγος ἰχθύων θαλασσίων πλήρης.

¹⁴ Probalinthus is a δῆμος of the Pandionis φυλὴ: in which were Myrrhinus, Prasiæ, Steiria, all locally near to, and south of Probalinthus: Marathon, Œnoe and Tricorythus are all in the tribe Æantis, which contained also Rhamnus, Aphidnæ, Perrhidæ, Titacidæ, and Psaphidæ, all in the same and more northern district. On the original classification of the demi, from local considerations, see the Dissertation in Vol. I. p. 652, of Dr Arnold's Thucydides. Valck. Herod. iii. 53. Siebel. Paus. I. 1, 3. Mr. Thirlwall's Greece, II. pp. 74, 392. Demi were subsequently removed from one tribe into another. Harpocrat. v. ii. Θυργωνίδαι. Niebuhr, R. H. i. p. 407. Müller (Art. Attika in Ersch. and Gruber Encycl. p. 227), observes, "Da nun die Kleisthenischen Phylen chorographisch waren, wie in Griechenland eben auch die Eleischen (Pausan. 5, 9) die Ephesischen (Steph. βέννα) die der Laconischen Periöken, (Orchomenos p. 314) so müssen die Demen einer Phyle wie Ortschafen eines Kreises zusammen gelegen haben."

¹⁵ A Greek who left Marathon the same morning as we did, but crossed Mount Pentelicus, was stopped by the klefts and plundered, as he informed us himself the morning after our arrival at Athens.

Chapter VII

¹ 'ΑΙΔ' ΕΙΣ' ΑΘΗΝΑΙ ΘΗΣΕΩΣ 'Η ΠΡΙΝ ΠΟΛΙΣ.

² I should also notice the German translation of this wok, published at Halle in 1829, which contains a valuable appendix from the pen of K. O. Müller, to whom Athenian topography is so deeply indebted for his article on Athens and Attika, in Ersch and Gruber's Encyclopædia, T. vi. p. 228 sqq. and for his "Brief nach Athens," 1833.

Chapter VIII

¹ Jamque adscendebant collem, qui plurimus urbi
Imminet adversasque aspectat desuper arces.

² See note 3.

³ Plat. Critia. 112. a. τὸ πρότερον (ἡ ἀκρόπολις) μέγεθος ἦν πρὸς τὸν Ἠριδανὸν καὶ τὸν Ἰλισσὸν ἀποβεβηκυῖα, καὶ περιειληφυῖα ἐντὸς τὴν Πνύκα καὶ τὸν Λυκαβηττὸν ὄρον ἐκ τοῦ καταυτικρὺ Πνυκὸς ἔχουσα... (Formerly the Acropolis stretched to the Eridanus and the Ilissus, comprising the Pnyx within its circuit, and reached to Mount Lycabettus, its limit on the opposite side to the Pnyx...)

⁴ 'Ες τὺν Πάρνηθ' ὀργισθεῖσαι, φροῦδαι κατὰ τὸν Λυκαβηττόν.

Hence the combination of the two mountains in Aristophanes' Ranæ 996, would become much more appropriate, if instead of ἦν οὖν σὺ λέγῃς Λυκαβηττοὺς καὶ ΡΑΡΝΗΣΩΝ ἡμῖν μεγέθη we were to read ΡΑΡΝΗΟΩΝ. The *distant Parnassus* did not offer a fit illustration to an Athenian audience, who saw *the neighbouring Parnes* daily. The confusion of Πάρνης and Παρνησὸς occurs in the MSS. of nearly every ancient Lexicon. See Ruhnken. Tim. v. Παρνησὸς (i.e. Πάρνης:) ὄρος μεταξὺ βοιωτίας καὶ'Αττικῦς. The reason why Parnassus has thus so frequently intruded itself into the place of Parnes, is obvious.

⁵ Pausan. I. 32, 2. Ἀγχεσμὸς ὄρος οὐ μέγα καὶ Διὸς ἄγαλμα Ἀγχεσμίου.

⁶ Xenoph. Œcon. xix. 6.

⁷ Pseudo-Plat. Eryx. 24.

⁸ On this custom of affixing ὄροι see Boeck. Mus. Crit. ii. 625.

Chapter IX

¹ Tellus habet in se corpora prima.

² ἀεὶ διὰ λαμπροτάτου
βαίνοντες ἁβρῶς αἰθέρος.   Eurip. Med. 829.

³ Critia. iii. B. οἷον νοσήαντος σώματος ὀστᾶ, περιερρηκνίας τῦς γῆς... like the bones of an emaciated body, the soil having collapsed about it.

⁴ These cisterns are the λάκκοι, of which such frequent mention is made in Athenian writers (ὕδωρ λακκαῖον Theoph. Charact. xx. 3.) They are well described in Photinus Lex. p. 203. Ed. Cant ... They are seen in great numbers on the western rocky range on which the Pnyx is. In the narrow valley between the hill of the Pnyx and the Museum there remain two ὑδρορρόαι or water-courses, channelled in the rock, one on each side of the road. Leading, as they do, toward the Peiræus, they call to mind the treasonable device for setting fire to the arsenal there, which was denounced by the informer in Arist. Acharn. 884.

........θρυαλλίδα
ἐνθεὶς ἂν ἐς τίφην ἀνὴρ Βοιώτιος
ἅψας ἂν ἐσπέμψειεν
δι' ὑδρορρόας...

........*a Bœtian*
Might ram into the funnel of a reed
A lighted wick, and shoot it to the docks
Along a water-course.

These water-courses have been in some places lined with cement (κονιατοί Demosth. 175. 5) ...The road itself is like a channel cut in a rock: the interval between the wheel-tracks in it is 3 feet 11 inches.

Chapter X

¹ Eum locum libenter invisit, ubi Demosthenes et Æschines inter se decertare soliti sunt.

² J. Pollux. viii. 132, well describes the Pnyx as χωρίον κατεσκευασμένον κατὰ τὴν παλαιὰν ἁπλότητα.

³ ἀγορᾶς κύκλος. Eur. Or. 917. Casaubon. Theoph. Char. ii. "Quod ait a formâ hoc forum *circuli* nomen nactum esse verum est."

⁴ By Cimon. Plut. Vit. p. 202. whence I think the allusion is to this act of *Cimon* in Aristoph. frag. Γεωργοὶ n. 162. Dindorf.

ἐν ἀγορᾷ δ' αὖ πλάτανον εὖ διαφυτεύσομεν.
We'll plant the Agora with rows of Plane-trees.

⁵ Demosthen. Androt. 618. See Harpocrat. in. προπυλαῖα ταῦτα.

⁶ ἀφ' ὧν κτήματα ἀθάνατα αὐτῷ ρερίεστιν, τὰ μὲν τῶν ἔργων ἡ μνήμη, τὰ δὲ τῶν ἀναθημάτων τῶν ἐπ' ἐκείνοις ἀνατεθέντων τὸ κάλλος, Προπύλαια ταῦτα, ὁ Παρθενὼν, Στοαὶ, Νεώσοικοι.

⁷ Compare Æschines de f. 1. (c. 21. Bremi.) ἀνιστάμενοι οἱ ῥήτορες ἀποβλέπειν εἰς τὰ Προπυλαῖα ἐκέλευον ἡμᾶς, καὶ τῦς ἐν Σαλαμῖνι πρὸς τὸν Πέρσην ναυμαχίας μεμνῆσθαι...

⁸ αὐτὴ γὰρ ἡ γῆ ξύμμαχος κείνοις πέλει. Æschyl. Pers. 778. A curious specimen of the *religious* feeling attached to this spot is preserved in an inscription engraved in the rock a little to the N.W. of the Pnyx.

HIEPON
ΝΥΜΦ[ΑΙΣ]
ΔΗΜΟΣ[ΙΑΙΣ]

SACRED TO THE POPULAR NYMPHS.

⁹ Demosth. c. Neær. 1375. 16.

¹⁰ Arist. Eq. 1105.

¹¹ See the comparison. Demosthen. π.π. 383. 7. Quintil. x. 3. 30. Demosthenes in litore, in quod se maximo cum sono fluctus illideret, meditans (μελετῶν) consuescebat *concionum fremitus non expavescere.* Cic. Fin. v. 2. in *Phalerico declamare solitum Demosthenem.*

¹² Which suggested the offer of the cushion to the Demus in the Equites. 783 −

ἐπὶ ταῖσι πετραῖς οὐ φροντίζει σκληρῶς σε καθήμενον οὕως
οὐχ ὥσπερ ἐγὼ ῥαψάμενός σοι τουτὶ φέρω· ἀλλ' ἐπαναίρου,
κᾆτα καθίζου μαλακῶς ...

¹³ Hence the use of the word ἄνω for, "in the Pnyx". Demosth. 285. 2. πᾶς ὁ δῆμος ἄνω καθῆστο. cf. Plutarch. Nic. 7. Euripides, in describing an *Argive* assembly, draws his picture of it from the Athenian Pnyx. Orest. 871 −ὁρῶ δ' ὄχλον στείχοντα, καὶ θάσσοντ' ἄκραν. Hence too the Pnyx was subsequently dedicated to Ζεὺσ ὕψιστος. Corp. Inscript. p. 475.

¹⁴ Pac. 673. ὅστις κρατεῖ νῦν τοῦ λίθου.

¹⁵ κατὸ τῶν πετρῶν ἄνωθεν τοὺς πόρους θυννοσκοπεῖν. Equites. 313.

¹⁶ διοσημία 'στιν καὶ ρανίς βεβληκέ με· Acharn. 171.

¹⁷ Plutarch. v. Themist. (i. p. 476. Reiske) τὸ βῆμα τὸ ἐν Πνυκὶ πεποιημένον ὥστ' ἀποβέπειν πρὸς τὴν θάλασσαν (i.e. so that *a person might look off from* it to the sea)

ὕστερον οἱ Τριάκοντα πρὸς τὴν χώραν ἀπέτρεψαν. On this sense of ἀποβλέπειν, see Buttmann. Excur. Platon. Alcib. i.

Chapter XI

[1] Curia Martis Athenis.

[2] Pausan. i. 28. 5. Eurip. Iph. T. 962. Orestes says:

ὡς εἰς Ἄρειον ὄχθον ἧκον ἐς δίκην δ'
ἔστην...ἐγὼ μὲν θἄτερον λαβὼν βάθρον
τὸ δ' ἄλλο πρέσβειρ' ἥτις Ἐρινύων.

When we had mounted to the hill of Ares,
We scal'd two adverse Steps; I took the one,
The eldest of the Furies trod the other.

[3] J. Pollux. viii. 10. ὑπαίθριοι ἐδίκαζον.

[4] Act. Apost. xvii. 34.

[5] Athens was emphatically *a city of Gods*, πόλις θεῶν. In the animated description of Hegesias quoted by Strabo (396. b.) ἐκεῖνο Λεωκόριον, τοῦτο Θησεῖον,...οὐ δύναμαι δηλῶσαι καθ' ἓν ἕκαστον· ἡ γὰρ Ἀττικὴ ΘΕΩΝ ἐστὶ κτίσμα καὶ προγόνων. A passage, it may be observed, which throws light upon the very similar expressions of Strabo which follow it (p. 396. d): ἐπ' ἄλλων πλειόνων ἐστὶν ἱστορεῖν πολλὰ, καὶ εἰσ τὸ Λεωκόριον καὶ τὸ θησεῖον· ΟΥΣ ἔχει καὶ τὸ Λύκειον καὶ τὸ Ολυμπιεῖον, – where instead of ΟΥΣ, the word ΘΥΣ (i.e. θεοὺς) seems to be required in the text. Concerning this *confusion*, see Bentley on Free-thinking, p. 118. Bast. Palæog. p. 812.

[6] ὅτι οὐκ ἐνχειροποιήτοις ναοῖς κατοικεῖ ὁ Θεός.

[7] By Bentley, Sermon ii.

[8] Herod. viii. 52.

[9] See Arrian Exped. Alex. vii. p. 470. Blancard. γέγραπται ἡ Αθηναίων καὶ Αμαζόνων μάχη πρὸς Κίμωνος (read by transposition, Μίκωνος, Aristoph. Lys. 678. τὰς Ἀμάζονας σκόπει, ἃς Μίκων ἔγραψ' ἐφ' ἵππων.)

[10] Thus the figure of Paris in the Æginetan pediment was a copy of a Persian archer. See Müller Phid. Vit. p. 58 and a further analogy in a monument illustrated by Millingen (Uned. Mon. ii. p. 15).

[11] Eumenid. 655.

πάγον δ' Ἄρειον τόνδ' Ἀμαζόνων ἕδραν,
when they besieged the Acropolis,
Ἄρει δ' ἔθνον ἔνθεν ἐστ' ἐπώνυμος
πέτρα, πάγος τ' Ἄρειος....

[12] Pausan. i. 14. 5.

[13] It has been attributed to Epimenides: but a temple of the Furies stood here before his visit to Athens. Compare Thuc. i. 126. Plut. Sol. 12.

[14] See Dobree Adversar. i. p. 47. Müller Eumenid. p. 179, and in his Appendix to Leake, p. 454.

[15] Perhaps alluded to Soph. Œd. Col. 157.

[16] Eur. Elect. 1272. πάγον παρ' αὐτὸν χάσμα δύσονται χθονός. Æschyl. Eumen. 908. θάλαμοι...κατὰ γῦς.

[17] Aristoph. Plut. 424. Cicero de Leg. i. 14.

[18] Eum. 908.
πρὸς φῶς ἱερὸν τῶν δε προπομπῶν
κατὰ γῆς σύμεναι.

Chapter XII

[1] ....πέτραι
κοῖλαι, φιλόρνεις, δαιμόνων ἀναστροφάι.

[2] Simonid. Poet. Min. i. p. 367. Gaisford. Herod. vi. 105.

[3] Schol. Ar. Lysist. 910. πλησίον τοῦ Πανείου ἡ Κλεψύδρα.

[4] Ister ap. Schol. Ar. Av. 1702. ἀρχομένων τῶν ἐτησίων...and ἀφθῆναι ἐν τῷ φαληρικῷ. In the conclusion of the Schol. Aristoph. Lysist. 913. Κλεψύδρα ἔχει τὰς ῥεύσεις ὑπὸ γῆν φέρουσα εἰς τὸν ΦΛΕΓΡΕΩΔΗ ΛΕΙΜΩΝΑ should be corrected to τῶν ΦΑΛΗΡΕΩΝ ΛΙΜΕΝΑ.

[5] 4 Lysist. 377.

[6] ΠΡΟΜΑΧΕΩΝΑ ΤΟΝΔΕ ΠΗΓΑΙΟΥ ΥΔΑ
ΤΟΣ ΑΝΗΓΕΙΡΕΝ ΕΚ ΒΑΘΡΩΝ ΟΔΥ
ΣΣΕΥΣ ΑΝΔΡΙΤΖΟΥ ΕΛΛΗΝΩΝ ΣΤΡΑΤΗΓΟΣ
ΕΤΕΙ ΑΩΚΒ ΚΑΤΑ ΜΗΝΑ
ΣΕΠΤΕΜΒΡΙΟΝ

[7] Eurip. Ion. 492.

ὦ Πανὸς θακήματα καὶ
παραυλίζουσα πέτρα
μυχώδεσι μακραῖς
ἵνα χοροὺς στείβουσι ποδῶν
Ἀγραύλου κόραι τρίγονοι
στάδια χλοερὰ πρὸ Παλλάδος
ναῶν.

The ναοὶ here are the Ereetheum and the Parthenon.

[8] Polyæn. Strat. i. 21.

[9] The position of which, assigned on the authority of Pausanias, is confirmed by the inscription found near the spot by Dodwell. i. p. 371.

[10] From Herod. viii. 52. through the Pelasgicum τὸ ὑπὸ τῇ ἀκροπόλει Thuc. ii. 14.

[11] ἐφήβων ὅρκος ἐν τῷ τῆς Ἀγραύλου Demosth. 438. 18.

[12] While this sheet is passing through the press a letter from Athens brings me the intelligence that "close to the Erectheum (Παλλάδος ναὸς. Eur. Ion. see note p. 85) a *subterranean way has been found* leading down to the cavern supposed of Agraulus, and leading out into the town from the centre of the northern face of the Acropolis rock."

Chapter XIII

[1] Credit miros audire Tragœdos
    In vacuo lætus sessor plausorque Theatro.

[2] In Philostrat. V. A. iv. p. 179. οἱ Ἀθηναιοι εἰς τὸ Θεάτρον τὸ ἐπι τῇ ἀκροπόλει is an error for ὑπὸ.

[3] Hence the act of the Κόλαξ, (Theoph. Char. ii) τοῦ παιδὸς ἐντῷ θεάτρῳ ἀφελόμενος τὸ προσκεφάλαιον αὐτὸς ὑποστρῶσαι is explained from the hardness of the seat.

[4]
```
ΗΛΙ . . . . . . . . .
ΜΑΞΙΜΟC  ΦΙΛΙΠΠΟC  ΓΑ. . . .
. . . . . ΟC  CΤΡΑΤΟΝΕΙΚΟC
```

There were therefore at this time three συγχορηγοί. Compare Clinton F. H. ii. p. 83.

[5] The rock above the highest seat in the Theatre which has been cut perpendicularly, was called, from this circumstance, Κατατομή. It is well illustrated by Harpocratio in

v. Κατατομὴ, who there notices tripods (such as these on the columns) above the Theatre, and inscriptions like those I have noticed, cut in the face of the rock.

6   ΜΗΤΡ
      ΟΒΙΟΥ

7
ΑΙ Π Ε Ι C ω Ν Ι
Α Ν Ο □ Κ Α Ι
Γ Ρ Ι Π Ο C ΑΝ Ε
Θ Ε C Α Ν

Compare Rose, Inscript. p. xxxix.

[8] It is called *Hecatompedum,* by Hesychius in υ. ἑκατόμπεδον, probably from its *symmetry* alone.

[9] Sympos. 175. e. (where Socrates is speaking of Agathon's dramatic victory in the theatre). ἡ δόξα σου ἐμφανὴς ἐγένετο ἐν μάρτυσιν Ἑλλήνων πλέον ἢ τρισμυρίοις.

[10] The passage of Dicærchus is (p. 8. Hudson. G. M. or Creutzer Melelemata iii. p. 80). Ὧδε ἦν τῶνἐν τῇ οἰκουμένῃ κάλλιστον Θέατρον ἀξιόλογον μέγα καὶ θαυμαστόν – where for ὧδε ἦν (which Dicæarchus would not have said, for it *still existed*), Hemsterhuis. in Wesseling. Probabil. p. 335. and Boissonade Philostr. 662. and on L. Holst. Epist. P. 14. note, have probably substituted Ὠδεῖον.

[11] The term τρισμύριοι was a general one employed to signify in round numbers the whole free adult population of Athens at the time; Boeck. Econ. i. p. 48, it is no more to be taken *literally* in the passage of Plato, than is Juvenal's similar expression '*Totam hodie Romam Circus* capit.' Compare Col. Leake's Morea ii. 535. It is curious that the term τρισμύριοι still remains in the Greek language as a general expression of the number, not indeed of the population of Athens, but of Greece. A. Soutzo, 1833, in his poem to King Otho (p. 80.) says

καὶ διέβης τῆς Ναυπλίας τὰς πρασίνους πεδιάς
ὁπαδοὺς κ'εὐχετὰςἔχων τρεῖς Ἑλλήνων μυριάδας,

which may be compared with the expression cited from Plato (Sympos. 175. d.), ἡ δόξα σουἐμφανὴς ἐγένετο ἐν μάρτυριν Ἑλλήνων πλέον ἢ τρισμυρίοις.

[12] The effect of this enchantment is fancifully illustrated in the topographical fragment on Athens (Dicæarchus p. 9) ἔστι ταῖς θέαις ἡ πόλις λήθην ἐμποιοῦσα (read ἐμπιοῦσα, i.e. imbibing oblivion, "longa oblivia *potans*" by means of public spectacles; compare Lucian. Tim. p. 170. κάθαπερ τό λήθης ὕδωρ ἐκπιὼν) τῆς τῶν σίτων προσφορᾶς. Dicæarchus here means to say, *"The city of Athens beguiles itself of hunger by means of its dramatic Spectacles."*

¹³ ὦ κλεινὰ Σαλαμὶς, σὺ μέν που
ναίεις ἁλίπλαγκος εὐδαίμων
πᾶσιν περίφαντος ἀεί
ἐγὼ δ' ὁ τλάμων &c.

¹⁴ ὁρᾷς τὸν ὑψοῦ τόνδ' ἄπειρον αἰθέρα
καὶ γῆν πέριξ ἔχονθ' ὑγραῖς ἐν ἀγκάλαις
τοῦτον νόμιζε Ζῆνα, τόνδ' ἡγοῦ θεόν.
                                    Eurip. frag. incert. i. 2.

¹⁵ Ζεὺς Πολιεύς. Pausan. i. 24. 4.

¹⁶ χαίρετ' ἀστικὸς λεὼς
ἴκταρ ἥμενοι Διὸς
Παρθένου φίλας φίλοι
σωφρονοῦντες ἐν χρόνῳ,
Παλλάδος δ' ὑπὸ πτεροῖς
ὄντας ἅζεται Πατήρ.

¹⁷ Pac. 165.

¹⁸ Av. 785.

¹⁹ Equites, 165. Steinbuchel Alterthumskunde p. 17, concludes some good observations on this subject with the remark that "Der Grieche waehlte vorzugsweise den Ort (for their Theatres) welcher zugleich die lohnendste Aussicht *uber Stadt* und *Hafen* und die naechste Umgebung both ...."

²⁰ Plato Repub. vi. 492. 6.

²¹ Ὅταν ξυγκαθέζομενοι ἄθροοι πολλοὶ εἰς ἐκκλησίας ἢ εἰς δικαστήρια ἢ θέατρα, ξὺν πολλῷ θορύβῳ τὰ μὲν ψέγωσι τῶν λεγομένων ἢ πραττομένων τὰ δὲ ἐπαινῶσιν, ὑπερβαλλόντως ἑκάτερα, καὶ κροτοῦντες· πρὸς δ' αὐτοῖς αἵ τε πέτραι* καὶ τόπος ἐν ᾧ ἂν ὦσιν ἐπηχοῦντες διπλάσιον θόρυβον παρέχωσι τοῦ ψόγου τε καὶ ἐπαίνου· ἐν δὴ τῷ τοιούτῳ τὸν νέον, τὸ λεγόμενον, τίνα οἴει καρδίαν ἴσχειν; ἢ ποίαν ἂν αὐτῷ παιδείαν ἰδιωτικὴν ἀνθέξειν, ἣν οὐ κατακλυσθεῖσαν ὑπὸ τοῦ τοιούτου ψόγου ἢ ἐπαίνου οἰχήσεσθαι φερομένην ἢ ἂν οὗτος φέρῃ;

* The πέτραι alluded to, are in the Theatre, the southern rocks of the Acropolis; in the Pnyx, those described above, pp.39-40.

Chapter XIV

¹   Ἀνίωμεν ἐς τὴν Ἀκρόπολιν αὐτὴν, ὡς ἂν ἐκ περιωπῆς ἅμα
      καταφανῆ πάντα ᾖ τὰ ἐν πόλει.

² Lysist. 484.

      ἄβατον Ἀκρόπολιν
      ἱερὸν τέμενος.

³ There is a particular allusion to the Acropolis in Dicæarchus (p. 9) where he calls the city of Athens a θαυμαστόν ΠΛΙΝΘΙΝΩΝ ζῴων διδασκαλεῖον; which expression has been corrupted by the transcribers: for what are ζῷα πλίνθινα? The true reading I conceive to be θαυῷμαστόν ΤΙ ΛΙΘΙΝΩΝ ΖΩΙΩΝ διδασκαλεῖον, i.e. "*a certain admirable Studio of Sculpture.*" That works of sculpture were called ζῷα λίθινα, is evident from Philemon. (Athenæi 605. f.).

ἀλλ' ἐν Σάμῳ μὲν τοῦ λιθίνου ζῴου πότε
ἄνθρωπος ἠράσθη τις.

At Samos too a man once fell in love
With the Statue in the Temple.

And Aristotle (in Diog. Laert. v. p. 277. quoted by Meineke), ζῷα λίθινα ἀναθεῖναι Διῒ καὶ 'Αθηνᾷ. Hence the *frieze* of a building is called its zophorus. In MSS., *ĩ* is equivalent to *w*. Hence arose the confusion.

⁴ Aristid. Panathen. ὡς ἐπ' ἀσπίδος, κύκλων εἰς ἀλλήλους ἐμβεβηκότων πέμπτος εἰς ὀμφαλὸν πληροῖ. I have no doubt that it is the *Acropolis* which is the ἄστεος ὀμφαλὸς θυόεις ἐν ταῖς ἱεραῖς Αθάναις. in Pindar. (frag. Dith. iv. p. 225, Dissen).

⁵ Cicero (at the end of his Proœm. Paradox). Opus, tale ut in *Arce* poni posset; quasi illa Minerva Phidiæ.

⁶ Polemon wrote four books on the Acropolis; Heliodorus fifteen. We read of Roman writers also, "quibus unum opus est intactæ Palladis Arcem Carmine perpetuo celebrare....."

⁷ Pausan. i. 22, 3. Comp. Boeck. Corp. Ins. i. p. 474.

⁸ This nearness of the Temple of Peitho to the Theatre gave additional force and boldness to an assertion of the same dramatist in another play acted in the same place:

οὐκ ἔστι ΠΕΙΘΟΥΣ ΙΕΡΟΝ ἄλλο πλὴν λόγος
καὶ ΒΩΜΟΣ αὐτῆς ἐστ' ἐν ἀνθρώπου φύσει.

Eurip. frag. *Antig.*

There is no other TEMPLE OF PERSUASION
Than Speech; and in Man's Heart her ALTAR *is.*

⁹ Πέτραν παρ' αὐτὴν Παλλάδος, κατόψιον
γῦς τῆσδε ναὸν Κύπριδος καθείσατο
ἐρῶσ' ἔρωτ' ἔκδημον, 'Ιππολύτῳ δ' ἔπι
τὸ λοιπὸν ὠνόμαζεν ἱδρύσθαι Θεάν.

Eurip. Hippol. 30.

[10] This association, as θεοὶ σύνναοι, in the same Temple, of Aphrodite and Peitho (*Suada Venusque*) is illustrated by Pausan. i. 24, 3. and the elegant fragment of Ibycus. Athen. 564. d. σὲ μὲν Κύπρις ἅ τ' ἀγανοβλέφαρος Πειθὼ ῥοδέοισιν ἐν ἄνθεσι θρέψαν, and by a group consisting of Helen, Paris, Peitho and Aphrodite in Winckelmann. Mon. Ined. p. 157. This union has been dissolved by the copyist in Pliny (N. H. xxxvi. 4.) "*Scopas* fecit *Venerem* et Pothon et *Phaethontem*," which has been quoted by Hirt in one place (Bildenkunste p. 210.) without suspicion; in another (in Sillig's Catalog. Artif. p. 488.) he has corrected the last word to *Phanetem*. But it ought to be PEITHUNTEM. I would confirm this (for Wolf's note on Hesiod Theogon. 987, may render a confirmation necessary) from Æschylus Suppl. 1025.

    ΚΥΠΡΙΔΟΣ δ' οὐκ ἀμελεῖ θεσ-
    μὸς ὅδ εὔφρων...
    μετάκοινοι δε φίλα μα-
    τρὶ πάρεισιν ΠΟΘΟΣ ᾇ τ' οὐ-
    δεν ἄπαρνον τελέθει θέλκ-
    τορι ΠΕΙΘΟΙ......

Where the members of the group are identical with those in that of Scopas mentioned by Pliny. Comp. Pausan. i. 42, 6. The Latin accusative *untem* has much perplexed transcribers. See the Latin Schol. in Runkel's Cratinus p. 82, where, for "Jupiter in *Ramum* evolavit Atticæ regionis," not Rhamn*unta*, but Rhamn*untem* (i.e. Rhamn*ūm*) is to be substituted.

[11] Thuc. ii. 14. τὸ πρὸ τούτου ἀκρόπολις ἡ νῦν οὖσα ἦν· Of which fact the citadel still preserved a record in its name, *Polis*. Thuc. ii. 15. καλεῖται δια' τὴν παλαιὰναν ταύτῃ κατοίκησιν ἡ ἀκρόπολις μεχρὶ τοῦδε ἔτι ὑπ' Ἀθηναίων πόλις.

[12]   At Pater ut summa prospectum ex *arce* petebat
  Anxia in assiduos absumens lumina fletus,
  Quum primum inflati prospexit lintea veli,
  Præcipitem sese scopulorum e vertice jecit
  Amissum credens inmiti Thesea fato.

[13] In order to give a name to the Ægean. (Serv. Æneid. iii. 74. Keightley Mythol. p. 349.) which etymology is refuted by the word Ægean alone. The sea is Αἰγαῖον πέλαγος: but the adjective from Ægeus is Αἰγεῖος. They both occur in Æschyl. Ag. 645. Eumen. 653. The accurate observation of the Scholiast on Apoll. Rhod. i. 831. might have cautioned the mythologists against this error.

[14] For, Aristoph. Aves 574. αὐτίκα Νίκη πέτεται πτερύγοιν χρυσαῖν.

[15] Pausan. iii. 15, 7. This Deity was also termed Νίκη 'Αθηνᾶ (on which see Dobree Advers. i. p. 482). Standing thus as she did at the exit from the Acropolis, she was properly implored, to aid them as an escort, (προπομπὸς) by persons starting on any dangerous enterprise, as in Soph. Philoct. 134.

Ἑρμῆς ὁ πέμπων δόλιος ἡγήσαιτο νῶν
Νίκη τ' Ἀθάνα Πολιὰς, ἥ σώζει μ' ἀεί.

[16] Whence the modern Greek word σιμὰ near, and "ἀποσιμόνω (éloigner) ἀποσιμοῦν ναῦν. Thuc. iv. 25." Koray. Atak. iv. p. 499.

[17] Lysist. 632.

φορήσω τὸ ξίφος τὸ λοιπὸν ἐν μύρτου κλαδὶ,
ἀγοράσω τ' ἐν τοῖς ὅπλοις ἑξῆς Ἀριστογείτονι
ὧδέ θ' ἑστήξω παρ' αὐτόν·

I will wield my sword hereafter braided with the myrtle spray,
Near Aristogeiton standing, arm'd, and in the Agora
Here will keep my post beside him.

This last trait is very characteristic and happy: for in ordinary cases when an honorary statue, to be placed in the Agora, was granted by the Athenian State, it was expressly provided by a clause in the grant itself, that the Statue should *not* be placed near that of Aristogeiton; but, in fact, *any where* else in the Agora *except* ἑξῆς Ἀριστογείτονι. This is proved by an honorary inscription, which I copy in the collection of Mr Finlay: to whom I beg here to express my gratitude for the assistance he rendered me at Athens in the prosecution of these enquiries.

. . ΔΟΥΝΑΙΔΕΑΤΩΙΚΑΙ[ΣΙΤ]
[Η]ΣΙΝΕΜΓΡΥΤΑΝΕΙΟΙΚΑΙ[ΓΡ]
ΟΕΔΡΙΑΝΕΝΑΓΑΣΙΤΟΙΣΑ[ΓΩ]
ΣΙΝΤΟΙΣΤΗΣΓΟΛΕΩΣΚΑΙ[ΕΓ]
[Γ]ΟΝΩΝΤΩΙΓΡΕΣΒΥΤΑΤΩΙΕ[Ι]
ΝΑΙΔΕΑΥΤΩΙΚΑΙΕΙΚΟΝΑΣΤ
ΗΣΑΙΕΑΥΤΟΥΧΑΛΧΗΝΕΦΙΠΓ
ΟΥΕΝΑΓΟΡΑΙΟΓΟΥΑΜΒΟΥΛΗ
ΤΑΙΠΛΗΝΠΑΡΑΡΜΟΔΙΟΝΚΑΙ
ΑΡΙΣΤΟΓΕΙΤΟΝΑ.

[Be it decreed]

to give him both maintenance
in the Prytaneum and a front-seat
at all the Games celebrated
by the State, and to the eldest
of his descendants for ever, and
that permission may be granted him to erect also
a Bronze Equestrian Statue of himself
in the Agora, wherever he may choose
except BY THE SIDE OF HARMODIUS AND
ARISTOGEITON.

Compare Cramer's Greece, ii. p. 304. Dio. Chrys. i. p. 637. on the especial honours, (τιμαὶ ἐξαίρετοι as the latter calls them), paid to Aristogeiton.

[18] Arrian. Exp. Alex. iii. p. 197. Blancard. ʽΑρμοδίου καὶ Ἀριστογείτονος χαλκαῖ εἰκόνες κεῖνται ἐν Κεραμεικῷ, ἧ ἄνιμεν ἐς πόλιν καταντικρὺ τοῦ Μητρῷ...

[19] Recent discoveries have brought to light this Temple of Victory. I owe the following communication on the subject to W. R. Hamilton, Esq. "The height of the columns, some of which are *in situ*, is 3. 58. French metres. The wall of the cella is replaced to the height of about two feet. The southern wing of the Propylæa, to the west of which the Temple stands, was within the line of the northern wing."

Chapter XV

[1] Adsta, atque Athenas antiquum opulentum oppidum
Contempla; age Templum Cereris ad lævam adspice.

The Temple of Ceres, (see Pausan. i. 22.) stood on the *right* of the entrance to the Propylæa. The Propylæa were probably depicted as the scenic decoration of this play of Ennius. To the actors, therefore, turning to the audience, the Temple of Ceres was on their *left*, as here expressed. For the same reason, it seems, the Heræum is placed to the *left* of Argos and Mycenæ by Sophocles, (Electr. 7) whereas, in fact to a person approaching these places, it was on the *right* of both.

[2] For it seems probable that this character for its profuse expenditure, as well as the distance of the epoch, recommended the year of Euthymenes to the choice of Aristophanes in Acharn. 67.

ἐπέμψαθ᾽ ἡμᾶς ὡς βασιλέα τὸν μέγαν
μισθὸν φέροντας δύο δραχμὰς τῆς ἡμέρας
ἐπ᾽ Εὐθυμένους ἄρχοντος...

i.e. in the most lavish times.

[3] Arist. Nub. 69.

ὅταν σὺ μέγας ὢν ἅρμ᾽ ἐλαύνῃς πρὸς Πόλιν
When you grow up, and to the Citadel
Shall guide your Car.

[4] Æschines. π. π. 29. Compare the catalogue of the mirabilia of Athens in Phœnic. Athenæi 652. e. whence it may be inferred that the Propylæa were sometimes simply termed Πύλαι, as the old entrance was by Herod. viii. 52. and that this is the case in the times of Alexis (Ath. 336. e).

τί ταῦτα ληρεῖς φληναφῶν ἄνω κάτω

Λυκεῖον, Ἀκαδήμειαν, Ὠδεῖον, Πύλας
λήρους σοφιστῶν; οὐδὲ ἓν τούτων καλόν.

The Propylæa could hardly have been omitted here. The *pediment* of the Propylæa seems to have attracted especial admiration. See Bekker's Anecd. p. 202, 20, and 348, 3. in ἀετὸς προπύλαιος.

[5] ὄψεσθε δέ· καὶ γὰρ ἀνοιγνυμένων ψόφος ἤδη τῶν
Προπυλαίων
ἀλλ' ὀλολύξατε φαινομέναισιν ταῖς ἀρχαί-
αισιν Ἀθήναις,
καὶ θαυμασταῖς καὶ πολυΰμνοις, ἵν' ὁ κλεινὸς Δῆμος
ἐνοικεῖ.
Aristoph. Equites 1326.

[6] Quale Te dicet tamen
Antehac fuisse, *tales cum sint Relliquiæ!*

[7] By Müller de Parthenonis Fastigio in his Comment. de Phidiæ Vita, p. 75. sqq. with a sketch of a proposed restoration. See also Col. Leake's Memoir on the Disputed Positions in Athens, p. 40.

[8] See this longing expressed in his Supplices, v. 487.

[9] κείσθω δόρυ μοι, μίτονἀμφιπλέκειν
ἀράχναις, μετὰ δ'ἡσυχίας πολίῳ
γήρᾳ ξυνοικοίην·
ἀείδοιμι δὲ στεφάνοις κάρα
πολιὸν στεφανώσας,
Θρηϊκίαν πέλταν πρὸς Ἀθάνας
περικίοσιν ἀγκρεμάσασ' θαλάμοις.
Eurip. Erecth. ap. Stob. ii. p. 403. Gaisford.

[10] ὡς πασσαλεύω κρᾶτα τριγλύφοις τόδε
Λέοντος, ὃν πάρειμι θηράσασ' ἐγώ.

Eurip. Bacch. 1206.

[11] Vitruv. iii. In cymis *capita Leonina* sunt scalpenda.

[12] Boeck. Inscr. p. 177. Hence the whole temple was sometimes called Παρθενὼν ἑκατόμπεδος. Plutarch v. Cat. ii. p. 555. Pericl. i. p. 619. and the remarkable passage de Glor. Athen. vii. p. 377. where he is summing up the splendid results of Athenian conquests, which are ὅλαι πόλεις, καὶ νῆσοι, καὶὐπειροι καὶ νηχοτάλαντοι, καὶ λάφυρα, ὧν ἀγάλματα καὶ σύμβολα, παρθενῶες ἑκατόμπεδοι, νότια τείχη, νεώσοικοι, Προπύλαια. I take this opportunity of suggesting ἤπειροι καναχοτάλαντοι in lieu of the unintelligible words in the text. χρυσοῦ καναχὴ is an expression well known from Soph. Antig. 130. whence ἤπειρος καναχοτάλαντος would be a country, '*auro quæ plurima fluxit.*' See Blomf. Gloss. Choeph. 146.

¹³ λαβὼν ὑφάσμαθ' ἱερὰ θησαυρῶν παρὰ
κατέσκιαζε, θαύματ' ἀνθρώποις ὁρᾶν·
ἐνῦν δ' ὑφανταὶ γράμμασιν τοιαίδ' ὑφαί.
V. 1143.

¹⁴ In the Peace of Aristophanes 555.

¹⁵ The prospect (ἄποψις) which the Parthenon commands, has called forth much admiration. Aristides well describes this view, especially the πεδίων κάλλη καὶ χάριτας πρὸ τῆς πόλεως εὐθὺς ἀπὸ τοῦ εἴχους μᾶλλον δὲ ἀπὸ τῆς ἀκροπόλεως κεχυμένων. It will serve to restore the right reading to Dicæarchus. 'Αθηνᾶς ἱερὸν πολυτελὲς ἀπόβιον, ἄξιον θέας, ὁ καλούμενος Παρθενὼν ὑπερκείμενος τοῦ θεάτρου. The corrupt word should probably be ἀπόψιον. Marx in Creuzer. Meletem. proposes κατόψιον.

Chapter XVI

¹ Diva triformis.

² Schol. Aristid. p. 320. τρία ἦσαν ἀγάλματα ἐν 'Ακροπόλει τῆς 'Αθηνᾶς,ἓν μὲν τὸ ἀρχαῖον καὶ διοπετές, ὕτερον τὸ χαλκοῦν, ὃ ἔθεσαν μετὰ τὰ Περσικὰ, τρίτον τὸ φειδίου, τὸ ἐκ χρυσοῦ καὶ ἐλίφαντος κατεσκευασμένον.

³ Demosth. 428. 15. ἡ χαλκῆ ἡ μεγάλη 'Αθηνᾶ.

⁴ ἀλλ' ἦλθεν,...ἰκὼν ὡς ὁρᾶν ἐφαίνετο·
Παλλὰς, κραδαίνουσ' ἔγχος ὑπολόφῳ κάρᾳ.
Herc. Fur. 1002.

⁵ Zosimus, v. p. 294.

⁶ This appellation had, in the time of Æschylus, acquired the character of a proper name: it did not require to be distinguished by the definitive article. See Eumen. 80, where Minerva says to Orestes,

ἵζου παλαιὸν ἄγκαθεν λαβὼν βρέτας.

7   ΕΥ.   τίς θεας
                 Πολιοῦχος ἔσται; τῷ ξανοῦμεν τὸν πέπλον;
    ΠΕΙ.   τί δ'οὐκ 'Αθηναίαν ἐῶμεν Πολιάδα;

Arist. Av. 826. (where Schol. τῇ Αθηνᾷ 'Πολιάδι οὔσῃ πέπλος ἐγίνετο παμποίκιλος ὃν ἀνέφερον ἐν τῇ πομπῇ τῶν Παναθηναίων...)

⁸ γέγηθε κόσμον προστιθεὶς ἀγάλματι
καλὸν κακίστῳ καὶ πέπλοισιν ἐκπονεῖ.
Hippolyt. 630.

[9] ...εἴτε χώρας ἐν τόποις Λιβυστικοῖς
τίθησιν ὀρθὸν ἢ κατηρεφῆ πόδα
φίλοις ἀρήγουσ'...
Æschyl. Eumenid. 282.

[10] Comp. Hym. Cerer. 182. ἀμφὶ δὲ πέπλος κυάνεος ῥαδινοῖσι θεῆς ἐλελίζετο ποσσίν. Hence κατηρεφῆ πόδαα in Æschylus. The statue of Polias seems to have been erect, (Aristoph. Αv. 827. πανοπλίαν ἕστηκ' ἔχουσα.) and the drapery of the Peplos to have fallen in full folds over the feet, thus covered or *roofed* over, (κατηρεφεῖς) as in that of the Æginetan Minerva. (Hirt. Wolf. Analek. iii. p. 170). The ὀρθὸς ποῦς on the contrary, seems to indicate the attitude in which the foot is not in repose, but projected with some exertion, (see this use of ὀρθὸς, Elmsl. Med. 1134. Dissen. Pind. Ol. xi. 4.) as in combat, which is the attitude of the Itonian Pallas. Millingen. Uned. Mon. ii. p. 9. and of that in the Athenian Vase.

[11]   ΚΛΕΩΝ

ἰδοὺ φέρω σοι τήνδε μαζίσκην ἐγώ.

'ΑΛΛΑΝΤΟΠΩΛΗΣ

ἐγὼ δὲ μυστίλας μεμιστυλημένας
ὑπὸ τῆς θεοῦ τῇ χειρὶ τῇ ἐλεφαντίνῃ.

ΔΗΜΟΣ

ὡς μέγαν ἄρ' εἶχες ὦ πότνια τὸν δάκτυλον.

'ΑΛΛΑΝΤΟΠΩΛΗΣ

ὦ Δῆμ' ἐναργῶς ἡ Θεός σ' ἐπισκοπεῖ,
καὶ νῦν ὑπέρεχει σου χύτραν ζωμοῦ πλέαν.

ΚΛΕΩΝ

ουδωκεν τουτὶ τέμαχος σ' ἡ φοβεσιστράτη.

'ΑΛΛΑΝΤΟΠΩΛΗΣ

ἡ δ' ὀβριμοπάτρα γ' ἐφθὸν ἐκ ζωμοῦ κρέας
καὶ χόλικος τε καὶ γαστρὸς τόμον.

ΔΗΜΟΣ

καλῶς γ' ἐποίησε τοῦ πέπλου μεμνημένη

Equites, 1165.

[12] i.e. The Chryselephantine Statue by Phidias, in the *Parthenon.* See the proposed restoration of this Minerva in Quatremère de Quincy Jupiter Olympius, p. 226. The face, feet, and hands alone of this statue were of ivory. Plat. Hipp. maj. 290. b.

ATHENS AND ATTICA 189

¹³ i.e. The Bronze Colossal Statue, also by Phidias, of Minerva *Promachus*:standing near the Propyl.æa (Πυλαίμαχος) on the north-east. The shield and spear, with which she was armed, are here ludicrously converted into a χύτρα and τορύνη (as χύτρα and ὀβέλισκος for a shield and spear in Aristoph. Aves, 388). Her gigantic form is described by ὑπερέχει.

It will, I think, be found that, when accuracy of distinction is required, the Athenian writers of the best age do not give to Minerva Polias the epithet of *Pallas*, but reserve it for the other two, especially for this statue of *Promachus*.

¹⁴ i.e. The Minerva Polias: the next line is a convincing proof that the Peplos was dedicated to her, and not to any other Minerva. As a single supplementary remark connected with this topic, we may notice the small images of Pallas (Παλλάδια) worn about the person, περιφερόμενα, as amulets. (See Millingen, U. M. ii. p. 13, and p. 73). The Scholiast on Aristides, p. 320, Dindorf, after distinguishing these three Minervas of the Acropolis, adds, λέγοι δ' ἄν τις περὶ ἄλλων Παλλαδίων, τοῦ τε κατ' Ἀλαλκόμενον τρισα τὸν αὐτεφυρῶν (from Müller's correction, Eumenid. p. 106). καὶ τῶν περὶ αὐτεφυρῶν (περιαυτοφόρων) λεγομένων. Παλλάδια περιαυτόφορα are, ἅ τις ἂν φέροι περὶ ἑαυτόν which both Ulysses and Diomed do, in the vase illustrated by Millingen.

Chapter XVII

¹ Ἵκετο δ' ἐς Μαραθῶνα καὶεὐρυάγυιαν Ἀθήνην
Δῦνε δ' Ἐρεχθῆος πυκινὸν δόμον.

² *Erecthei Athenis delubrum vidimus.*

³ See the Plan in the map of Athens.

⁴ διπλοῦν οἴκημα. Pausan. i. 26, 5.

⁵ Pausan. i. 27, 2. τῷ ναῷ τῆς Ἀθηνᾶς Πανδρόσον ναὸς συνεχής ἐστί.

⁶ In Philochor. Atthid. Siebel. p. 2, a dog is described as entering the shrine of Polias, and thence *penetrating* (δῦσα) into that of Pandrosus: (hence the shrine of Pandrosus was the *interior* chamber, i.e. the *western* of the two, and the *central* of the three), in which was the sacred olive, and beneath it the altar of Ζεὺς ἑρκεῖος. This altar was properly placed in the *centre* of this building, as of a public αὐλή. The words of Virgil

Ædibus in *mediis*, nudoque sub ætheris axe
Ingens ara fuit, juxtaque veterrina *laurus*
Incumbens aræ atque umbrâ complexa Penates,

give a good picture of this spot and its features. The triple division of the Erectheum might have suggested Ovid's description (Metam. ii. 737.) of the chambers of the daughters of Cecrops

> Tres habuit thalamos, quorum tu Pandrose dextrum,
> Aglauros lævum, medium possederat Herse.

[7] It could not be part of the Cecropium, for its western exterior wall is described in the inscription cited below as πρὸς τοῦ Πανδροσείου, (not τῷ Πανδροσείῳ), nor could it be the Pandroseum, for that was συνεχὲς to the shrine of Polias: it was a neutral ground, without any other specific name than στοὰ, by which I believe it to be described in the inscription.

[8] Boeck. C. i. 261. Wilkins Atheniensia. p. 195. Rose, Inscr. p. 144.

[9] On this ground; the Κόραι (so the Caryatides are termed in the inscription), are described there as standing ἐν τῇ πρὸςτάσει (portico) τῇ πρὸ τῷ Κεκροπίῳ, whereas the *northern* portico is described as πρὸς τοῦ θυρώματος. In the former, the *dative* case signifies that the *Caryatid* portico was a part of, and attached to the Cecropium: while in the latter, the *genitive* indicates that the northern portico was only in the direction of or *towards* the portal.

[10] Æschylus (Suppl. 218.) seems to draw his picture from this object in the Athenian citadel, when he says of an Argive Temple,
> ὁρῶ ρίαιναν τήνδε σημεῖον θεοῦ.

Hegesias (in Strabo p. 396.) applies this identical expression to the trident in the Erectheum. ὁρῶ τὴν ἀκρόπολιν καὶ τὸ περὶ τῆς τριαίνης ἔχει τι σημεῖον.

[11] See Bentley, Hor. Od. i. 7, 5.

[12]
> οὐκ ἔσθ', ἑκούσης τῆς ἐμῆς ψυχῆςἄνερ
> προγόνων παλαιὰ θέσμι' ὅστις ἐκβαλεῖ,
> οὐδ' ἀντ' ἐλάας χρυσέας τε Γοργόνος
> τρίαιναν ὀρθὴν στᾶσαν ἐν πόλεῆως βάθροις
> Εὔμολπος οὐδὲ Ὀρῆξ ἀναστέψει λεὼς
> στεφάνοισι, Παλλὰς δ' οὐδαμοῦ τιμήσεται.

Frag. Eur. Erecth. ap. Lycurg. p. 161. 24. p. 264. Bekker. See Dobree Aristophanic. p. 76. who from a reference to the locality of these objects, has very happily restored this passage, once deemed irremediably corrupt.

[13] Pausan. 1. 27, 4.

[14] Herod. v. 82. Inscr. Anthol. ii. p. 773. Hesych.
Ἐρεχθεὺς· Ποσειδῶν ἐν Ἀθήναις...

[15] Ister. ap Schol. Œd. Col. 701. Some fanciful etymologies of the term Μορία have been assigned (Schol. Nub. 1002). The word seems to me to contain an allusion to this their supposed origin: it is an historical expression of this very propagation or *partition* of these olives from the one stock in the Erectheum. μορία ἐλαία is olea *partitiva*. The word itself (from μείρω, μόρος, &c.) still survives in its compound συμμορία, a *class*.

[16] Herod. viii. 55. δευτέρῃ ἡμέρῃ..ὅσον πηχυαῖν, but Pausan. i. 26, 7. αὐθήμερον...ἐπὶ δύο πήχεις. Thus in the interval of time between these two writers, in order that the miracle might become more marvellous, the days and cubits changed their respective numbers.

[17] Æd. Col. 667.

[18] That they have passed to Athens from Colonus appears from v. 708. That they have passed to 708. τᾷ ματροπόλει.

[19] Which they call ἀχείρωτον αὐτοποιὸν, παιδοτρόφον: the former epithets in allusion to its regermination after the Persian invasion: the last to its general propagation.

[20] θάλασσα, Herod. viii. 55. hence εὐθάλασσον, v. 711. κῦμα τὸ ἐν ἀκρπόλει. Pausan. viii. 20. 4.

[21] See Boeck. C. I. p. 481.

[22]
```
                O ΔΗΜΟΣ
       [ΣΩΚΡΑ]ΤΗ ΣΩΚΡΑΤΟΥΣ ΘΟΡΙΚΙΟΝ
   [ΟΥΝΕΚΑ Σ]ΑΣ ΕΔΑΗΣΑΝ ΑΠΟ ΦΡΕΝΟΣ ΑΞΙΑ ΜΟΙΣΑΝ
       [ΣΩΡΑΤΕ]Σ ΩΓΥΓΙΩΝ ΥΙΕΣ ΕΡΙΧΘΟΝΙΔΑΝ
   [ΤΟΥΝΕΚΑ ΣΟΙ] ΣΟΦΙΑΣ ΕΔΟΣΑΝ ΓΕΡΑΣ ΑΙ ΓΑΡ ΑΘΑΝΑΙ
         [ΟΙΑΙ ΙΣΑΝ]ΤΟΙΩΙΔ ΑΝΔΡΙ ΤΕΚΕΙΝ ΧΑΡΙΤΑ
```

Nossis Anthol. i. p. 526. χάριτας τίκτεν ἴσας...

[23] [ΚΕΚ]ΡΟΓΙΣ ΓΑΙΔ[ΩΝ ΕΝΙΚΑ]
      [ΚΤΗ]ΣΙΓΓΟΣΧΑΒΡ[Ι ΟΥΕΧΟ]
      ΡΗΓΕΙ ΔΑ......

[24] Concerning whom see Plut. v. Phoc. p. 302. v. Demosth. p. 717. Athenæus iv. 165. Wolf proleg. Lept. p. 29. Bremi.

[25] Dio Chrysostom indeed (i. p. 635.) asserts that *Leptines was condemned*: (ἑάλω γραφῆς). This we know to have been impossible from the nature of the suit. The legal term (προθεσμία) in which Leptines was subject to prosecution, had expired. He was ἀνεύθυνος (see Arg. Dem. Lept. 453. 9). It is singular that F. A. Wolf should have approved this statement of D. Chrysostom, when he himself observes in the next

page, that the title πρὸς Λεπτίνην, and not κατὰ Λεπτίνου, prefixed to the oration "Leptinem *præsentem* in judicio signat non reum factum." Proleg. p. 152.

[26]
Ο ΔΗΜΟΣ
ΓΝΑΙΟΝ ΑΚΕΡΡΩΝΙΟΝ
ΠΡΟΚΛΟΝ ΑΝΘΥΠΑΤΟΝ
ΤΗΖ ΕΙΣ ΕΑΥΤΟΝ ΕΥΝΟΙΑΣ
ΚΑΙ ΚΗΔΕΜΟΝΙΑΣ ΕΝΕΚΑ

[27] Pausanias thus speaks of that change, i. 18. 2. τὰς εἰκόνας τῶν ἱππέων εἴτε οἱ παῖδές εἰσιν οἱ Ξενοφῶντος εἴτε ἄλλως εἰς εὐπρέπειαν πεποιημέναι. It has been thought that Pausanias used the above obscure expressions for fear of giving offence: for one of the above statues became an Agrippa; as the inscription on its base still indicates - the other probably an Augustus. But (I conceive) he had another meaning. The statue, be it remembered, remained the same; the inscription alone was altered. The statue was like an actor (see Die. Chrys. i. 647.) playing successively different parts on the same stage. Hence Pausanias might well say, he could not tell very clearly who the statue really was. If the statue itself was to be believed, it was a son of Xenophon: if the inscription, an Agrippa. By recording this his dilemma, he tacitly censures the folly of the Athenians in thus conferring honorary distinctions, which denoted nothing, but the weakness of those who conferred them. Pausanias writing under the Antonines, had little to fear from indulging in sarcasm on Agrippa. Pliny satirized Augustus, and dedicated his satire to Trajan. Pausanias too (ii. 18.) says openly enough of a similar statue, τὸν ἐπίγραμμα ἔχοντα ὡς εἴη Αὔγουστος, Ὀρέστην εἶναι λέγουσιν.

[28] Pausan. i. 18, 3. Other instances at Athens of the same practices are recorded in Paus. i. 2. 4. (and Siebelis note.) i. 22. 4. Hence when Phædrus said (Epil. lib. ii.)
Æsopi ingenio statuam posuere Attici
Servumque collocarunt æternâ in basi,
he wrote with a significant allusion to the practice of his times in this city: the epithet has been suspected without reason. Hence also perhaps it was that Theophrastus has put into the mouth of his flatterer the speech ἡ εἰκών σου ὁμοία ἐστί. (Char. ii).

[29]
[ΑΓΑ]ΘΗΙ [ΤΥΧΗΙ]
[ΑΠΟ]ΛΛΩΝ[ΙΟΣ]
[Α]ΦΙΔΝΑΙΟ[Σ ΤΗΝ]
[ΘΥΓ]ΑΤΕΡΑ ΑΝΘΕΜΙΑ[Ν]
[ΚΑΙ]Ο ΘΕΙΟΣ ΟΥΛ[ΠΙΑΝΟΣ]
[ΚΑΙ]Η ΜΗΤΗΡΔΙΦΙΛΩ[ΝΗ]
[ΚΑΝ]Η ΦΟΡΗΣΑΣ[ΑΝ]
[Α]ΝΕΘΗΚΑΝ

[ΕΓ]Ι ΙΕΡΕΙΑΣ ΠΕΝΤΕΤΗΡΙ[ΔΟΣ]
[ΙΕ]ΡΟΚΛΕΟΥΣ ΦΛΥΕΩΣ
[ΚΑΙ]ΚΟΣΘΕΝΗΣ
[ΚΑΙ].......ΕΓΟΗΣΑΝ

I have here supplied Καικοσθένης as one of the sculptors of this statue from a fragment of another inscription beneath the N.E. of the citadel, where we read

ΚΑΙΚΟΣΘΕΝΗΣ ΕΠΟΙΗΣΕΝ.

```
30  1    ΠΑΡΑΔΙΔΩΜΙ ΤΟΙΣ
         ΚΑΤΑΧΘΟΝΙΟΙΣ ΘΕ
         ΟΙΣ ΤΟΥΤΟ ΤΟ ΗΡΩ
         ΟΝ ΦΥΛΑΣΣΕΙΝ ΠΛΟΥ
    5    ΤΩΝΙ ΚΑΙ ΔΗΜΗΤΡΙ
         ΚΑΙ ΠΕΡΣΕΦΟΝΗΙ
         ΚΑΙ ΕΡΙΝΥΣΙ ΚΑΙ ΠΑΣΙ
         ΤΟΙΣ ΚΑΤΑΧΘΟΝΙΟΙΣ
         ΘΕΟΙΣ ΕΙΤΙΣ ΑΠΟΚΟ
   10    ΣΜΗΣΕΙ ΤΟΥΤΟ ΤΟ ΗΡΩ
         ΟΝ Η ΑΠΟΣΚΟΥΤΛΩΣΕΙ
         Η ΕΙ ΤΙ ΚΑΙ ΕΤΕΡΟΝ ΜΕΤΑ
         ΚΕΙΝΗΣΕΙ Η ΑΥΤΟΣ Η
         ΔΙ ΑΛΛΟΥ ΤΟΥ ΤΟΥΤΩ ΜΗ
   15    ΓΗ ΒΑΤΗ ΜΗ ΘΑΛΑΣΣΑ
         ΠΛΩΤΗ ΑΛΛΑ ΕΚΡΕΙ
         ΖΩΘΗΣΕΤΕ ΠΑΝ ΓΕΝΕ[Ι]
         ΠΑΣΙ ΤΟΙΣ ΚΑΚΟΙΣ ΠΕ[Ι]
         ΡΑΝ ΔΩΣΕΙ ΚΑΙ ΦΡΕΙ
   20    ΚΗ ΚΑΙ ΠΥΡΕΤΩ ΚΑΙ ΤΕ
         ΤΑΡΤΑΙΩ ΚΑΙ ΕΛΕΦΑ[ΝΤ]
         [ΙΑΣΕΙ ΚΑΙ] ΟΣΑ ΚΑΚΑ [ΚΑΙ ΠΑ]
         ΘΗ ΑΝΘΡΩ[ΠΩΙ ΓΙ]
         ΓΝΕΤΑΙ ΤΑΥΤΑ [ΓΙΓΝΕΣ]
   25    [ΘΩ] ΤΩ ΤΟΛΜΗΣΑΝΤΙ
         ΕΚ ΤΟΥΤΟΥ ΤΟΥ ΗΡΩ
         ΟΥ ΜΕΤΑΚ ΕΙΝΗΣΑΙ ΤΙ
```

Compare the inscriptions of a similar purport in Boeck. p. 531, 542. See also p. 919, where a transcript is offered of this inscription. In v. 11. ἀποσκουτλώσει, is connected with σκοῦλαι; κνῆσαι in Hesychius. In v. 17. ἐκρειζωθήσετε is for ἐκρειζωθήσεται, by the common confusion of ε for αι.

Chapter XVIII

[1] Ὀρῶμεν ὡς τὸν Παρθενῶνα, ὄυτω καὶ τὸ Θησεῖον ἅπαντας προσκυνοῦντας.

[2] Plutarch. v. Cimon. iii. p. 189. Reiske.

[3] It has been hence argued, that at the time of the erection of the Theseum, the *labours of Hercules* were not *twelve* but *ten*. This might have been a just inference had it been possible to have introduced *twelve* metopes on the frieze of a hexastyle portico, such as that of this temple.

[4] Here. fur. 1323. Theseus addresses Hercules just dying:

ἕπου δ' ἅμ' ἡμῖν πρὸς πόλισμα Παλλάδος
δόμους τε δώσω, χρημάτων τ' ἐμῶν μέρος.

Chapter XIX

[1] ἔνθαδε μιστύλλουσι δρόμον φαεθοντίδος αἴγλης
ὕδασι δ' ἠελίοιο ταλαντεύουσι κελεύθους.

[2] The order is this: Boreas, Kaikias, Apeliotes, Euros, Notus, Libs, Zephyrus, Skiron.

[3] Eubul. Athen. 8. c. Menander. Ath. 243. a. Arist. Eccles. 652. where Schol. τὸ παλαιὸν καλοῦντες ἐς δεῖπνον καὶ καλούμενοι παρεσημαίνοντο τὴν σκιὰν· οὐδ' ὑποτηρήσεως οὔσης αἰτίας (read ἐτέιας, i.e. since there was then (τὸ παλαιὸν) no indication even of the year, much less of the day, to intimate) εἰς πόσας ὥρας προήκει τὸ ἔτος. αἰτίας and ἐτείας were identical in sound, when this Scholion was transcribed, as they are in Greece now. The same confusion existed in Eurip. Stob. p. 141. 　— οἱ δ' ὄλβου μετὰ
φθίνουσ' αἰτίοις προσφερεῖς μεταλλαγαῖς;
where Valckenaer (Diatr. p. 6.) has well restored ἐτείοις. The expression ὥρας ἐτείους occurs in Diog. Laert. ix. 10.

[4] ὅταν ἡ δεκάπουν τὸ στοιχεῖον λιπαρὸν χωρεῖν ἐπὶ δεῖπνον.

[5] Pausan. i. 20, 1. ἐστὶν ὁδὸς καλουμένη Τρίποδες· ἀφ' οὗ δὲ καλοῦσι τὸ χωρίον, ναοὶ θεῶν μεγάλοι, καί σφισιν ἐφεστήκασι τρίποδες— But the ναοὶ were *not* μεγάλοι, as this surviving fabric shews; therefore it has been proposed to insert οὐ before that word. Yet even then is the difficulty removed? Houses became a street, not by being great or not great, but by being continuous. The word ΜΕΓΑΛΟΙ should therefore, I think, be altered into ΜΕΤΑΛΛΟΙ (Theocr. 1. 134. has the form ἔναλλα) or ΜΕΤΑΛΛΗΛΟΙ, i.e. one after another, in a line. Compare Plato Gorg. 472. a. Τρίποδες ἐφεξῆς ἑστῶτες ἐν Διονυσίῳ, speaking of this same street.

Connected with the Dionysiac Theatre on the west and this street of the Tripods on the east was the Temple of Dionysus. At this spot I find the following inscription.
ΠΛΕΙΣΤΑΙΝΟΝ ΣΟΚΛΕΟΥΣ ΚΕΦΑΛΗΘΕΝ
Η ΓΥΝΗ ΠΛΕΙΣΤΙΣ ΚΑΙ Η ΘΥΓΑΤΗΡ ΣΟΣΙΝΙΚΗ
ΑΡΧΟΝΤΑ ΓΕΝΟΜΕΝΟΝ ΔΙΟΝΥΣΩΙ ΑΝΕΘΗΚΑΝ.

And connected with the street of Tripods the following:

ΤΙΜΟΔΗΜΟΣ ΤΙΜΟΔΗΜΟΥ
ΠΑΙΔΩΝ ΕΝΙΚΑ..........

The inscription on the Monument of Lysicrates is on the *eastern* part of its curved architrave: the street therefore ran on that side of it.

Chapter XX

¹ λάμπει δε σαφὴς ἀρετὰ
ἕν τε γυμνοῖσι σταδίοις
σφίσιν ἕν τ' ἀσπιδοδούποιιν ὁπλίταις δρόμοις.

² The average length of the Greek Stadium was 600 feet (ἓξ πλέθρα), equal to about 612 English. The interior of the Athenian Stadium is found to measure 630 English feet. The distance of its *course* itself cannot now be precisely ascertained; but it was necessarily something less than the length of the interior.

³ Soph. Elect. 686. ἰσώσας τῇ ἀφέσει τὰ τέρματα.

⁴ οὐχ οἱ μὲν δεινοί τε καὶ ἄδικοι, he enquires, δρῶσιν ὅπερ οἱ δρομεῖς ὅσοι ἂν θέωσιν εὖ ἀπὸ τῶν κάτω, ἀπὸ δε τῶν ἄνω μή; τὸ μὲν πρῶτον ὀξέως ἀναπηδῶσιν, τελευτῶντες δὲ καταγέλαστοι γίγνονται, τὰ ὦτα ἐπὶ τῶν ὤμων ἔχοντες καὶ ἀστεφάνωτοι ἀποτρέχοντες;

It has been supposed that this Panathenaic Stadium was not constructed till the administration of the orator Lycurgus, about 350 B.C. But the assertion of the pseudo-Plutarch (Vitt. x. Oratt.) on which this supposition rests, is merely to this effect; that Lycurgus *completed* (ἐξειργάσατο) the Stadium, by constructing a podium (κρηπὶς), and levelling the bed (χαράδρα) of the Stadium. Sophocles would never have ventured to make an *Athenian* charioteer victorious over *nine* competitors at Delphi (as he does in his Electra, 707 sq.) had Athens not possessed a Stadium in his time: and there is no evidence of there having been ever *more than one* at Athens.

⁵ See Phot. Lex. v. περιαγειρόμενοι, and Ruhnk. Tim. p. 216.

⁶   ἤδη δ' ἂν ἕλκων κῶλον ἐκπλέθρου δρόμου
       ταχὺς βαδιστὴς τερμόνων ἂν ἥπτετο.

⁷   θᾶσσον δὲ βύρσαν ἐξέδειρεν ἢ δρομεὺς
       δισσοὺς διαύλους ἵππιος.

⁸ The Stadium is no doubt referred to above in the term ἔκπλεθρος δρόμος, for the πλέθρον was ἄκτον μέρος σταδίου. Tim. Lex. Platon.

⁹ An inscription, which I copy, in another part of Athens, affords so pertinent an illustration of the contests which once took place on this spot that it is inserted here.

[............]ΙΠΠΟΘΟΩΝΤΙΔΟΣ ΦΥΛΗΣ
[ΠΩΛΙΚΗΙ ΞΥΝΩ] ΡΙΔΙ ΑΚ[ΑΜ] ΠΙ[ΟΝ]
[(ὁ δεῖνα τοῦ δεῖνα)] ΚΛΕΟΥΣ ΑΙΑΝΤΙΔΟΣ ΦΥΛΗΣ
[ΠΟΛΙΚΗΙ ΞΥΝΩΡΙ]ΔΙ ΔΙΑΥΛΟΝ
[............]ΚΛΕΟΥΣ ΠΤΟΛΕΜΑΙΔΟΣ ΦΥΛΗΣ
[ΞΥΝ ΑΣΠΙΔ]Ι ΔΙΑΥΛΟΝ ΕΝ ΟΠΛΟΙΣ
[ΕΚΤΩΝΙΠΠΙ]ΕΩΝ
[ΑΙ] ΓΕΙΔΟΣ ΦΥΛΗΣ

[ΕΚΤΩ]Ν ΙΠΠΕΩΝ
[ΙΠ]ΠΟΘΟΩΝΤΙΔΟΣ ΦΥΛΗΣ
[............]ΕΚ ΤΩΝ ΦΥΛΑΡΧΩΝ
[............]ΟΟΣ ΠΤΟΛΕΜΑΙΔΟΣ ΦΥΛΗΣ
[............]Ν ΕΚ ΤΩΝ ΙΠΠΕΩΝ
[............]Υ ΟΙΝΕΙΔΟΣ ΦΥΛΗΣ
[..........]ΕΚ ΤΩΝ ΦΥΛΑΡΧΩΝ
[.........Κ]ΕΚΡΟΠΙΔΟΣ ΦΥΛΗΣ
[.........]ΘΕΩΝ ΛΑΜΠΑΔΙ
[.........]ΔΟΣ ΦΥΛΗΣ
[ΕΚ ΤΩΝ ΖΕΥΓ]ΙΤΩΝ
[ΑΡΜΑΤΙ ΠΟΛΕΜΙ] ΣΤΗΡΙΩ
[..........ΠΤ]ΟΛΕΜΑΙΔΟΣ ΦΥΛΗΣ
[ΑΡΜΑΤΙ ΤΕΛΕΙ]ΩΙ
[........ΑΙΑ]ΝΤΙΔΟΣ ΦΥΛΗΣ
[ΔΙΑΥΛΟ]Ν
[ΛΕΟΝ]ΤΙΔΟΣ ΦΥΛΗΣ
[ΑΚΑΜΠ]ΙΟΝ
[ΛΕ]ΟΝΤΙΔΟΣ ΦΥΛΗΣ
[ΑΠΗΝΗΙ ΠΟΛΕ]ΜΙΣΤΗΡΙΑΙ
[ΛΕΟΝ]ΤΙΔΟΣ ΦΥΛΗΣ
[Ι]ΠΠΟΘΩΝΤΙΔΟΣ ΦΥΛΗΣ
[ΑΚΑΜ]ΠΙΟΝ
[........]ΠΤΟΛΕΜΑΙΔΟΣ ΦΥΛΗΣ
[ΕΚΤΩΝ ΙΠΠΙ]ΕΩΝ ΙΠΠΕΩΝ ΙΠΠΩ ΠΟΛΥΔΡΟΜΩ
[..........]ΑΙΓΕΙΔΟΣ ΦΥΛΗΣ
[........]ΙΠΠΟΘ..ΟΦΩΝ
[.............]ΒΑΣΙΛΕΩΣ ΑΝΤΙΟΧΟΥ [ΕΠΙ]ΦΑΝ[ΟΥΣ]
[ΑΡΜΑΤΙ ΠΩ]ΛΙΚΩ
[...........]ΑΛΕΞΑΝΔΡΕΥΣ
[ΑΡΜΑΤ]Ι ΤΕΛΕΙ[ΩΙ]
[...........]ΛΑΟΔΙΚΕΥΣ ΤΩΝ ΠΡΟΣ ΘΑ[Λ]Α[ΣΣ]ΗΙ
ΠΩΛΙΚΩΝ
Σ ΜΥΝΔΙΟΣ
ΑΡΜΑΤΙ ΤΕΛΕΙΩΙ
[.............]ΒΑΣΙΛΕΩΣ ΑΝΤΙΟΧΟΥ ΕΠΙΦΑΝ[ΟΥΣ]
ΕΛΕΥΣΙΝΙΩΝ ΑΜΜΩΝΙΟΣ ΑΜΜΩΝΙΟΥ
[......]Σ ΙΕΥΓΕΙ ΕΓΒΙΒΑΙΩΝ
ΚΕΚΡΟΠΙΔΟΣ ΦΥΛΗΣ
[ΔΟΛΙΧ]ΟΝ
ΑΚΑΜΠΙΟΝ
[........]ΚΕΚΡΟΠΙΔΟΣ ΦΥΛΗΣ
ΑΚΑΜΠΙΟΝ
Κ.. Φ..
ΑΡΜΑΤΙ ΠΟΛΕΜΙΣΤΗΡΙΩΙ
[......]ΟΥ ΚΕΚΡΟΠΙΔΟΣ ΦΥΛΗΣ
[ΟΛΥ]ΜΠΙΚΩΙ..
....

The different species of courses in the Stadium, mentioned here, are as follows:

(1) The στάδιον, or ἀκάμπιον, *one* course from the starting-place to the καμπτήρ. Pindar. Ol. xi. 64.

(2) δίαυλος; two.

(3) δίαυλος ἵππιος; four. Musg. Eur. Elect. 825.

(4) δόλιχος; seven.

(5) δόλιχος ἵππιος; twenty-four? Boeck. Insc. p.703.

They are well described by Tzetzes Chil. p.22. Kiessling. Comp. Pausan. iii. 14. 3. v. 8. 6. See Dissen. Pindar. i. p.267. on ἀπήνη, (of mules) πώλων συνωρίς, ἅρμα τέλειον; πολεμιστήριον Aristoph. Nub. 28.

Chapter XXI

[1] καναχοῦσι πηγαὶ δωδεκάκρουνον τὸ στόμα
Ἰλισσὸς ἐν τῇ φάρυγι.

[2] Which seems to have been an ancient practice here: for near this spot a sculptured marble was found in 1759 with an inscription beginning with Οἱ πλυνῆς Νύμφαις εὐξάμενοι. Paciaudi Mon. Pel. i. p. 207. Millin. Gal. Myth. n. 327.

[3] The only passage, as far as I am aware, in the extant works of the Athenian dramatists, in which there is a shadow of allusion to the Ilissus is in the Œdipus Coloneus, v. 687. Here, however, as the MSS. and the context show, Κηφισοῦ, and not Ἰλισσοῦ, is the true reading. The latter was probably introduced into his own MS. by a scribe who was a little angry at the preference universally given to the Cephisus. As a sort of revenge for this, another copyist has attempted to make room for the Cephisus, by ejecting the Ilissus from its proper place in Apollon. Rhod. i. 215. and by inserting the name of the former. We may here observe, in connexion with this topic, that the Athenian dramatists never speak of Phalerum or Peiræus as Athenian harbours, but of *Munychia* only. (Eur. Hippolyt. 760). Whence it may be that the port of Munychia had then fallen into disuse: for it would only have begun to be of use to poets, when it had ceased to be so to merchants and sailors.

[4]
        ἔνθα, ποθ' ἁγνὰς
ἐννέα Πιερίδας Μούσας λέγουσι
ξανθὰν Ἁρμονίαν φυτεῦσαι,
τοῦ καλλινάου τ' ἀπὸ Κηφισοῦ ῥοὰς
τὰν Κύπριν κλῄζουσιν ἀφυσσαμέναν
χώραν καταπνεῦσαι μετρίας ἀνέμων
ἡδυπνόους αὔρας......

[5] Par. Reg. iv. 249.

[6] Ep. vii. p. 398. ed. Francof.

⁷ Ἔοικας, ὦ παῖ, τὸ ἄνθος τοῦτο ἰδεῖν ἐθέλειν...(ἀλλ' ἐγώ τε σοι δ' ἐπιδείξω ΤΙΧΟΥΣ πρὸς τὸν ΙΛΙΣΟΝ ἅμα ἄμφω βαδίσαιμεν;) ἀλλ' ἐγώ τε σοί γ' ἐπιδείξω· ἔξω τείχους πρὸς τὸν Ἰλισὸν ἅμα ἄμφω βαδίσωμεν.

The word ἔξω was absorbed by the last syllable of the preceding one, ἐπιδείξω. See the passages, to which Fronto alludes, in the Phædrus, p. 227. a. πορεύομαι ἔξω τείχους; and p. 229. a. κατὰ τὸν Ἰλισσὸν ἴωμεν. Fr. Jacobs, in Wolf's Analekten, i. p. 115, had before restored Ἰλισσὸν, to the passage in Fronto: but for τίχους he proposes τάχος.

⁸ Bekker. Anec. p. 326.

Chapter XXII

¹ Ποῦ τὶν ἐκκλησίαν ὄψομαι, ποῦ Κεραμεικόν, Ἀγορὰν, Δικαστήρια, τὴν καλὴν Ἀκρόπολιν, τὰς Σεμνὰς Θεάς;

² Thuc. ii. 14. τὸ πρὸ τούτου (Theseus) ἀκρόπολις ἡ νῦν οὖσα πόλις ἦν, καὶ τὸ ὑπ' αὐτὴν πρὸς νότον μάλιστα τετραμμένον.

³ Pausan. i. 3. 5. sqq. and 1. 5. 1.

⁴ See Boeck Inscr. n. 525. Thuc. vi. 54. Aristoph. Aves, 1008.

⁵ They stood on the eastern verge of the Agora on a platform, probably a ἡμικύκλιον, called ὀρχήστρα. Tim. Lex. Plat. in. v. p. 196. and Phot. p. 351. πρῶτον ἐκλήθη ἐν τῇ ἀγορᾷ. It is to this orchestra, and not, I think, to that of the Theatre, that Diocleides alludes, (Andoc. Myst. p. 112. Bekker), when he asserts that he saw by the light of the moon, when standing in the Lenæum, the three hundred men whom he accuses of having mutilated the Hermæ, as they were descending from the Odeum, and going towards the Orchestra. He implies that they were just at the eastern verge of the Agora, and were going to cross it toward the stoa of the *Hermæ* at its other extremity, which was their main object.

⁶ Plat. Menexen. init.

⁷ Harpocrat. v. βασίλειος Στοά. See also Plato. Charmid. p. 55. Heindorf. The speech of Praxagora in Ecclesiaz. 685. is a very descriptive one, and replete with topographical information;

> Β. τὰ δὲ κληρωτήρια ποῖ τρέψεις; Π. εἰς τὴν ἀγορὰν καταθήσω,
> κᾆτα στήσασα παρ' Ἁρμοδίῳ κληρώσω πάντας, ἕως ἂν
> εἰδὼς ὁ λαχὼν ἀπίῃ χαίρων ἐν ὁποίῳ γράμματι δειπνεῖ,
> καὶ κηρύξω τοὺς ἐκ τοῦ βῆτ' εἰς τὴν στωὰν ἀκολουθεῖν
> τὴν βασίλειον δειπνήσοντας, τὸ δὲ θῆτ' εἰς τὴν παρὰ ταύτην.

ATHENS AND ATTICA 199

The θῆτα cannot refer to the *Theseum*, which is not a Stoa, as has been supposed; but it refers to the Stoa of Zeus Eleutherios, which stood parallel to the Stoa Basileios, or παρὰ ταύτην. (Harpocr. in βασίλειος στοά· δύο στοαὶ ἦσαν παρ' ἀλλήλας, ἡ τοῦ Ελευθερίου Διὸς καὶ ἡ βασίλειος). And this was parallel to the Stoa Basileios in *site*, As θῆτα is to βῆτα in *sound*.

[8] Paus. i. 2 4.

[9] Ibid.

[10] Pausan. i. 2. 4. Hence the Temple of Ceres, and the statue of Proserpine, the Eleusinian deities, were placed near it: hence, too, it seems, Alcibiades selected the house of Polytion, which stood close by, for the scene of his counterfeit of the Eleusinian mysteries.

[11] The latter passed through the Thriasian gate; for that gate was called Thriasian, as leading to Thria near Eleusis: and the Thriasian gate was the same as Dipylum (Plutarch. Pericle, T. i. p. 651). αἱ Θριάσιαι πύλαι αἳ νῦν Δίπυλον ὀνομάζονται. Also the Dipylum was the communication from the outer to the inner Cerameicus: hence Plutarch called the latter τὸν ἐντὸς τοῦ Διπύλου Κεραμεικόν. Plut. Syll. T. iii. p. 104. That the Panathenaic procession entered the city from the outer Cerameicus, appears from Thuc. vi. 57. It therefore passed through Dipylum.

[12] Polyb. xvi. 25. Attalus passes from the Peiræus through Dipylum. That the Dipylum was the main entrance from the Peiræus is evident from Lucian Navig. 17. 24.

[13] T. Liv. xxxi. 24. A Dipylo accessit, porta, quæ velut in *ore urbis* posita major aliquanto patentiorque quàm cætaræ.

[14] It must not be forgotten, that when writers speak of the *inner Cerameicus*, they use a term which was not known at Athens till many years after the Peloponnesian War. Then there was but one Cerameicus, that namely *outside the walls*. The adoption of the term *inner Cerameicus*, and the foundation of the *new* Agora, were probably contemporary. The *old* Agora, whose splendours could only remind the inhabitants of Athens of the degradation to which they were reduced, was then disused: its very name was merged in the more general one of Cerameicus. Hence it is only by *later* writers that the statues of Harmodius and Aristogeiton are described as in the *Cerameicus*; by *earlier* authors they are placed in the *Agora*.

[15] The Leocorium was in μέσῳ τῷ Κεραμεικῷ, but was on the verge of the *agora*. See note 20 below.

[16] Thuc. vi. 56. Harpocrat. Λεωκόριον· ἐν μέσῳ τῷ Κεραμεικῷ.

[17] Plutarch. Cimon. iii. p. 189. Reiske.

[18] Cimon going as it seems from his house to the citadel passes through the Cerameicus. Plutarch. iii. p. 181.

[19] The πόλαι Μελιτίδες (Marcellin. v. Thuc. p. ix.) were πρὸ τοῦ ἄστεος (Herod. vi. 103.) i.e. north of the city; (so Herodotus says πρὸ τῆς ἀκροπόλεως, for, *north* of the Citadel. viii. 52). Melite also joined Colonus. (Schol. Av. 998). Colonus was on the north side of the Agora. Hence the north and southern limits of Melite are determined: between these the *Theseum* stands. That the Theseum stood in Melite is rendered still more probable by the fact, that in Melite stood the Melanippeion, or Μελανίππου τοῦ Θήσεως ἡρῶν, and also by the promise of Theseus to Hercules quoted above (δόμους τε δώσω χρημάτων τ' ἐμῶν μέρος), which was I conceive realized in the inauguration of Hercules into Melite near the Theseum (comp. Ar. Ran. 502), or, in the mythological language of Athens, in his receiving *Melite in marriage* (Schol. Ran. 502). Thus the Theseum being in Melite, Theseus was associated with his friend and his son.

[20] As Harp. v. Ευρυσακεῖον· ἐν Μελίτῃ· and Harpocr. v. Κολωνίτας· Κολωνὸς, πλησίον τῆς ἀγορᾶς, ἔνθα τὸ Ευρυσακεῖον. Cp. Schol.

[21] Harpocrat. v. Κολωνίτας.

[22] Marcellin. v. Thuc. ix. Herod. vi. 103.

[23] Herod. vi. 103. Cp. Ælian. H. A. C. xii. 40. Marcellin. v. Thuc. ix. which passages afford an additional proof that Melite was where we have placed it: Herodotus places the cemetery just outside the walls north of Cœle: Ælian, in the exterior Cerameicus: Marcellinus, outside the gates leading into Melite. Hence Cœle was contiguous to the southern limit of the outer Cerameicus, and Melite to that of Cœle.

[24] Plat. Parmenid. 127. a. c.

[25] Demosth. c. Con. p. 1258. 25.

[26] τὸ φερρεφάττιον. That this temple was in the *Agora* may be proved from Hesychius v. (φερσέφαττιον·. that the Λεωκόριον was also in the Agora, is shewn from this passage of Demosthenes, p. 1258. 23. and 25). That they were the extremes of the Agora, may be inferred from their being specified as the opposite limits of an evening's walk in the Agora; and that the Leocorion was the *northern* extreme appears from Harpocrat in. v. Λεωκόριον· ἐν μέσῳ τῷ Κεραμεικῷ.

[27] With this inscription: Τοῦτο ἐστὶ Κολλυτὸς, τοῦτο δὲ Μελίτη. Strabo, p. 65. c.

[28] Toup. Hesyc. iii. p. 525. Steph. Byz. Διόμεια. Diomeia was a borough of the Ægeid Tribe, in Bekker. Lex. Seg. p. 240. for ΔΕΙΟΜΝΑ: δῆμος 'Αιγηΐδος is to be read ΔΙΟΜΕΙΑ. Collyttus, Melite and Diomeia are properly combined in Plutarch Exil. T. viii. p. 372. Reiske.

29 In Milton's description of Athens (P. R. iv. 283.) the only topographical inaccuracy consists in the site there assigned by him to the Lyceum. It is there placed within instead of without the walls.

30

ΟΥ ΤΑΔΕ ΘΕΛΞΙΜΕΛΗΣ ΑΜΦΙΟΝΙΣ ΗΡΑ[ΤΟ ΜΟΥΣΛ]
ΟΥΔΕ ΚΥΚΛΩΠΕΙΑΣ ΧΕΙΡΟΣ ΕΛ[ΑΣΣΕ ΒΙΛ.]

31 Æschin. c. Ctes. p. 163. προσέλθετε τῇ διανοίᾳ εἰς τὴν Ποικίλην, ἁπάντων γὰρ ὑμῶν τῶν καλῶν ἔργων τὰ ὑπομνήματα ἐν τῇ ἀγορᾷ ἀνάκειται.

32 Pausan. i. 15. 4. These were preserved there with great care, being ἐπαληλιμμέναι πίσσῃ, μὴ σφᾶς ὅ τε ρόνος λυμαίνηται καὶ ὁ ἰός, when they were seen there by Pausanias. Cp. Aristoph. Equit. 843.

33 Meton, the celebrated astronomer, lived near the Pœcile, (Ælian. V. H. xiii. 12.) and near the Colonus in the city. Schol. Arist. Av. 998.

34 Lucian. Jov. Tragæd. ii. p. 681. Ἑρμῆς ὁ ἀγοραῖος, ὁ παρὰ τὴν Ποικίλην.

35 πρεσβεύσασ παρὰ Φίλιππον, καὶ ἐρομένου (τοῦ βασίλεως) ποταπαί εἰσιν αἱ Ἀθῆναι, ἐπὶ τῆς τραπέζης αὐτὰς κατέγραψε.

Hermog. Invent. c. 2.

Chapter XXIII

1 Κἀκεῖνα περὶ τῶν Παναθηναίων τούτων ἤκουον, πέπλον
μὲν ἀνῆφθαι τῆς νεώς, ἡδίω γραφῆς, σὺν οὐρίῳ τῷ κόλπῳ,
δραμεῖν δὲ τὴν ναῦν, οὐχ ὑποζυγίων ἀγόντων, ἀλλ' ἐπιγείοις
μηχαναῖς ὑπολισθείνουσαν, ἐκ Κεφαμεικὸν ἄρασαν χιλίᾳ
κώπῃ, ἀφεῖναι δὲ ἐπὶ τὸ Ἐλευσίνιον· καὶ περιβαλοῦσαν
αὐτὸ παραμείψαι, καὶ κομιζόμενον παρὰ
τὸ Πύθιον ἐλθεῖν, οἷ νῦν ὥρμισται.

2 Hence its motion is described by a nautical term. Plat. Euthyph. 6. a. πέπλος ἀνάγεται εἰς τὴν ἀκρόπολιν.

3 Philostrat. v. Herod. as above.

4 This is asserted here on the authority of an extract from Strattis, the comic poet, (preserved by Harpocrat. v. τοπεῖον), in which it is shown below that the Panathenaic Peplus is alluded to: Harpocratio there says,

τοπεῖα· τὰ σχοινία. Στράττις Μακεδόσι,
τὸν Πέπλον δὲ τοῦτον ἕλκουσιν, δονεύοντες τοπείοις
ἄνδρες ἀναρίθμητοι
εἰς ἄκρον, ὥσπερ ἱστίον, τὸν ἱστόν.

So the last words of these verses should, I think be written, instead of ἱστίον τὸν εἰς τόν... as the words stand in all the editions: for the vertical mast which supported the Panathenaic *peplos* was called ἱστός (see Phot. Lex. v. ἱστός καὶ κεραία, and Bekker. Anecdot. p. 267. 5.), and the transverse one was termed κεραία. The gloss referred to is, ἱστὸς· τὸ ἐπίμηκες ξύλον, κεραία δὲ τὰ πλάγια, ὥστε γενέσθαι γράμμα τὸ ταῦ, (i.e. in this form, **T**), διετείνετο δὲ πολλάκις ὁ τῆς Ἀθηνᾶς πέπλος εἰς τοῦτο τὸ σχῆμα καὶ ἐπόμπευσεν. Strattis meant to say, that the crowd draws the peplos along, hauling it up with ropes to the top of its masts like a sail. (Since writing the above, I have found the following note on the article in Harpocration, in Dobree's Adversaria, i. p. 589: τοπεῖον. Stratt. Legerim τὸν ἱστόν—Sed non expedio.—Qu. εἰς ἄκρον τιν' ὥσπερ ἱστόν *aliquem quasi malum.*")

[5] Denon, Voyage de la Sicile, iv. p. 144. See the representation of the car in Capt. W. H. Smyth's Sicily, p. 85. The 9th to 13th of July are occupied by the festival of S. Rosalia. The great Panathenæa were celebrated on the 28th of Hecatombæon. Cp. Clinton, F. H. p. 325.

[6] Thuc. vi. 57.

[7] Bekker. Anecd. i. p. 22. v. βασίλειος στοά.

[8] Bekker. Anecd. i. p. 242. v. δρῦν φέρειν διὰ τῆς ἀγορᾶς. Compare Himerius quoted by Schneider Xen. Mag. Eq. c. 3. and Menander p. 165. Meineke.

[9] Suid. v. μεχρὶ τοῦ Ελευσινίου.

[10] Hence Virgil has imagined a convenient shifting of the wind to aid it on its course. Ciris. v. 21. sq.
> Sed magno intexens, si fas est dicere, *Peplo*
> Qualis Erectheis olim portatur *Athenis*
> Cum levis *alterno Zephyrus* concrebuit *Euro,*
> Et prono gravidum provexit pondere *Currum.*

[11] ἀνὰ δ' ἐβόασεν λεὼς
Τρωάδος ἀπὸ πετρας σταθείς·
πᾶσα δὲ γέννα φρυγῶν
πρὸς πύλας ὡρμάθη.
τίς οὐκ ἔβα νεανίδων
τίς οὐ γεραιὸς, ἐκ δόμων;
κλωστοῦ δ' ἀμφιβόλοις λίνοισι, ναὸς ὡσεὶ
σκάφος κελαινὸν εἰς ἕδρανα
λάϊνα Παλλάδος θέσαν θεᾶς.

[12] By these arguments. The ship was seen by Pausanias in a spot near the Areopagus (i. 29. I). But it was preserved in the *Pythium* (Philostrat. V. S. p. 537. as above, p. 100.) or temple of Apollo Pythius: further, Apollo Pythius was called Patrous at Athens.

Aristid. i. p. 112. ἡ πόλις προσλαβοῦσα ἑαυτῇ πατρῷν 'Απόλλωνα τὸν Πύθιον, and Harpocrat. v. 'Απόλλων Πατρῷος, ὁ Πύθιος. Cp. Schol. Ar. Av. 1527. and Demost. Coron. 274. 25. Now there was a temple of Apollo *Patrous* at the southern base of the Areopagus. (Pausan. 1. 2. 5). As the Father-Deity of Athens he was properly placed in the Agora: (Pseudo-Plut. v. Lycurg.) βωμὸς Απόλλωνος ἐν τῇ ἀγορῇᾳ, and near the Metrourn: the ship was seen by Pausanias near this spot. This temple, therefore, I conceive to have been the Pythium, in which the Panathenaic ship was preserved.

There were two other temples called by the same name, Pythium, which, are not to be confounded with this: one stood near another Metroum ...for the connection of these two deities is as usual as it is natural ... on the right bank of the Ilissus, in the region termed Agriæ, (Pausan. i. 19.) probably the Pythium of Thucyd. ii. 14. The other was on Mount Pames not far from Phyle. Strabo. 40 4. C. and 392. C. φιλόχορος τὴν Νισαίαν, or (the eastern Megaric boundary) ἀπὸ ἰσθμοῦ μεχρὶ Πυθίου διήκειν φησίν. See Müller Dorians. i. p. 267.

At Athens, in the church of Υπαπάντη (200 yards below the grotto of Pan under the Acropolis), I find a fragment of an inscription which perhaps came from the Pythium of which we have first spoken.

[ΣΤΕΦ]ΑΝΗΦΟΡΗΣΑΣ
[ΤΩΙΠΥΘΙ]ΩΙ ΑΠΟΛΛΩΝΙ
ΤΗΝ ΠΥΘΑΙΔ[Α]

Chapter XXIV

[1] Theseæ brachia longa Viæ.

[2] B.C. 456. Thuc. i. 108. τὰ μακρὰ τείχη, τό τε Φαλήρονδε καὶ τὸ ἐς Πειραιᾶ—the last words are well added to distinguish these pair of μακρὰ τείχη from that pair which afterwards bore the same name.

[3] After B.C. 445. (Æschin. π. π. p. 51. 57. Andoc. p. 24. 23.) which exactly corresponds with the time in which Pericles began to have the direction of public affairs. Clinton, F. H. B.C. 444.

[4] Thuc. ii. 13. τὸ μεταξὺ τοῦ τε μακροῦ καὶ του Φαληρικοῦ. The Phaleric wall had therefore now ceased to be regarded as μακρὸν τεῖχος.

[5] Liv. xxxi, 26. Murus qui *brachiis duobus Peirœum* Athenis jungit.

[6] This wall was the most important of the three: it was the only one that was guarded in the Peloponnesian war. (Thuc. ii. 13. τὸ ἔξωθεν). It abutted on the city-wall to the north of the Theseum, not far from the Melitensian gate. Compare Plutarch. Themist. p. 481. Reiske, with Plato Rep. 439. d. which passages prove also that near it were the πύλαι Δημιάδες.

[7] Pausan. viii. 10. 4. calls it twenty stadia. The length of the two long walls (τὰ μακρὰ τείχη ρπὸς τὸν Πειραιᾶ) was *forty.* Thuc. ii. 13. Strabo, p. 606. and Villoison Anecd. i. 55.

[8] Plato, Gorg. 456. A. Harpocrat. τοῦ διὰ μέσον τείχους. Plutarch, who is very circumstantial on this point, clearly identifies the διὰ μέσου τεῖχος with a μακρὸν τεῖχος. Compare his expression in Vit. Pericl. p. 620. with those in his de Glor. Ath. p. 383. (Reiske). He agrees with Plato in attributing its commencement to Pericles.

[9] Cratin. ap. Plutarch. vii. p. 383. Reiske.

[10] See some of the analogies traced in Süvern's Essay, p. 28. of Mr. W. R. Hamilton's translation.

[11] The following are the details of an excursion from Athens towards the south-west, made with a view of tracing the vestiges of the long walls:

		H.	MIN.	
At	VIII.		45.	(A.M.) leave the temple of Theseus.
	IX.			On brow of Pnyx hill.
			4.	Walls there, abutting on κύκλος ἄστεος.
			20.	Cross Ilissus.
			30.	Fall into road to Phalerum.
			37.	Vestiges of a long wall (the Phaleric?) of a hard coarse pudding-stone.
			42.	Other vestiges.
	X.			Church on r. Blocks: from wall? pass over a low ridge; cistern: Marsh. Bear to right, and find a wall, (τὸ διὰ μέσου τεῖχος?) of white and soft Phaleric stone: bear further to the north; after 219 paces come to another similar wall of soft Phaleric stone. These two the Πειραικὰ σκέλη.
			39.	Cross over the middle wall: proceed toward the N.E. of Phalerum: go along the flat beach toward the eastern point of Phalerum: here the apex of Mount Lycabettus is seen just over the Propylæa.
	XI.			At eastern foot of Phaleric Hill. Gate of Phalerum: descend over rocky hill to the eastern χήλη of the Phaleric harbour: the substructions of this χήλη are very massive: breadth of its wall from 8 to 10 yards: some of the blocks of stone 11 feet long: attached to it, a tower, 12 yards square: further on, 60 paces, another tower, at the extremity of the χήλη, to defend the entrance. Pass along the brink of the harbour toward the western χήλη: A distance of 200

paces, near the μυχὸς, are vestiges of wall skirting the harbour: at 450 from this point, is western χήλη. The beauty of the Phaleric basin is very remarkable. There are fewer vestiges on the Phaleric hill than on that of Munychia.

Upon the whole, I should conclude, from our observations this morning, that the traces of the long wall which we saw on the south of the Ilissus, are too far to the south of the line of the Peiraic σκέλη, to have any connection with either of them. The former also is of a different stone: it tends to the east of Phalerum, and is probably lost in the Phaleric marsh. Compare Plut. v. Cimon. iii. p. 202. εἰς τόπους ἑλώδεις τῶν ἔργων ἐμπεσόντων, ἐρεισθῆναι διὰ Κίμωνος, χάλικι πολλῇ καὶ λίθοις τοῖς βάρεσι ἑλῶν πιεσθέντων.

A very interesting inscription was discovered at Athens in 1829, which exhibits a public contract with certain individuals for the repair of the Long Walls. This inscription is inserted in the Bullettino dell' Institute Archeologico di Roma, 1835, pp. 49-64. It says nothing of the repair of the *Phaleric* Wall, while it specifies both the north and the southern ones.

Chapter XXV

[1] Nympharum Domus.

[2] The offerings with which the sides of this cave were once hung, rurally described in a picture of a pastoral grotto, similar to the present: (Longus, Pastoral, i. p. 5. *Villois*, ἀνέκειντο δὲ γαυλοὶ καὶ αὐλοὶ πλάγιοι καὶ σύριγγες καὶ κάλαμος, πρεσβυτέρων ποιμένων ἀναθήματα; which I quote at length, and suggest also that γαυλοὶ should there be altered into αὐλοὶ, on the authority of Theocritus, xx. 29.

κἤν αὐλῷ λαλέω, κἤν δώνακι, κἤν πλαγιαύλῳ.

Liquids were offered in γαυλοὶ, (Theoc. v. 58.) but the γαυλοὶ themselves were not hung up as ἀναθήματα.

[3] σπήλυγγες Νυμφῶν εὐπίδακες, αἵ τόσον ὕδωρ
 εἴβουσαι σκολιοῦ τοῦδε κατὰ πρέονος,
Πανός τ' ἠχήεσσα πιτυστέπτοιο καλιή
 τὴν ὑπὸ βησσαίης ποςςὶ λέλογχε πέτρης,
αὐταί θ' ἱλήκοιτε καὶ εὐθήροιο δέχεσθε
 Σωσάνδρου ταχινῆς σκῦλ' ἐλαφοσσοΐης...
  Crinagor. Anthol. i. p. 269. Jacobs.

[4] Even after that which they have received from Boeck. C. Ins. Gr. 456.

[5] ΑΡΧΕΔΗΜΟΣΟΦ
  ΗΡΑΙΟΣΟΝΥΜΦ

ΟΛΗΓΤΟΣ ΦΡΑΔ
ΑΙΣΙΝΥΜΦΟΝΤ
ΑΝΤΡΟΝΕΞΗΡΓ
Α[Ξ]ΑΤΟ.

[6] Compare Elmsl. Med. 31. not. c. We have two other dialectic forms, κᾶπον, and 'Αρχέδαμος, in another inscription found in this cave:

['Αρχέ]δαμος ὁ Φερ—
[αῖος] κᾶκον Νύμ[φ]
αις ἐφύτευσεν.

[7] 'Αρχέδημος ὁ Φηραῖος ὁ νυμφόληπτος
ὁπαδαῖσι Νυμφῶν τἄντρον ἐξηργάξατο.

The metre of the first line is Choriambic.

$$\text{Ἀρχέ}||\overset{\_}{\delta\eta}\overset{\cup}{\mu}\overset{\cup}{o}s \;\; \overset{\_}{\overset{}{\delta}} \; \overset{\_}{\Phi\eta} \;|\; \overset{\_}{\rho}\overset{\cup}{\alpha\hat{\iota}}\overset{\cup}{o}s \; \overset{\_}{\overset{}{\delta}} \; \overset{\_}{\nu\nu\mu\phi} \;|\; \overset{\cup}{o}\overset{\_}{\lambda\eta\pi}\overset{\cup}{\tau o}s.$$

My conjecture that this inscription is intended to be *metrical* is confirmed by the character of the *other two*, which were found here, and of which only the latter now remains on the spot. They are both anapæstic.
(1)

$$\text{Ἀρχέδη}||\overset{\cup}{\mu}\overset{\cup}{o}s \;\overset{\_}{\overset{}{\delta}}\; \overset{\_}{\Phi\eta}|\overset{\_}{\alpha\hat{\iota}o}s \;|\; \overset{\_}{\kappa\alpha\hat{\iota}}\; \overset{\_}{\chi o\lambda}|\overset{\_}{\lambda\epsilon\hat{\iota}\delta\eta}s \;|\; \overset{\_}{\tau\alpha\hat{\iota}s}\;\; \overset{\_}{\text{Νύμ}}|\overset{\_}{\phi\alpha\iota s}\;\overset{\_}{\dot{\omega}}\;|\; \overset{\cup}{\kappa o}\overset{\cup}{\delta o}\overset{\_}{\mu\eta}|\overset{\cup}{\sigma\epsilon\nu}:$$

which is an Aristophanic anapæstic tetrameter, with a trisyllabic base:
and (2)

Ἀρχέδημος ||

$$\overset{\cup}{\overset{}{\dot{o}}} \;\overset{\cup}{\Phi\epsilon}\overset{\_}{\rho\alpha\hat{\iota}}|\overset{\_}{o}s \;\overset{\_}{\kappa\hat{\alpha}}|\overset{\_}{\pi o\nu}$$

$$\overset{\_}{\text{Νύμ}}\overset{\cup}{\phi\alpha\iota}s \;\overset{\cup}{\epsilon}\overset{\_}{\phi\acute{\upsilon}}\overset{\_}{\tau\epsilon\upsilon}|\overset{\cup}{\sigma\epsilon\nu};$$

of which the two latter lines are hypercatalectic anapæstic monometers. It was perhaps designed, in these metrical prolusions, that the syllables Αρχε—, Αρχεδη—, Ἀρχέδημος, should thus stand successively as a base *extra metrum*. It will be observed that the word Νύμφαις occurs with the article ταῖς in one of these and not in the other; which is another confirmation of the above conjecture.

[8]   ἐν δὲ κρητῆρές τε καὶ ἀμφιφορῆες ἔασιν
       λάϊνοι.
                          Odyss. xiii. 105.

[9]   Θῆσσαν τράπεζαν αἰνέσασ, Θεός περ ὤν.
                          Eur. Alc. init.

[10] Welcker. Æschyl. Tril. p. 240, considers Ἔρσος as a form of Ἔρος, Ἔρως, the principle of increase, and adds, p. 286. Man statt des Regens den Than setz
Vos date perpetuos teneris sementibus *auctus* (ἔρσας) die dann der Pallas zum Dank in der *Ersephorien* dargebracht werden. Cp. Buttmann. Lexilog. ii. p. 170.

[11] See an instance of abbreviation in the Elean Inscription. Boeck. p. 29.

[12] τ' ἀντ[ρον] Ε[ρ]
σου κλύ[ει]
καὶ τῶν [χ—]
θονε[ων]

[13] εὔχεσθάι τε Διῒ χθονίῳ Δημήτερι θ' ἁγνῇ
Hesiod O. and D. 457.

[14] αἰγιβάτῃ τόδε Πανὶ καὶ εὐκάρπῳ Διονύσῳ
καὶ Δηοῖ χθονίῃ ξυνὸν ἔθηκα γέρας,
αἰτέομαι δ' αὐτοὺς καλὰ πώεα καὶ καλὸν οἶνον,
καὶ καλὸν ἀμῆσαι καρπὸν ἀπ' ἀσταχύων.
Incert. Anthol. i. p. 195. (Jacobs).

[15] Νυμφῶν τινῶν ἱερὸν ἀπὸ τῶν κορῶν τε καὶ ἀγαλμάτων ἔοικεν εἶναι— Plat. Phædr. 230. 6. Compare his description of the allegorical Cave. Repub. vii. init.

[16] Olympiodor. v. Plat. p. 1. τὸν Πλάτωνα λαβόντες οἱ γονεῖς τεθείκασιν ἐν τῷ Ὑμηττῷ, βουλόμενοι ὑπὲρ αὐτοῦ τοῖς ἐκεῖ Θεοῖς Πανὶ καὶ Ἀπόλλωνι νομίῳ καὶ Νύμφαις θῦσαι.

Chapter XXVI

[1] Ἀποθνήσκουσιν, ὦ πορθμεῦ, καὶ πόλεις, σπερ ἄνθρωποι.

[2] On this name Stuart well remarks, (iii. p. 37. new edit.) "Legrana or Lagriona, perhaps Λαύριον, the υ is frequently changed into γ; for instance, Ἔγριπος from Εὔριπος: and the termination α is added: for the modern Greeks never finish a word with a consonant."

[3] Plutarch. v. Thes. p. 26. Reiske. Philochor. ap. Schol. Eur. Hippol. 39.

[4] Steph. Byz. v. Σφηττός and v. Ἀνάφλυστος.

[5] Steph. ubi sup.

[6] τῆς δὲ γῆς τὸ πρὸς νότον

ὁ σκληρὸς οὗτος καὶ γίγαντας ἐκτρέφων
εἴληχε Πάλλας...
        Ap. Strabo. 392. C.

[7] Philochor. ap Schol. Hippol. 39. Plut. Thes. p. 26.

[8] In our way there we leave on the left, Mount Elymbo, Balmá (on l. at *metochi Anáphyso*), with ruins on it, and beyond it Mount Pani with cave, 1½ hours off.
To r. here is Mount Σκωρί: behind is Mount Ιζουρδά: in front of us is Μεσχώρι, a ridge of low mountains running round Σκωρί: behind is Σαντειρῆνα and Θερικό.
To l. just before arriving at Lagrona is Καταφήκη.

Chapter XXVII

[1] Diva quibus retinens in summis urbibus arces.

[2] Schol. Aristid. Dind. p. 27. Πρόνοια 'Αθηνᾶ ἐκλήθη...ἐπ' ἄκρας τῆς Αττικης, ἤγουν τοῦ Σουνίου.

[3] Odyss. iii. 278. Ar. Nub. 400.

[4] πολλοὶ δὲ νῦν μὲν εἰσὶν οὐκ ἐλεύθεροι
εἰς αὔριον δὲ Σουνιεῖς.
        Anaxand. Athenæi. 263. c.

[5] Dernosth. 238. 19.

[6] Cicer. Ad Attic. viii. 3. *in* (Sunio), non ut *oppido*, præposui sed ut *loco*. But see Ernest Ind. δῆμοι.

[7] And lead also, Aristot. Œcon. ii. Πυθοκλῆς Ἀθηναῖος Ἀθηναίοις συνεβούλευε τὸν μόλυβδον τὸν ἐκ τῶν ΤΥΡΙΩΝ παραλαμβάνειν, where Boeck (Diss. de Laureo Econ. Ath. ii. p. 429. English Translation) proposes to πῶς ὁρμήσειαν ἂν ἐπὶ τὰ μέταλλα; ἀπέχει γὰρ τῶν ΑΡΓΥΡΙΩΝ ἡ ἐγγύτατα πόλις Μέγαρα, *&c*.

[8] λαύρα in ancient Greek is a street or lane; λαυρεῖον, a place formed of such lanes; i.e. a mine of shafts, cut as it were into streets like a catacomb. Hence in the modern language of Greece, λαῦραι (pronounced lávrai) are applied to monasteries, and are "rnonachorum *cellæ* quæ cum sejunctæ sint, *vias* et angiportus quodammodo formant." DuCange. Gloss. in. v. Compare Welcker, Trilog, p. 212, who refers λαβύρινθος to the same root: to which opinion the modern pronunciation of the word (lávrinthos) would seem naturally to lead.

[9] Juvenal, iii. 178.

¹⁰ Cp. Ruhnkeniana, p. 38.

¹¹ Veteres ineunt *proscenia* ludi,
Præmiaque ingeniis *pagos* et compita circum
Theseidæ posuere, atque inter pocula læti
Mollibus in pratis unctos saluere per utres...
                                            Virg. Georg. iii. 381.

¹² Schol. Arist. Plut. 1130. ἐν μέσῳ τοῦ θεάτρου ἐτίθεντο ἀσκοὺς πεφυσημένους, &c. Ruhnk. Tim. v. ἀσκωλιάζω. This theatre bears a strong resemblance to the representation of the theatre on a fictile vase found at Aulis, described by Millin. Vases Antiques, ii. 55, 56. and Stuart, Athens, ii. p. 86.

¹³ Φρουρὰ παρ' ἀκτήν τεταμένη, νῆσον λέγω·
'Ελένη τὸ λοιπὸν ἐν βροτοῖς κεκλήσεται.
                                            Eur. Helen. 1689.

¹⁴ v. ad Eur. Hippol. 455.

—ἀνήρπασεν
ἡ καλλιφεγγὴς Κέφαλον εἰς θεοὺς Ἕως,
ἔρωτος οὕνεκ,...

from Thoricus, Apollodor. ii. 4. 7. See the representation on the vase in Millin. Gal. Myth. i. p. 23.

¹⁵ Œd. Col. 1590.

ἐπεὶ δ' ἀφῖκτο τὸν καταρράκτην ὁδόν,
χαλκοῖς βάθροισι γῆθεν ἐρριζωμένον,
ἔστη κελεύθων ἐν πολυσχίστων μιᾷ,
κοίλου πέλας κρατῆρος, οὗ τὰ Θησέως
Περίθου τε κεῖται πίστ' ἀεὶ ξυνθήματα·
ἀφ' οὗ μέσος στὰς, τοῦ τε Θορικίου πέτρου,
κοίλης τ' ἀχέρδου κἀπὸ λαΐνου τάφου,
καθέζετ'...

¹⁶ The interpretation adopted by Kruse, (Hellas, ii. 1. p. 252.) where he supposes the Θορίκιος πέτρος of Sophocles to be a *promontory* at *Thoricus*, had been properly guarded against, even on grammatical grounds, by the remark of Elmsley, i. c. 'Male nonnulli *rupem*, Θορικίας πέτρας quasi scripserit poeta.'

Chapter XXVIII

¹ Σὲ δ' ἀμφὶ σεμνὰς Ἰφιγένεια κλίμακας
Βραυρωνίας δεῖ τῆσδε κληδουχεῖν θεᾶς.

² Athenæi. p. 689. c. where Schweighæuser interprets the expression as if it signified τοιχώρυχοι or fossores murorum.

³ ἐπικατατέμνοντες τῶν μέτρων ἐντός, and συντρήαντες εἰς τὰ τῶν πλησίον. Demosth. c. Pantæn. p. 977. 7.

⁴   [λοι]μῷ θανούσης εἰμὶ [σ]ῆμα Μυρίνης.
Compare the epitaph,
    γηρᾷ θανοῦσαν τάφος ἔχει φιλοξένην,
copied by Mr. Hughes at Athens, inserted in Welcker's Sylloge Epigr. p. 23.

I take this opportunity of quoting another inscription of a very early date, and similar to that in the text. I copied it at Athens from two separate fragments of stone, found not far from each other.

    ΕΜΑΦΙ   ΟΠΑΙΔΟΣ ΤΟΔΕ
    ΕΘΕΚΕΝ   ΣΤΕΣΙΟΗΟΝΘΑΝ
    ΟΕΣΚΑ   ΤΕΙ

Which, with the supplementary additions from conjecture, may be thus exhibited in an elegiac distich:

    [σ]ῆμα [φ]ίλου παιδὸς τόδε [Πενθεσίλαος] ἔθηκεν
    Στησίου, ὃν Θάν[ατος δακρυ]όεις κα[τέ]χει

⁵ Perhaps Μαρώνεια. Bekk. Anec. 279. 32. τόπος Ἀττικῆς, ὅπου τὰ μέταλλα. Demost. 967. 17. There must be some error in Fourmont's assignation of his Myrrhinusian inscription to Meronda: (Boeck. C. I. i. p. 138). Myrrhinus stood much further to the north than Meronda. Strabo 399. a. places it between Brauron and Probalinthus.

⁶ Eurip. Iph. T. 1461.

⁷ From Braóna a village is visible, lying at about two miles distance to the north, another almost double the distance, in nearly the same direction. They are called Bála and Spata. Their names suggest the conjecture that they may have succeeded to the Attic demi Kephalæ, and Prospalta. Further north, and near to Marathon, were the demi of Plotheis and Semachidæ (Boeck. Insc. i. p. 122). At Kephalæ was a Temple of Venus; for Κεφαλαῖσιν, is to be written instead of Κεφαλαίωσιν (i.e. Κεφαλαῖσιν) in Isæus. p. 24. Bekker.

⁸ . . ἐκ τῆςδ' ἕδρα
ἔξελθ', ἔχεις γὰρ χῶρον οὐχ ἁγνὸν πατεῖν. . .

⁹ Εἶναι ὑπανδρευμένος, καὶ ἡ νύμφη του εἶναι τόσον εὐμόρφη, νὰ τὴν γράψῃς.

¹⁰ Cleisthenes, to whom the demi owed their existence, (Herod. v. 66-69.) in order to ingratiate himself with the popular party, incorporated in his new tribes both foreigners and those resident aliens who had been excluded from the old tribes by his predecessor. So I would propose to understand a difficult passage in Aristot. Politic. iii. 2. Κλεισθενὴς μετὰ τὴν τῶν τυράννων ἐκβολὴν πολλοὺς ἐφυλέτευσε ξένους καὶ ΑΦΥΛΟΥΣ μετοίκους, and not ΔΟΥΛΟΥΣ μετοίκους, as the text now stands, without any meaning, in all the editions. In Plutarch (P. Æemil. i.) the words σύμφυλα and ἀφύλους are contrasted in the same way as I conceive φυλετεύω and ἀφύλους to be here.

¹¹ Of these two co-ordinate divisions, that into φυλαὶ and δῆμοι was of a political, that into φρατρίαι and γένη of a religious and domestic character. Cp. Meier de Gentilitate Attica, p. 10 and 14.

¹² This following long inscription admits of much more copious illustration than is appropriate in this place. The Εἰκαδεῖς v. 5. are probably connected with the τριακάδες, into which the φρατρίαι and γένη were divided (cf Hesych. v. τριακάς and ἀτριάκαστοι, and Meier. i. c. p. 21). On the similarity and confusion of θ and β (v. 5.) see Bast, Comment. Pal. p. 709. The judicial words συνδικεῖν and ἐπίσκηψις are illustrated, the former, in a restricted sense, by Elmsl. Eur. Med. 155; the latter, by Bentley on Phalaris, p. 267. These religious corporations, of which the Eikadensian was one, are noticed incidentally in Theophrast. Char. xi. 5. Cp. Meier. p. 34. The ἐφηγήσιος ἄρχων (v. 22.) was superintendent of the ἐφηγήσεις, which were properly suits against the harbourers of outlaws. Suidas v. ἐφήγησις. Wachsmuth. ii. 294. In v. 25, we have the decision of the question of orthography of Παρνήσσιος, which is canvassed by Elmsl. Acharn. 348.

I take this opportunity of quoting from another inscription, which I copied at Athens, another illustration of the text of this same play. In this inscription, which consists of about fifty Athenian names, occur the words:

ΛΑΚΡΑΤΕΙΔΗΣ ΣΩΣΤΡΑΤΟΥ ΙΚΑΡΙΕΥΣ

proving, against the more recent editor, that Bentley was right in substituting the first word for the unmetrical form of it which is found in all the editions of the Acharnians v. 220.

[Ε]ΠΑΜΕΙΝΩΝ ΑΜΕΙΝΙΟΥ ΕΙΠΕΝ ΕΓΕΙΔΗ ΤΙ-
ΝΕΣ ΕΝΑΝΤΙΑ ΤΩΙ ΟΡΚΟΙ ΟΝ ΩΜΟΣΑΝ ΚΑΙ ΤΕΙ
ΑΡΑΙ ΗΝ ΕΙΚΑΔΕΥΣ ΕΠΗΡΑΣΑΤΟ ΔΙΑΤΕΛ
ΟΥΣΙ ΓΡΑΤΤΟΝΤΕΣ ΚΑΙ ΛΕΓΟΝΤΕΣ ΚΑΤΑ Ε
5 ΙΚΑΔΕΩΝ ΕΠΙ ΘΛΑΘΕΙ ΤΩΝ ΚΟΙΝΩΝ ΤΩΝ
ΕΙΚΑΔΕΩΝ ΑΦ ΩΝ ΤΑ ΙΕΡΑ ΤΟΙΣ ΘΕΟΙΣ Θ
ΥΟΥΣΙΝ ΕΙΚΑΔΕΕΣ ΚΑΙ ΤΟΙΣ ΔΙΚΑΖΟΜΕΝ-
ΟΙΣ ΕΙΚΑΔΕΥΣΙΝ ΣΥΝΔΙΚΟΥΣΙΝ ΥΠΕ
ΝΑΝΤΙΑ ΤΟΙΣ ΕΙΚΑΔΕΥΣΙΝ ΚΑΙ ΜΕΜΑΡ
10 ΤΥΡΗΚΑΣΙΝ ΕΠΙ ΤΟΥ ΔΙΚΑΣΤΗΡΙΟΥ Ε
ΠΙ ΘΛΑΘΕΙ ΤΟΥ ΚΟΙΝΟΥ ΤΩΝ ΕΙΚΑΔΕΩΝ
ΨΕΥΔΕΙΣ ΜΑΡΤΥΡΙΑΣ ΕΛΕΣΘΑΙ ΤΡΕΙΣ
ΑΝΔΡΑΣ ΗΔΗ ΕΞ ΕΙΚΑΔΕΩΝ ΟΙ ΤΙΝΕΣ
ΣΥΝΑΓΩΝΙΟΥΝΤΑΙ ΤΩΙ ΕΠΕΣΚΗΜΜΕΝ-
15 ΩΙ ΤΑΙΣ ΜΑΡΤΥΡΙΑΙΣ ΠΟΛΥΞΕΝΩΙ ΟΠΩ
Σ ΑΝ ΔΙΚΗΝ ΔΙΔΩΣΙΝ ΟΙ ΤΑ ΨΕΥΔΗ ΜΑΡΤ
ΥΡΟΥΝΤΕΣ ΕΠΑΙΝΕΣΑΙ ΔΕ ΠΟΛΥΞΕΝΟΝ
ΔΙΟΔΩΡΟΥ ΚΑΙ ΣΤΕΦΑΝΩΣΑΙ ΧΡΥΣΩΙ ΣΤ
ΕΦΑΝΩΙ ΟΤΙ ΔΙΚΑΙΟΣ ΕΣΤΙ ΓΕΡΙ ΤΑ ΚΟΙ-
20 ΝΑ ΤΑ ΕΙΚΑΔΕΩΝ ΚΑΙ ΕΠΕΣΚΗΨΑΤΟ ΤΟΙΣ
ΜΑΡΤΥΣΙΝ ΑΝΑΓΡΑΨΑΙ ΔΕ ΤΟ ΨΗΦΙΣ
ΜΑ ΤΟΥΣ ΑΡΧΟΝΤΑΣ ΤΟΥΣ ΕΦΗΓΗΣΙΟΥ ΑΡ
ΧΟΝΤΟΣ ΕΙΣ ΣΤΗΛΗΝ ΛΙΘΙΝΗΝ ΚΑΙ ΣΤΗΣ
ΑΙ ΕΝ ΤΩΙ ΙΕΡΩΙ ΤΟΥ ΑΠΟΛΛΩΝΟΣ ΤΟΥ ΠΑ
25 ΡΝΗΣΣΙΟΥ

Chapter XXIX

[1] παρδακὸν τὸ χωρίον

[2] Hesych. Κῦκαλα: δῆμος Αἰαυτίδος φυλῆς.

[3] τὸ μεγάλο θηριὸ ἔχει τήν φωλεάν του ἐπάνω εἰς τὰ βουνὰ.

[4] Strabo. 399. c. τοὺς ἐν τῇ μεσογαίᾳ δήμους τῆς Αττικῆς μακρὸν εἰπεῖν διὰ τὸ πλῆθος.

[5] Στειριακὴ ὁδός. (Plato) Hipparch. 229. a.

Chapter XXX

[1] παλαιὸν εἰς ἴχνος μετέσταν.

[2] 'Στὸν Ὄλυμπον, 'στον κόλυμβον,
'στὰ τρία ἄκρα τουρανοῦ
ὅπου αἱ Μοῖραι τῶν Μοιρῶν,
ὦ ἡδειὰ μοῦ Μοῖρα
ἃς ἔλθη τώρα νὰ μ' ἴδη—

³ See below, p. 131. Some of the other villages visible in the route are Καλογρέσι under Lycabettus, on the north-cast of it: Bracháni, ten minutes to the south-west of Pellicó: a stream here is called Πισπύρι (qu. Εὐπυρίδαι?): Logothéti, ten minutes south of Bracháni.

⁴ The church is about two hundred yards south of the village of Pellicò. There are three other small churches near it.

HOPOS : APTE
MIAOS : TEME
NOS : AMAPV
SIAS

or,   Ὄρος Ἀρτέ–
μιδος τεμέ–
νους Ἀμαρυ–
σίας..

Limit of the sacred precincts of Amarusian Artemis.

⁵ Pausan. i, 31. 5.

⁶ Arist. Pac. 190.

⁷ Τρυγαῖος Ἀθμονεὺς ἀμπελουργὸς δεξιός.

⁸ οὐκέτι Κολαινὶς ἀλλ' ἀκαλανθὶς Ἄρτεμις,

Av. 871. ἐν Ἀμαρύνθῳ ἡ Κολαινὶς Ἄρτεμις. οἱ Μυρρινούσιοι Κολαινίδα ἐπονομάζουσιν, ὥσπερ Πειραιεῖς τὴν Μουνυχίαν, Φιλιᾶται δὲ τὴν Βραυρωνίαν. Schol. ad loc.

⁹ See his will in Diog. Laert. v. Plut. iii. 30. Cp. Bentley, Epist. Socr. p. 407. (ed. 1777.)

¹⁰ Welcker. Trilog. p. 293. Von dem alten verbande der Ergadeis scheint noch die Phyle *Akamantis* gleichsam ein Ἀκμόνιον rastloser Arbeiter, worin der Demos Hephæstiadæ mit einem Tempel des und Hephæstos, so wie in dessen Naehe der Demos Εὐπυρίδαι, und dann die beyden andern Demen Δαιδαλίδαι und Αἰθαλίδαι Ueberreste zu seyn. He would probably connect the Ἀθμονεῖς (at Marousi) as Αἰθμονεῖς with the same class. The Δαιδαλίδαι were subsequently removed into the Cecropid Tribe. In Bekker, Anecd. p. 240, for ΔΑΔΑΜΑΤΑΙ: δῆμος Κεκροπίδος should be written ΔΑΙΔΑΛΙΔΑΙ.

¹¹ Herod. i. 62.

¹² Andocid. Myst. p. 14. νικήσαντες τοὺς τυράννους ἐπὶ Παλληνίῳ (Cp. Sluiter Lect. Andoc. pp. 9 and 53, for the history, Herod. v. 64). Elms. Heracl. 849, proposes to

read Παλλήνῳ, thinking that the name of the demus was Πάλληνον; but it was really Pallene. Antig. Caryst. c. 12.

[13] Eur. Heraclid. 1030. See a similar fable with respect to the body of Orestes, Herod. i. 68. Pausan. iii. 3. 7; and of Hesiod, viii. 54; cf. Aristid. iii. p. 284. Canter, who says that these ὑποχθονίους φύλακας τῶν Ἑλλήνων ῥύεσθαι τὴν χώραν οὐ χεῖρου ἢ τὸν ἐν Κολωνῷ κείμενον Οἰδίπουν. Œd. Col. 576. 621.

[14] ἀλλὰ δεῖ ζητεῖν τὸν ἄνδρα καὶ βλέπειν Βαλλή–ναδε.   Acharn. 222.

[15] Inscript. ap. Boeck. p. 235. In Diog. Laert. Theophr. v. 57. ΠΕΛΑΝΕΥΣ is an error of the text for ΠΕΛΛΗΝΕΥΣ.

[16] Pallene was near Gargettus; for Eurystheus, who was buried at Pallene (Eur. Heraclid. 1030), is said to be interred near Gargettus (Strabo, 377. Hesych. v. Γαργηττός). Hence is explained the story of Plutarch, Vit. Thes. c. 13, that the Pallenians would not intermarry with the Agnusians, because of an act of Agnusian treachery committed at Gargettus that is, near their *own village of Pallene*. See Bentley, Phalaris, p. 145. The same story would lead us to suppose that Agnus was near to Pallene, and Agnus was not far from Athens (Alciphro, Ep. xxxix). On the whole, therefore, I would place Gargettus beneath the northern extremity of Hymettus, not far from the cross road called Stauró. This would exactly tally with the narrative, that when Pallas marched on Athens by the direct road from Sphettus, his sons were sent by him with a secret detachment of armed men to lie in ambush at Gargettus (Plutarch. Them. 13.), in order to take Theseus in the rear when he had marched southward from Athens towards Sphettus, to encounter their father.

[17] Antig. Caryst. c. 12. See Müller, Brief nach Athen. p. 19. Leake's Memoir, p. 35.

[18] On the connection of Pallas with Hephæstus, see Plat. Critia, 109. c. Cic. N. D. iii. 22, 23, where the Apollo Patrous of Athens is spoken of as their son.

[19] In Athenæus, 234. f. Two of the three Parasiti there mentioned are *Gargettians*, which confirms the opinion above stated, p. 131. that Gargettus was near Pallene.

[20] Ten stadia. Thuc. viii. 67.

[21] Soph. Œ. C. 670.

[22] The Academy was six stadia from Dipylum. Cic. de Fin. V. init.

[23] Also a church at the bottom of another hill, of the Agio-'Ακίνδυνοι, who are also said to resemble Eumenides in character.

[24] Œ. C. 55.

²⁵ Pausan. i. 28. 7.

²⁶ Compare the passage in Valer. Max. v. 3, which is remarkable for its local accuracy: Œdipodis ossa inter ipsum *Areopagum* et excelsam Præsidis Minervæ Arcem honore aræ decorata quasi sacrosancta colis. This connection of Œdipus with the Areopagus explains the allusion in Soph. Œ. C. 947.

²⁷ V. 1600, where the Scholiast well observes, ἱερὸν πρὸς τῇ ἀκροπόλει; and to this temple belongs the inscription found near the spot, and still visible there, which records a dedication ΔΗΜΗΤΡΙ ΚΑΙ ΚΟΡΗΙ. Boeck. Insc. p. 467.

²⁸ Cp. Eur. Phœniss. 1707, where Œdipus dies at *Colonus*.

Chapter XXXI

¹ Καὶ τοὐρανοῦ γ', ὡς φασὶν, ἔστιν ἐν καλῷ.

² Dio. Chrys. ii. p. 197.

³ Ibid. p. 197. εἶναι τὴν χώραν ἀραιὰν, ὡς μήτε ὕεσθαι πολλάκις μήτε ὑπομένειν τὸ ΠΙΝΟΜΕΝΟΝ ὕδωρ; where Casaubon transposes the last words: but the last but one ought to be, I conceive, simply ΓΙΝΟΜΕΝΟΝ. Xen. Œcon. 17. 12. ἐν χειμῶνι πολλὰ ὕδατα γίγνεται. Aristop. Vesp. 265. δεῖται τὰ κάρπιμα ὕδωρ γενέσθαι.

⁴ A. δέσποιν' ἁπασῶν πότνι' Ἀθηναίων πόλι!
B. ὤνθρωπε, μὴ λέγ', οὐκέτ' εἰσὶ δεσπόται.
A. ὥς μοι καλόν σου φαίνεται τὸ νεώριον!
B. ἄλλῳ μεθ' Ἑλλήσποντον αἰσχρὸν φαίνεται
καὶ τὸν Λύσανδρον. A. ὡς καλὸς δ' ὁ Πειραεύς.
B. ἔτι γὰρ μετὰ τῶν πρὶν τειχέων αὐτὸν βλέπεις;
A. ἄλση δὲ τίς πω τοιάδ' ἔσχ' ἄλλη γύν;
B. εἶχεν μὲν, ἴσως δ' ἐπὶ συμφοραῖς ἀπεκείρατο.
A. καὶ τοὐρανοῦ γ', ὡς φασὶν, ἔστιν ἐν καλῷ.
B. πῶς; οἵ γε λιμώττουσι, καὶ νοσοῦσι, καὶ
τὸ πλέον ἀπόλλυται μέρος ἐκ τῶν ἀέρων
ἢ τῶν πολεμίων.

Vet. Com. ap. Dio. Chrysos. tom. ii. p. 334. As I have taken some liberties with the text of this passage, in order to restore its metrical character, I will transcribe it as it stands in the text of Reiske. ii. p. 334. δέσποινα δ' ἁπασῶν πόλεων πότνια Ἀθηναίων πόλι, μί λέγε ἄνθρωπε, οὐκέτ' εἰσὶν ἐκεῖνοι. ὡς καὶ καλόν σου φαίνεται τὸ νεώριον. ἀλλὰ μεθ' Ἑλλήσποντον καὶ Λύσανδρον αἰσχρόν. καλὸς δ' ὁ Πειραιεύς, ἔτι δὲ μέτα τῶν τειχέων αὐτὸν βλέπεις· ἄλση δὲ τίς πω τοιάδ' ἔσχ' ἄλλη γυνή; (γύη Valcken. Hippol. 186.) εἶχε μὲν δὴ, σωθεῖσα δὲ (Valcken. δηωθεῖσα, but ΔΗCΩΘ ΕΙΣΑ ΔΕ seems to be only a combination of two readings: ΙCΩCΔ' ΕΙΤΑ ΔΕ) ὡς ἐπὶ συμφοραῖς ἀπεκείρατο.

⁵ Compare Xen. Vectigal. c. i. and Aristoph. Athen. ix. 372. c. on the climate and seasons of Attica.

⁶ Τῶν μὲν αὐτοφυῶν, ἀήρ τε οὗτος ἐξαίρετος τοῦ πολλοῦ, καὶ λιμένες τοιοῦτοι· ἔτι δὲ αὐτῆς τῆς Ἀκροπόλεως ἡ θέσις, καὶ τὸ ὥσπερ αὔρας εὔχαρι πρόσβαλλον πανταχοῦ· τοῦ γὰρ τῆς πάσης Ἀττικῆς ἀέρος οὕτως ἔχοντος, ἄριστος καὶ καθαρώτατός ἐστιν ὁ τῆς πόλεως ὑπερέχων. γνοίης δ' ἂν αὐτὴν, ἐπὶ τῇ πόρρωθεν, ὡς περιαυγῇ* τῷ ὑπὲρ τῆς κεφαλῆς ἀέρι...

*For ὥσπερ αὐγῇ (i.e. ὡς ΠΕΡΑΥΓΗΙ), which is the reading of all the editions, I have here substituted in the text, ὡς ΠΕΡΙΑΥΓΗ. In Aristot. de Mundo ἅλως περιαυγὴς is, a *circumlucent* halo; which is the sense required here.

Chapter XXXII

¹ Ἀγορὰ 'ν Ἀθάναις χαιρε.

Chapter XXXIII

¹ ὄψει γὰρ αὐτοὺς καὶ σφόδρ' ὄντας Ἀττικούς.

² It is there entitled Εὐχὴ ἐπὶ ἔχθρας εἰρηνευούσης. Eucholog. p. 685.

³ Ἐγὼ πεισθεὶς ὑπὸ τῶν φίλων διηλλάγην τούτοις ἐν τῇ πόλει ἐναντίον μαρτύρων, οἵτινες διήλλαττον ἡμᾶς πρὸς τῷ νεῷ τῆς Ἀθηνᾶς. (Andoc. 146. 3.)

⁴ As an indication of the public feeling now entertained here, and as a specimen of modern oratory, I transcribe a copy of the Bishop's address:-

 'Ομιλία σύντομος, ῥηθεῖσα παρὰ τῷ Ναῷ τοῦ Ἁγίου Γεωργίου, (Θησέως) εἰς τὴν δοξολογίαν γινομένην, ὅτε ἀπεστάλη τὸ ά. διάταγμα τοῦ κραταιωτάτου καὶ θεοφυλάκτου ἡμῶν Βασιλέως Ὄθωνος, ἐν Ἀθήναις, παρὰ τοῦ ταπεινοῦ Ἐπισκόπου Ταλαντίου Νεοφύτου, καὶ Τοποτηρητοῦ Ἀθηνῶν, συναθροισθέντος παντὸς τοῦ λαοῦ.

 '''Εχάρι ποτὲ ὁ Ἰσραηλιτικὸς λαὸς ὅτε ἐπέστρεψεν, ἐκ τῆς αἰχμαλωσίας τῆς ἐν Βαβυλῶνι, εἰς Ἱερουσαλήμ. Πολὺ περισσότερον ἐχάρημεν ἡμεῖς σήμερον, εὐλογημένον μου ἀκροατήριον, ἀγαπητοί μου ἀδελφοὶ καὶ συμπολῖται, διότι, διὰ τοῦ θείου ἐλέους, ἔπειτα ἀπὸ τόσους ἀγῶνας, τοσαύτας θλίψεις, ἀπὸ τόσα βάσανα, ἀπὸ τόσους κινδύνους, λενλασίας, σφαγάς, πυρκαϊὰς, φεύγοντες, διεσπάρημεν τῇδε κἀκεῖσε, ἠδηἐπεστρέψαμεν εἰς τὴν ποθεινοτάτην πατρίδα μας, καὶ ἐπατήσαμεν εἰς τὸ ἔδαφος τῆς πατρῷας μας γῆς, περιφερόμενοι εἰς τὰ ἐρείπια, ὡς εἰς παλάτια, χαίροντες. "Εὐλογητὸς ὁ Θεὸς ὁ παιδεύων καὶ πάλιν ἰώμενος!" Ὁ πανάγαθος Θεός, ὡς ἐλεήμων, ὡς συμπαθής καὶ οἰκτίρμων, παρέβλεψε τὰ πλήθη τῶν ἁμαρτιῶν μας, καὶ μᾶς ἠλέησεν. Ἔνευσεν εἰς τὰς καρδίας τῶν τριῶν κραταιωτάτων Ἀνάκτων, οἵτινες ἑνωθέντες, τῇ θείᾳ δυνάμει, ἀπέστελλον ἡμῖν τὸν κραταιότατον καὶ γαληνότατον ἡμῶν Βασιλέα Ὄθωνα, οὗ τὸ κράτος καὶ ἡ ἰσχὺς αὐτοῦ εἴη ἄμαχος καὶ ἀκατατρόπωτος εἰς αἰῶνας. Ναί, Χριστὲ Βασιλεῦ! πάλιν λέγω τὸ, "εὐλογητὸς ὁ Θεὸς ὁ παιδεύων καὶ πάλιν ἰώμενος!" Ὢ δόξα! ὢ λαμπρότης! ὢ εὐφροσύνη! ὢ ἀγαλλίασις! Δεδοξασμένον τὸ πανάγιόν σου ὄνομα, Βασιλεῦ τῶν βασιλευόντων, ἐπουράνιε Θεὲ, Κύριε Παντοκράτωρ! Διὸ εἶναι πρέπον ἡμεῖς, ὡς ἀληθεῖς χριστιανοὶ, νὰ ὑμνολογήσωμεν, ἀπὸ καρδίας καὶ ψυχῆς, ἄνδρες τε καὶ γυναῖκες, τὸν ὕψιστον

Θεὸν, καὶ νὰ ἄρωμεν χεῖρας ἱκετίδας πρὸς αὐτόν, δεόμενοι ἀεννάως ὑπὲρ τῆς ὑγιείας καὶ ἐνισχύσεως τοῦ θεοσυντηρήτου, καὶ γαληνοτάτου, καὶ κραταιωτάτου ἡμῶν Βασιλέως, ὃν διέποι καὶ συντηροῖ, ὡς κόρην ὀφθαλμοῦ ἀκλόνητον, καὶ ἀκράδαντον. Ναὶ, πανάγιε Βασιλεῦ! Καθὼς ἡ Α. Μ. νουθετεῖ καὶ συμβουλεύει, διὰ τοῦ Β. αὐτοῦ διατάγματος, ὡς κοινὸς πατὴρ, νὰ παύσῃ τοῦ λοιποῦ ἀπὸ ἡμᾶς ἡ διχόνοια, ἡ σατανικὴ ἔχθρα, ἣν ἐγέννησεν ἡ φορὰ τοῦ καιροῦ, καὶ αἱ δειναὶ περιστάσεις (διότι τὸ ἀποτέλεσμα τῆς ἔχθρας καὶ τῆς σατανικῆς διχονοίας ἄλλο οὐκ ἔστιν, εἰ μὴ ἀφανισμὸς, ὄλεθρος, καὶ ἐξόντωσις πάντων), ἂς ἀκούσωμεν τοῦ ἱεροῦ Εὐαγγελίου, τὸ ὁποῖον εἶναι τὸ νέκταρ τὸ οὐράνιον, ἡ δεσποτικὴ διδασκαλία (ὅσοι ἐπαγγέλλονται τὸν ἀληθῆ χριστιανὸν, κατὰ τὸ, "Σὺ εἶ Πέτρος, καὶ ἐπὶ ταύτῃ τῇ πέτρᾳ οἰκοδομήσω μου τὴν ἐκκλησίαν, καὶ πύλαι ᾅδου οὐ κατισχύσουσιν αὐτῆς." Ἂς ἐναγκαλισθῶμεν τὴν κατὰ θεὸν ἀγάπην, ἀγαπητά μου τέκνα. καὶ ἂς ἀπορρίψωμεν, δίκην κονιορτοῦ, τὴν διαβολικὴν ἔχθραν, προσφέροντες δοξολογίας εἰς τὸν παντοδύναμον καὶ ὕψιστον Θεὸν, ποιοῦντες τὰς ἐντολὰς τοῦ ἀπαραβάτως καὶ ἀπαραμειώτως, διὰ ν' ἀκούσωμεν τῆς μακαρίας καὶ ἀψευδοῦς ἐκείνης φωνῆς, τῆς λεγούσης· "Εὖ, δοῦλε ἀγαθὲ καὶ πιστὲ, ἐπ' ὀλίγα ἧς πιστὸς, ἐπὶ πολλῶν σὲ καταστήσω, εἴσελθε εἰς τὴν χαρὰν τοῦ κυρίου σοῦ·"καὶ, τοιουτρόπως, νὰ ζήσωμεν καὶ ἐνταῦθα εἰρηνικῶς, τιμίως, καὶ ἐνδόξως ὑπὸ τὴν βασικὴν προστασίαν καὶ σκέπην, διότι "καρδία Βασιλέως ἐν χειρὶ Θεοῦ," καὶ εἶτα ν' ἀξιωθῶμεν καὶ τῆς ἐπουρανίου αὐτοῦ Βασιλείας.
Ζήτωσαν αἱ κραταιώταται συμμαχικαὶ δυνάμεις!
Ζήτω ὁ κραταιώτατος καὶ γαληνότατος ἡμῶν Βασιλεὺς Ὄθων!
Ζήτω ἡ Ἑλλάς! Ἀμήν."

Ἐν Ἀθήναις.
τῇ 2. (14) Φευρ. 1833.

Chapter XXXIV

[1] χαλεπὸν ἦν πορεύεσθαι ἀπὸ τῆς Πελοποννήσου τὴν εἰς Ἀθήνας ὁδὸν, οὐδὲν μέρος καθαρὸν ἀπὸ λῃστῶν κακούργων ἔχουσαν.

[2] This excursion was made before King Otho's arrival in Greece.

[3] The same with Παιονίδαι, according to the conjecture of Stuart, on account of the similarity of sound. Cp. Leake Demi, p. 134. Perhaps however the Ποιμενίδαι (Meier de Gent. Attic. p. 50.) have a stronger claim on this head to be identified with Μενίδι.

[4] The following picture by Professor F. Thiersch (Etat Actuel de la Grèce, i. p. 237.) of the state of Greece at this time, is as true as it is sad. "L'administration est dissoute. Les préfets envoyés dans les eparchies par les gouvernemens, ont été ou chassés ou changés en agens des Capitaines (Vassos, &c.), dont les soldats occupant tout l'intérieur du pays et vivent aux dépens des habitans. L'action des lois a cessé. Des actes de violence l'ont remplacée. Dans les villages il n'y a presque plus personne, les paysans s'étant retirés des rnontagnes et dans les cavernes. Voici les auspices sous

lesquels la Regence arrive, parcequ'au lieu d'être en functions au mois de Mai 1832, elle n'y entre qu'en Février 1833. Ces neuf mois d'angoisses ont ruiné la Grèce."

Chapter XXXV

[1] Ἴομεν εἰς Σαλαμῖνα

[2] Lib. ii. ep. 3; and in Menander p. 342, ed. Meineke.

[3] τὰ μυστήρια, τὴν γειτνιῶσαν Σαλαμῖνα, τὰ ΣΤΗΝΑ, τὴν Ψυττάλειαν...ὅλην ἐν ταῖς Ἀθήναις τὴν Ἑλλάδα;

[4] στήνια by Dorville, Chariton. p. 449; and Σιλήνια by Meineke, Menand. p. 346.

[5] C. Nepos. v. Themist. 4. Barbarus adeo *angusto* mari conflixit (Æschyl. Pers. 412. πλῆθορ ἐν στενῷ νεῶν ἤθροιστο) ut ejus multitudo navium explicari non potuerit.

[6] αἰτιώτατος ἐν τῷ ΣΤΕΝΩΙ ναυμαχῆσαι ἐγένετο, ὅπερ σαφέστατα ἔσωσε τὰ πράγματα...Thuc. i. 74. Comp. Themistocl. Apophtheg. H. St. p. 98. μὴ πείθων ὁ Θεμιστοκλῆς τὸν Εὐρυβιάδην ἐν ΤΟΙΣ ΣΤΕΝΟΙΣ ναυμαχῆσαι κρύφα πρὸς τὸν βάρβαρον ἔπεμψε.

[7] In which κουτάλι signifies a spoon, and, as applied to this small flat island, expresses nearly the same idea as the ancient name did, which seems to be nothing more than a corruption of Ψῆττα λεία. Coulouri, the modern name of Salamis, is in the same way expressive of its *circular* form. Κουλοῦρι is interpreted by ὄφις in Eustath. ad Dionys. Perieget., and is the same word as the Latin *coluber* and *colurus*: hence it means a circular cake (κόλλυρα. Aristoph. Pac. 122.), which is its signification in Greece now; and hence the iron ring which encircles the pole of a plough is now called κολλοῦρα.

[8] Æschyl. Pers. 465.

Ξέρξης ἀνώμωξεν κακῶν ὁρῶν βάθος·
ἕδραν γὰρ εἶχε παντὸς εὐαυγῆ στρατοῦ,
ὑψηλὸν ὄχθον ἄγχι πελαγίας ἁλός,
ῥήξας δὲ πέπλους κἀνακωκύσας λιγύ
ἤϊξ' ἀκόσμῳ ξὺν φυγῇ.

The position of his throne seems to have been on the southern side of the hill now called *Κερατόπυργο*, and formerly Ægaleos. Schol. Aristid. p. 183. Dindorf. *Ξέρξης καθῆστο ἐπὶ τῆς ἠπείρου εἰς τὸ ἀυγάλεον* (read *τὸν Αἰγάλεων*) *ὄρος καταντικρὺ Σαλαμῖνος*. Cp. Harpocrat. v. *ἀργυρόπους δίφρος*.

Chapter XXXVI

¹ Ὦ πότνια Μοῖσα,
τὰν πολυξέναν ἵκεο
Δωρίδα νᾶσον
Αἴγιναν.

² λήμη τοῦ Πειραιῶς. Aristot. Rhet. iii. 10. 7. Cp. Cic. Off. iii. 2.

³ Demosth. c. Aristocr. 691.

⁴ Pausan. ii. 29.

⁵ The only evidence in favour of this supposition is furnished by the two words ΔΙΙ ΠΑΝΕΛΛΗΝΙΩΙ, which are said to have been inscribed on the portico of the temple. If this inscription ever existed there, the dialect alone proves it to have been a forgery. Again, the Greek deities did not write their names over the doors of their temples, "comme des marchands les leurs sur les portes de leur boutiques;" or, as it is elsewhere expressed, τούς Θεοὺς (ἐν τοῖς ἱεροῖς) ἐπιγράφειν οὐκ ἐστὶν εἰκός. Dio. Chrysost. i. p. 615.

⁶ ὅρος τεμένους 'Αθηνάιας.

⁷ Cp. A. Mustoxydi in Αἰγιναία. No. 1. July 15, 1831.

⁸ Pausan i. 44. and ii. 29. and 30.

⁹ Theophrast. de Signis pluv. p. 419. ἐὰν ἐν Αἰγίνῃ ἐπὶ τοῦ Διὸς τοῦ Ἑλλανίου νεφέλη καθίζηται, ὡς τὰ πολλὰ ὕδωρ γίγνεται—

¹⁰ See Grose's Local Proverbs. arts. Yorkshire and Leicestershire.

¹¹ See the instances in Middleton's Letters from Rome, p. 163. Mr. Blunt's Vestiges, p. 91; and his Reformation, p. 13.

¹² ὅτι Αἰακὸς τῷ Πανελληνίῳ Διῒ θύσας καὶ εὐξάμενος τὴν Ἑλλάδα γῆν ἐποίησεν ὕεσθαι. (Pausan. ii. 29).

¹³ ὅτι Ἠλίας προσηύξατο καὶ ὁ οὐρανὸς ὑετὸν ἔδωκε, καὶ ἡ γῆ ἐβλάστησε τὸν καρπὸν αὐτῆς. (Epist. St James, v. 18).

¹⁴ See Müller Æginetica p. 163. Heyne Excurs. Virg. Cir. 220. 295.

¹⁵ ‛Ὸς τόδ' ἄγαλμ' ἀνέθηκε, φιλόστρατός ἐστ' ὄνυμ' αὐτῷ,
    Πατρὶ δὲ τῷ τήνω Δαμοφόων ὄνυμα.

BIBLIOGRAPHY

Christopher Wordsworth – a select bibliography

Christopher Wordsworth was a prolific and successful writer - the Bodleian Library at Oxford University has nearly 200 entries for him in their catalogue. Indeed, he was still busy writing at 70, and his new edition of Theocritos (1877) was highly praised: "...*if he had devoted himself to the work of editing the classics he might have stood in the very first rank of European scholars*" (Elizabeth Wordsworth). His *Latin Grammar* was a bestseller for years, only superseded by Kennedy's famous work in 1866.

Christopher's early publications - those directly connected with classical studies and often reprinted during his lifetime - are still of considerable interest today, for example his studies on the inscriptions at Pompeii and investigations at Dodona were models of their kind and frequently commended and referred to by contemporary scholars.

Wordsworth's titles of interest to this volume

1836 *Athens and Attica*
1837 *Pompeian Inscriptions (Inscriptiones Pompeianæ)*
1839 *Greece, Pictorial, Descriptive and Historical*
1841 *King Edward VI Latin Grammar*
1843 *Theophilus Anglicanus*
1851 *The Memoirs of William Wordsworth*
1863 *Journal of a tour in Italy*
1877 *Theocritos*
1883 *Conjectural Emendations of Passages in Ancient Authors, with Other Papers*

Biography and background

Collections of Wordsworth's personal papers are to be found at Lambeth Palace, Harrow School, Lincoln Cathedral Library, Pusey House, Oxford, Trinity College, Cambridge.

Beeson, T., *The Bishops*, London 2002

"Christopher Wordsworth (1807-1885)", *Dictionary of Literary Biography*, 166, Detroit 1996
The Dictionary of National Biography, Oxford University Press
Overton, J.H., Wordsworth, E., *Christopher Wordsworth*, London 1890
Perry, G.G., Overton, J.H., *The Bishops of Lincoln*, Lincoln 1900
Strudwick, V., *Christopher Wordsworth, Bishop of Lincoln 1869-1885*, Lincoln 1987

Other works and sources

(From among 19th-century, and earlier, travellers, historians, and topographers)

Clarke, E.D., *Travels in Various Countries of Europe, Asia and Africa* (1816)
Cramer, J.A., *A Geographical and Historical Description of Ancient Greece* (1828)
Dodwell, E., *Classical and Topographical Tour in Greece* (1819); *Views in Greece* (1821); *Views and Descriptions of Cyclopian or Pelasgic Remains in Greece and Italy* (1834)
Gell, W., *The Itinerary of Greece* (1819); *Narrative of a Journey in the Morea* (1823)
Gordon, T., *History of the Greek Revolution* (1832)
Lampriere, J.L., *Classical Dictionary of Proper Names mentioned in Ancient Authors* (1788)
Leake, W.M., *Researches in Greece* (1814)
The Topography of Athens (1821)
Travels in The Morea (1830)
Travels in Northern Greece (1835)
Peloponnesiaca (1846)
Mure, M., *Journal of a Tour in Greece and the Ionian Islands* (1842)
Pittakes, K.S., (First Greek 'Conservator of Antiquities' under
L. Ross. See pp. 35, 164), *L'ancienne Athènes* (Athens 1835)
Stuart, J., Revett, N., *The Antiquities of Athens and Other Monuments of Greece* (1762-1816,1841)
Thirlwall, C., *History of Greece* (1835)
Wheler, G., *A Journey into Greece* (1682)

Classical topographers and commentators

Aristophanes, *Lysistrata* (for his observations of the Acropolis)
Cyriac of Ancona, *Later Travels* (ed. W. Bodnar, Harvard 2003)
Dicaearchus (fragments only)
Pausanias (ed. Frazer, J.G.), *Guide to Greece*, 1900
Pausanias (ed. Levi P.), *Guide to Greece* (Vol. 1, Central Greece), Harmondsworth 1971
Strabo, *Geography*

Modern travellers and contemporary studies

Andrews, K., *Athens*, London 1967
Braudel, F., *The Mediterranean*, London 1992

Braudel, F., *The Mediterranean in the Ancient World*, Harmondsworth 1998
Drinkwater, G. C., Sanders, T.R.B., *The University Boat Race, Official Centenary History*, London 1929
Hammond, N. G. L., *A History of Greece to 322 BC*, Oxford 1986
Jenkins, R., *The Dilessi Murders*, London 1961; *The Victorians and Ancient Greece*, Oxford 1980
Kurtz, D., *The Reception of Classical Art in Britain*, Oxford 2000
Leigh Fermor, P., *Roumeli*, London 1966
Morris, J. (ed.), *Travels with Virginia Woolf*, London 1993
Roessell. D., *In Byron's Shadow: Modern Greece in the English and American Imagination*, Oxford 2002
Roller, D., *Early Travellers in Eastern Boiotia*, Amsterdam 1988
Stoneman, R. *Land of Lost Gods*, London 1987; *A Literary Companion to Travel in Greece*, Harmondsworth, 1984
Woolf, V. (ed. Dick, S.), *A Dialogue upon Mount Pentelicus* (The Complete Shorter Fiction of Virginia Woolf), London 1985

Guides and maps

Barber, R., *Greece, Blue Guide*, London 1995
Mee, C., Spawforth, A., *Greece* , Oxford 2001
Greece, Baedeker, Leipzig 1889
Greece, A Hand-Book for Travellers in Greece, John Murray, London 1854
G*reece*, Rough Guides, London 2002
Paradissis, A., *Fortresses and Castles of Greece*, Athens 1975
Rupprecht Goethe, H., *Athens, Attica and the Megarid*, London 2001

1:60000 Road Editions (Attiki Odos A.E., Athens, 2004 'Olympic Games' edition)

Mythology

Graves, R., *Greek Myths*, London 1955

Natural history

Atchley S.C., *Wild Flowers of Attica*, Oxford 1938
Baumann, H. (trans. Stearn and Stearn), *Greek Wild Flowers*, London 1993
Polunin, O., *Flowers of Greece and the Balkans*, Oxford 1987
Rackham O., and Moody, J., *The Making of the Cretan Landscape*, Manchester 1996

Greek and Latin texts

The following is a select list of the authors of Greek and Latin literature, history, and topography referred to by Wordsworth. Works particulary featured by Wordsworth are added in italics works; bilingual editions of most of these are in the *Loeb Classical Library* series.

Aeschines
Aeschylus, *Eumenides; Persians*
Anaxandrides
Antigonus of Carystus
Aristophanes, *Acharnians;*
    Assemblywomen; Birds;
    Knights; Lysistrata
Aristotle, *Oeconomica; Rhetoric*
Arrian, *Alexander*
Athenaeus

Callimacus
Cicero, *De Finibus; De Legibus;*
    Letters to Atticus
Crinagorus

Demosthenes
Dio Chrysostom, *Discourses*
Diodorus Siculus, *Histories*
Diogenes Laertius, *Lives of Eminent*
    Philosophers
Dionysius

Eubulides
Euripides, *Alcestis; Bacchae; Children*
    of Heracles; Electra;
    Helen; Hippolytus; Ion;
    Iphigenia at Aulis; Medea;
    Phoenician Women; Trojan
    Women

Harpocration Valerius
Hegesias
Heliodorous
Herodotus, *The Persian Wars*
Hesiod, *Works and Days*
Homer, *Iliad; Odyssey*

Juvenal

Livy

Longus
Lucian
Marcellinus Ammianus
Menander

Olympiodorus

Pausanias, *Greece*
Philochorus
Philostratus, *Lives*
Photinus
Pindar
Pliny the Younger
Plato, *Charmides; Critias; Epistles;*
    Euthyphro; Gorgias;
    Menexenus; Parmenides;
    Phaedrus; Republic;
    Symposium; Timaeus
Plutarch, *Lives; Moralia*
Pollux, Julius
Polybius, *The Histories*
Polemon
Ptolemy

Scylax Periplus
Scymnus of Chios
Seneca, *Hercules Furens*
Simonides
Sophocles, *Electra; Oedipus Colonus*
St Paul, *Acts*
Stephen of Byzantium
Strabo, *Geography*

Theocritus
Theophrastus, *Weather*
Thucydides

Virgil, *Georgics; Metamorphoses*
Vitruvius, *On Architecture*

Xenophon

Editors and Commentators

(The following is a select list of the contemporary commentators and editors of Greek and Roman studies either referred to by Wordsworth, or otherwise relevant.)

Arnold, T.
Bekker, I
Bentley, R.
Boeck, de, A.
Clinton, F.H.
Cramer, J.A.
Dobree, P.P.
Dindorf, W.
Elmsley, P.
Hamilton, W.R
Holst. L.
Hudson, G.M.
Jacobs, F.W.
Keightley, T.
Kennedy, B.H.

Leake, W.M.
Mai, A.
Millingen, J.
Muller, K.O.
Paciaudi, P.
Reiske, J.J.
Rose, H.J.
Runkel, M
Thirlwall, C.
Tozer, H.F.
Valckenaer, L.C.
Wilkins, W.
Welcker, F.G.
Wolf, F.A.

Sidetrack 1

Wordsworth in context

After the following outline, the two lists provide the key dates relating to regional/political events and the development of antiquarian studies in Greece during Wordsworth's time. (See also Christopher Wordsworth's life, page xxiv and Bibliography).

Intrepid Britons, on some mission or another, were already criss-crossing the eastern Mediterranean early in the second millennium AD; Richard Coeur de Lion was in Rhodes in 1191. In the centuries that followed, the adventurers and pilgrims were joined by diplomats and traders, and from the 16th and 17th centuries scholars and enquirers (as well as 'collectors') began to explore the lands and seas of what is now modern Greece. These men (very rarely women) were interested in classical ideals and arts and wanted to contextualize the locations of Theseus and Pericles within the philosophies of Socrates and Plato. By 1676, George Wheler was compiling notes for his (and Jacob Spon's) influential early accounts, and the 18th century saw the founding of the Society of Dilettanti in London and the notion of the Grand Tour for Europe's wealthy sons – a chance to sample the various delights of the 'Enlightenment' in the sunshine of Italy and Greece.

The members of the Society of Dilettanti, in particular, were driven by the values of the ancients and their arts, and this fuelled a desire to map and chronicle the sites and explore their cultures, in many cases replicating the art and architecture in the cities and countryside of Europe. Soon after, 'classics faculties' in the great universities (and private schools) perfected the study of ancient literature (always somewhere in the curricula for a thousand years) and the cultivated man, suitably attired, was swapping sword for the words of Homer and Virgil and thinking of himself as an antiquary. In Greece, Turkish control and a subdued Greek identity facilitated the wholesale looting of treasures. Lord Elgin was one, but the Russians, Germans and French all helped themselves to the shiploads of marbles and ceramics that are now mournful captives in state museums.

At the same time, some visitors were prepared to take away only sketches, and the architects Stuart and Revett began their long project to publish the *Antiquities of Athens*; their set of four monographs did as much as anything to bring the classical features of Greece to Britain and to promote the 'Greek Revival'.

The early decades of the 19th century, with the end of the French wars and the slowly evolving independence of Greece, greatly facilitated the development of the skills of topography, epigraphy, and the appreciation of artefacts as objects within their contexts, and by the mid-19th century the foundations of the science of archaeology as we understand it today were laid. King Otho in Athens was advised by the brilliant Ludwig Ross, who did more than anyone to foster a true appreciation and respect for the antiquities of Athens and the territories of the new Greece. He also saw the need to encourage Greek academics to assume responsibility for their patrimony and the first Conservator of Antiquities, under Ross, was Kyriakos Pittakes, who published a worthy study on Athens (*L'ancienne Athènes*) in 1835. His work preceded Wordsworth's *Athens and Attica*, and he was a colleague and associate of the Cambridge scholar during his 1832/33 stay (see references on pages 35 and 164). Pittakes' slim volume is memorable for its pages of rare inscriptions and the author's plaintive and century-echoing comments on Lord Elgin: "*Jamais nous n'avons senti plus vivement la tyrannie des barbares que lorsque nous nous vîmes trop faibles pour empêcher un Ecossais d'enlever ce que les Goths, les Turcs, et les siècles avaient épargné. Je crois que dans l'état d'independence où nous entrons, nous aurons le droit de réclamer auprès de la nation Anglaise les chefs d'oeuvres de nos ancêtres, pour les remettre à la place que le divan Phidias leur avait choiseé.*"

One day these paradigms will return to Athens, but there is no doubt that the arrival of such talismanic stones to the new museums of Europe played a large part in stimulating both a popular and scientific appetite to reveal and explain what lay beneath the reach of a few spade thrusts. The opening up of the new Greece to the influences of the 'European' academic establishment, and Athens' reciprocal needs, meant that within fifty years Schliemann was excavating at Mycenae, and all the permanent institutions responsible for antiquities and archaeology had been established (in essence the Greek Archaeological Service and the 'Schools' of the French, Germans, Americans, and British).

The archaeological context (important contemporary publications are shown in italics)

(1435   Cyriac of Ancona begins noting the antiquities of the Levant)
1801   Visits to Greece by Dodwell and Clarke
1807   (30 October) Christopher Wordsworth born
1809   W.M. Leake begins his surveys in Greece
1811   The Society of Dilettanti in Attica
          Cockerell at Aegina and Bassae
1815   Elgin Marbles sold to British Museum
1816   *Travels*, E.D. Clarke
1817   *Unedited Antiquities of Athens*, Society of Dilettanti
1819   *Classical and Topographical Tour in Greece*, E. Dodwell
          The Itinerary of Greece, W. Gell
1820   The Mílos 'Venus' is found and starts her journey to Paris
1821   *The Topography of Athens*, W.M. Leake
1830   *Travels in the Morea*, W.M. Leake
1832   Edward Noel creates his estate at Achmetága (Prokópi), Euboea
1832   Ludwig Ross begins his work in Greece for King Otho
1833   Wordsworth tours Italy and Greece
1833   Wordsworth is the first Englishman in Greece to be presented to King Otho
1835   *Travels in Northern Greece*, W.M. Leake
1836   *Athens and Attica*, Christopher Wordsworth
1837   *Inscriptiones Pompeianæ*, Christopher Wordsworth
1837   Early stages of the 'Greek Archaeological Service'
1839   *Greece, Pictorial, Descriptive and Historical*, Christopher Wordsworth
1846   'French School' founded in Athens
1846   *Peloponnesiaca*, W.M. Leake
1848   *Reisen des Königs Otto und der Königin Amalia in Griechenland*, L. Ross
1863   Champoiseau digs on Samothraki
1870s   The French School begin excavations on Delos
1874   'German School' founded in Athens
1875   Carapanos works at Dodona
1876   Schliemann excavates at Mycenae
1882   'American School' founded in Athens
1884   *The Cyclades, or Life Among the Insular Greeks*, J.T. Bent
1885   Arthur Evans first visits Crete
1885   Christopher Wordsworth dies
1886   British School of Archaeology founded in Athens
1890s   Christos Tsountas excavates on Syros

The geopolitical context

(1456   Athens and Attica annexed to the Ottoman Empire)
1790s   Velestinlis tries to foment a Balkan-wide uprising against the Turks
1803   Ali Pasha crushes the Souliot revolt

1814	*The Philiki Etairia* (Friendly Society) forms in Odessa to focus the armed struggle
1815	Napolean loses at Waterloo
1821	Ypsilantis defeated at Dragatsani
1821	Archbishop Germanós raises Greek standard at Kalavryta, coinciding with a general revolt against the Turks and the beginnings of the War of Independence
1822	Massacre at Chios
1822	Ali Pasha executed at Ioánnina
1824	Byron dies at Mesolóngi
1827	Battle of Navarino
	Siege of Athens
1828	Last stand of Ibrahim Pasha outside Patras
1830	State of Greece recognized by European Powers
	The State boundaries were limited to a section of the mainland (roughly a line east-west between Vólos and Préveza), Attica, Euboea, the Peloponnese, and the Cyclades
1831	'President' Capodistrias assassinated in Navplio
1832	Christopher Wordsworth in Attica; he witnesses the final stages of the peaceful Turkish withdrawal and the last Ramadan to be celebrated from the Acropolis
1833	Imposition of the 17-year-old King Otho of Bavaria by the Powers
1843	Coup, and eventual abdication of Otho
1844	First Constitution
1845	George I appointed king (from Denmark; he reigned until 1913)
1864	Britain cedes the Ionian Islands to Greece, from Kérkira to Kíthira
	Revised constitution
1870s	Balkan wars
1881	Turkey cedes regions in Thessaly and Epirus, and the Sporádes
1890s	Economic downturn results in mass emigration
1896	Cretan uprising against Turks suppressed
1913	The state boundaries now include all northern Epirus and Macedonia (with Thessaloníki), Crete, and major islands (including Thásos, Lésvos, Sámos and Chíos)
1920	Eastern Thrace returns to Greece
1947	With the restitution of the Dodecanese, the modern geopolitical outlines of Greece are determined

Sidetrack 2

Athens and Attica:
Christopher Wordsworth's tour in 36 chapters and 5 months

From almost any compass point, geographical, cultural, metaphorical, the lands and seas that now comprise modern Greece were not easy to negotiate in the 19th (or any earlier) century.

By the 1820s, the Turkish occupiers of the mainland were at last against the ropes and being repeatedly 'jabbed' by the Greek resistance movement; but it needed the combined and self-interested muscle of the western 'Protecting Powers' to deliver the volley of punches that led to retreat of the Turks (after nearly 400 years) and the imposition of King Otho in 1833. For a cinematic, early and enjoyable history, seek out Thomas Gordon's *History of the Greek Revolution* (1832). His two-volume account, ending just before the arrival of King Otho, elucidates most of Wordsworth's contemporary historical references, such as the fate (1824) of the hapless General Odysseus (see pp. 50, 51). Before the Bavarian monarch landed at Navplio, the nominal 'President', Count Capodistrias, was assassinated, and over the following decades the lives of individuals in their local communities, those subsisting in uncompromising rural landscapes, were anything but romantic. And along these valleys and over these mountains came small parties of riders on muleback: the wealthy sons of the gentlefolk of Britain and Europe.

These parties were to need the services of dragomans, guides, and musket-bearing escorts, until the end of the century; armed gangs of 'klephts' (literally 'robbers') lurked in impenetrable lairs ready to kidnap, and worse. Today's Colombia is a possible parallel. The more 'civilized' regions might well have had garrisons of British or French troops and officers; for a period in 1855 these countries even felt it necessary to occupy the harbours of Piraeaus to secure their interests in the wider region. The Powers assured that they maintained a diplomatic and military eye on the infant modern Nation. Ministers and their staffs were installed in the neo-classical mansions that arose grandly in stone between the shanties, mosques, and beautiful Byzantine chapels that were all that remained of medieval Athens after the slow Ottoman withdrawals of 1830-1833.

Our author, Christopher Wordsworth, was among these young men who, far from the comforts of Winchester and Cambridge, literally risked their lives (he was indeed stabbed by brigands on his return from a trip to Delphi) to walk with Pausanias, Strabo, and Pliny. Inspired by these travellers of a few hundreds of years before and after Christ - and more recently by contemporary figures such as William Martin Leake - they took to their mules and swung on precarious wooden saddles through pines and olives, rivers and rocks, reciting the lines of the ancients and arguing over anapæstic tetrameters and the laws of verse (page 206, note 7).

Wordsworth never confides what he paid for a day on muleback or horse, but ten years after his own expedition, Mr. William Mure of Caldwell enjoys a lengthy two-volume visit over many of the same trails and notes that a man hires himself out for the daily rate of four shillings and sixpence, and that: "*One horse per day is three and a half drachms...This is the sum commonly paid by the natives, and includes every species of entertainment or allowance, either for man or horse, except the customary perquisite of a share in the wine provided for use on the road.*" (There were then 25 drachmas (100 leptá) to the English pound, and the Dílessi ransomers wanted £50,000 for the safe release of poor Lord Muncaster's party thirty years later. William Mure of Caldwell also gives the 1838 population of Athens as 20,000, or about one third of a good-sized English football crowd today.)

The full account of Wordsworth's 1832/33 travels is retold in full in his *Greece, Pictorial, Descriptive and Historical* (1839); this is now a much sought after work, with over 400 engravings by Copley Fielding and other artists. As well as a general history and archaeological introduction, the two volumes contain many detailed topographical accounts of the young scholar's travels from Epirus (then still Turkish) to Attica and the Peloponnese, via Phocis, Locris, Boeotia, Thessaly, Acarnania, Aetolia, and the Ionian Islands.

The production demands of this extensive work induced the author and his publishers (the publisher of Byron and, later, the first modern guidebook to Greece) to pre-release his account of Attica to meet the growing needs of tourists. Wordsworth decides not to present *Athens and Attica* (1836) chronologically in strict journal form, and there are few actual references to dates or events: those he does chronicle are noted below.

Early in October 1832 the travellers cross from Euboea to Attica, in the vicinity of Iphigenia's Aulis. We visit the major sites of northern Attica before taking mules to Athens. After settling in for a few days (in a now-demolished house close to the Thesíon) the party embarks for Aegina

– perhaps because any later and they might have found the seas of the Argo-Saronic too unreliable. Back in Athens, Wordsworth leisurely shares his thoughts on the great landmarks with us (Chapters VII-XXIV) over the chilly months of November and December 1832. Christmas and the New Year are spent in the town – Athens was not made the capital of independent Greece until 1834.

October 1832

Day	Itinerary
9	Aulis to Oropus (Chapter I)
10	Oropus to Tanagra and back (Chapters II & III)
11	To Athens via Marathon and the Temples of Rhamnus (Chapters IV, V, and VI)
12	At Marathon
14	Arrives in Athens and soon begins excursions to Aegina and "some of the Islands of the Aegean"
19	To Piraeus and Salamis (Chapters XXXIV & XXXV)
21-23	In Aegina (Chapter XXXVI)

November 1832

In Athens

December 1832

27	To the Nymphaeum on Mount Hymettus (Chapter XXV)
28-30	Excursions from Athens to Laureium, via Lagrona and the Sphettian way; Sunium, Thoricus, Keratiá, Prasiae (Pórto Ráfti), Brauron, Markopoulo, and return to Athens (Chapters XXVI, Chapter XXVII, XXVIII, XXIX)

January 1833

3	Musings on the Ilissus and Cephisus (Chapter XXI)
7	Walk towards Mount Pentelicus and the "two white knolls of Colonus" and return via Cephissia and Marousi (Chapter XXX)
30	The new king, Otho of Bavaria, aged 17, lands in Navplio (Chapter XXXIII). (Later, Christopher is the first Englishman in Greece to meet the new king.)
31	Christopher returns from a long trip to Delphi, on which he is attacked and wounded by 'klephts' (Chapter XXXI)

February 1833

1	A cold winter in Athens (Chapter XXXI)
14	The Bishop of Athens addresses the citizens in the Agora (Chapter XXXIII)

Sidetrack 3

Gazetteer

Many travellers are put off from discovering modern Attica by their first impressions of modern Athens, and consequently miss out on a great deal. In Wordsworth's day Attica was a must-see destination in itself, the only deterrent being the fear of brigands; today there are other distractions and tourists hurry to see the great sites of Athens, and perhaps make excursions to Sounion and Marathon, before leaving for other more immediately hedonistic locations or home. Perhaps this book will encourage visitors to take time to explore the lesser known antiquates such as Amphiaraus, Brauron, or Rhamnus ("*If Nicolas Poussin had ever left Italy to travel in Greece, and given himself to the delineation of Greek landscape, he would have chosen Rhamnus as one of the first scenes to exercise his pencil.*" (p. 24)). Using the author's maps as a starting point, there are any number of routes, coastal or mountainous and within easy reach of the city, that will find you directly in Wordsworth's foot or mule steps.

Of course, present-day travellers will have to make allowances for the developments of the last two hundred years or so. It is surreal to imagine Wordsworth's party, speculating on the remains of Brauron, cresting a pine-clad hill to see the millions of tons of rock and earth that have been shifted in the construction of the new airport at Spáta, and the network of highways around it.

A point also to remember is that Wordsworth could occasionally err in his topographical hypotheses; a case in point is on Aigina, where he confuses the sites of the temples. However, these mistakes are rectified in the modern guides and are quickly forgiven when you stumble over some stones, inscription, small chapel, or panorama that will have set Christopher off on a passage from Stephen of Byzantium or Xenophon.

The place-name index that follows is based on Wordsworth's nomenclature (and includes other locations he mentions beyond Attica): the problems of phonetics and accents will be well known to modern travellers to Greece. In most cases it is not difficult to associate the author's spellings with the modern Anglicised eqivalent; in some cases the contemporary name is added in square brackets and rounded brackets show where Wordsworth has included an alternative name for the location or site. (A modern road map should be referred to for the Greek spellings if required.)

Ægina, 31, 148 ff.
    Ai Asomatos (Temple of Aphaea), 154
    Bilikáda (Church of S. Athanasius), 151
    Marathóna (island), 155
    Panhellenium, 151-153
    Pertica (Church of S. Michael), 155
Acharnæ [Achárnes], 12, 13, 42, 68, 117, 131, 144
Ai Apostólus (Delphinium) [also Oropó (Oropus)], 13
Ambryssus, 136
Ampelákia (Salamis), 146
Amphiaraus, Temple of (Ai Apostólus)[Amphiáreion], 1, 15, 21
Anagyrus [see Bári]
Anaphlystus (Anáphyso) [Anávissos], 113, 116
Aphidnæ [associated with Kotróni], 16
Argalíki [Agrilíki], 28
Argos, 185 n.1
Ascra, 1
Asopus, River [also Borién], 5 ff., 137
Assyria, 136
Athens:
    Academy, 69, 77, 90, 96, 132
    Acropolis, 33, 39 ff., 118, 131 ff., 150, 157 ff.
    Agora, 31, 36 ff., 92 ff., 139
    Agra (district), 91
    Agraulus, Cave, 12, 51, 52
    Anaceium (Temple of the Anakes or Dioscuri), 52
    Apollo Patrous, Temple, 94
    Areopagus [Church of S. Dionysius (the Areopagite), caves of Apollo and Pan], 39 ff., 92 ff., 133, 134
    Basileios, Stoa, 94
    Callirhoe, fountain, 89
    Caryatides (also Minerva Polias, Temple), 75
    Cecropium, 75
    Cephisus, river, 76, 89, 90
    Cerameicus ('Inner'), 92, 95, 100, 102
    Cerameicus ('Outer'), 96, 97
    Ceres, Temple, 63, 94
    Clepsydra, fountain, 49, 50, 79
    Cœle (district), 97
    Collyttus (district), 98
    Colonus (Churches of S. Æmilian Panagia Eleousa, and S. Nicolas) ('Suburban'), 68, 77, 78, 96, 97, 132, 133
    Colonus ('Urban') (Agoræus), 96
    Cynosarges, 98
    Diomeia Gate (district), 98
    Dipylum, 95, 96, 101
    Eleusinium, 100, 101
    Erectheum (also Minerva Polias, Temple), 74, 75, 77, 159

Eumenides, Temple, 46-48, 133
Furies, Temple, 92, 133, 134
Hephæstus, Temple, 96, 99
Ilissus, river, 34, 55, 87 ff., 164
Jupiter (Zeus) Eleutherios, Stoa, 36, 94
Jupiter Olympius, Temple, 83, 85
Leocorium, 96, 97, 101
Limnæ, valley, 101
Long Walls, 24, 103, 104
Lycabettus, mount (also St George's Hill), 34-36, 131, 160
Lyceum, 98
Lysicrates' Choragic Monument, 83, 85
Mars, Temple, 93
Melite (district), 96-98
Mercury Agoræus, Statue, 99
Metroum, 94
Minerva Polias, Temple (Erectheum), 67 ff., 100, 102, 159
Minerva Parthenos, Temple, 67, 70
Museum, 67, 70
Odeum, 55
Olympieium, 89
Panathenaic Stadium, 83
Pandrosus, Temple (Pandroseium), 74-76
Parthenon, 157-160
Pnyx, 33 ff., 58, 92 ff., 141
Pœcile, Stoa, 27, 98, 99
Pompeium, 94, 95
Propylæa, 41, 50, 61, 63, 64, 70, 78, 102, 159

Semnai, Temple, 47
St George's Hill (also Lycabettus), 33-35
Stadium of Athens, 87, 88
Ten Heroes, Statues, 93
Theatre of Athens, 53, 55, 57
Theatre of Bacchus, 85
Theseus, Temple (also Thesíon), 30, 31, 81-83, 96, 142
Tholus, 93
Tower of the Winds, 83
Tripods, Street of, 54, 85
Venus Pandemus and Peitho, Temple, 60
Victory, Temple, 61, 62
Aulis (also Vliké) [Avlidha], 2, 4

Bári (Anagyrus) [Cave of Pan], 106
Barnaba, mount, 17
Boiáti, hills of, 8
Bœotia, 1 ff., 137, 164
Borién [see Asopus, river]
Bratchi, 10
Brilessus, mount (Tirlos), 17, 34
Brauron (Braóna)[Vravróna], 122, 123

Calamo (Kalamo), 15, 17
Cephissiá [Kifisia], 128, 129
Chæroneia, 136
Chalcis, 1, 4
Chalcomatádes (Hepaestia), 130
Ceos (Zia) (island), 122
Cithæron, mount (also Elaté, mount), 10
Corinth; Acrocorinthus, 136, 143, 148
Coroneia, 136
Crete, 61

Daulis, 136, 137
Deceleia [Tatóï/Dhekélia], 16

Delphi, 136
Delphinium (Ai Apostólus) [also
　　Oropó (Oropus)], 13
Délisi (Delium) [see also Dramisé],
　　5, 6
Delos (island), 28, 122
Dramisé (Δραμισή), St George
　　Dramisé, 55

Egripo, 5
Eleusis, 94, 95
England, 142
Epikeráta, 29
Erasinus, river, 122
Eubœa, 1, 3, 13, 17, 163
Euripus (river), 2, 3

France, 142

Gargettus [near Stavrós], 29, 129
Garitó, 129
Gerilé (Γεριλή), 5

Gliáthi [Mitsári], tower [north of the
　　town of Varnávas], 17
Graimáda (Γραιμάδα) (also Tanagra)
Grammaticó, 18, 20

Haliartus, 136
Haraklí (Heracleum), 130
Helicon, 1, 91
Hephæstia (district), 130, 132
Heracleium (Temple of Hercules),
　　132
Hymettus, mount, 34, 106, 107, 110,
　　111, 121, 126, 140, 150

Kalamo [Kálamos] (see Calamo)
Kalandra [Halandri], 130, 132
Kangiá, 126, 127
Kato-Suli (also Tricorythus), 28
Kea (see Ceos)
Keratiá, Church of S. Demetrius,
　　120, 121
Kokáli (hill), 8
Kókla (also Platæa and Plataiai), 126
Kotróni (hill), 28
Kourúgni (peninsula) [Kouroúni], 122

Krabáta (Κραβάτα), 29, 127
Church of the Madonna
　　(Παναγία) [Pikermi], 29
Kykala (district), 126

Lágrona [Legrená], 112, 114, 115
Lári (river), 8
Laureium [Lávrio], 116
Lebadeia, 136
Leontári, Church of S. Nicolas, 126
Leuctra, 136
London (British Museum), 159,
　　170 n.4,
Lópesa [Paianía/Liópesi], 126

Macaria (spring), 27
Macedonia, 1, 99
Macri (ancient Helena)
　　[Makrónisos], 118
Maleventi, mount, 122
Malizé [Maléxi], 121
Marathóna (Marathon) [Marathónas],
　　17, 21 ff., 47, 49, 74, 98,
　　131, 159; Βάλτος [Great
　　Marsh], 28; Βρεξίσι
　　[Brexisa/Little Marsh], 28;
　　Δρακονερὰ, 27
Marcópoulo, 122 ff.
Marousi, 129 ff.
Media, 136
Menídi, 144
Merónda [Merénda], 121
Mesogæa ('Interior' district)
　　[Mesogía], 127
Metropísi [Mitropísi], 120
Munich (Museum), 148
Mycenæ, 185 n.1

Nauplia (Napoli), 31, 139, 141, 156
Noziá (Noseá), mount (see also
　　Parnes), 10

Œnoe [Kalétzi], 28
Orchomenus, 136
Oropó (Oropus) (see also
　　Ai Apostólus
　　(Delphinium))[Oropós], 11,
　　13, 14

Pallene (Temple of Pallas), 131
Paní, mount [Pánio], 120
Parnassus, mount, 137
Parnes, mount (see also Brilessus,
　　Noziá (Noseá), and
　　Parnes) [Párnitha], 8, 10,
　　17, 35, 58, 125, 131, 137
Peiræus (see also Phalerum), 1, 70,
　　103, 138, 143
Pellikó (Pallene), 131, 132
Pentelicus, Mount [Pendéli], 29, 34,
　　128, 129, 150
Peraté, mount [Peratí], Church of
　　S. Spyridhon, 122
Perrhidæ, 16
Phalerum, 42, 50, 103
Pheræ, 108, 109
Phyle, pass of, 68, 137
Platæa (also Plataiai and Kókla), 137
Pompeii, 66, 158
Porto Mandri (see Thericó), 118
Port Raphté (Prasiæ (Prasá)
　　[Pórto Ráfti], 122
　　Chapel of S. Nicolas, 122
Probalinthus [Néa Mákri], 28
Psaloútha (Ψαλούθα), 5
Psyttaleia (island) (Lipsokoutáli)
　　[Psitália], 147 Pylos

Rhamnus, Temple of Nemeseos
　　[Rámnous], 17, 20 ff.
Russia, 142

Salamis, 56, 146
Saronic Gulf, 17
Scori (hill), 116
Sinope, 136
Skyros (island), 81, 96
Sparta, 61, 62, 99
Sphettus; Sphettian Way
　　(nr. Anáphyso
　　(Anaphlystus) [Anávissos],
　　113
Staníati (tower), 8
Staurokoráki, mount
　　[Stavrokoráki], 28
Stavro (Cross, Σταυρό) [Stavró], 127

Steiria (the old Steirian road) [Agh.
　　Triada], 127
Strongúle (hill)(Στρογγύλη)
　　[Strongíli], 122
Sunium [Sounio], 112, 115, 116
Switzerland, 163
Sycaminó (Sikámino/Συκάμινο), 8

Tanagra (also Graimáda (Γραιμάδα))
　　[Tanágra], 7 ff., S.
　　George, S. Nicolas, & S.
　　Theodore, 10
Thasos, 1
Thebes, 12, 64, 82, 136, 137
Thericó (Thoricus) [Thoriko],
　　79, 116 ff.
Thermopylæ, 139, 141
Thespiæ, 9
Thessaly, 1
Thrace, 1
Tibári, mount, 120
Tirlos, mount (also Brilessus), 17
Tiryns, 27
Titacidæ, 16
Tricorythus (also Kato-Suli), 27
Trivla, mount, 122
Troezen, 60

Venice, 81
Vliké (see Aulis)

Zephíri [Mákari], 29

A SELECT INDEX (see also Bibliography and Gazetteer)

Æschines, 39, 98, 99
Æschylus, 46-48, 55-57, 72, 79
Agave, 67
Alaric, 71
Alcibiades, 167 n.19, 199 n.10
Alciphron, 145,
Anaxandrides, 208 n.4 (XXVII)
Andocides, 169 n.11
Antigonus of Carystus, 214 n.12 & 17
Antiphon, 25, 97
Apollonius Rhodius, 90, 197 n.3
Aristogeiton, 16, 62, 93, 95
Aristophanes, 35, 42, 50, 57, 62, 69, 71, 72, 116, 117, 126, 129, 130, 139, 141
Aristotle, 15
Arnold, T., 173 n.14
Arrian, 177 n.9, 185 n.18
Athenæus, 192 n.24, 214 n.19
Aulus Gellius, 169 n.6

Barthélèmy, Abbé, 15
Bassano, 20
Beaufort, R.N., IV
Bekker, I. (Endnotes *passim*)
Bentley, R., (Endnotes *passim*)
Boeck, A. (Endnotes *passim*)
Breitstein, Ehren, of Coblentz, 59

Callicrates, 103
Callimacus, 170 n.12, 172 n.2
Catullus, 61, 115
Cecrops, 51, 75, 76, 189 n.6
Chabrias, 78, 79
Cicero, 116, 178 n.17, 182 n.5
Cimon, 44, 54, 81, 96, 97
Cockerell, C.R., IV
Cramer, J.A., 184 n.17
Cratinus, 12, 89, 104, 183 n.10
Crinagorus, 206 n.3
Ctesippus, 78, 79

Demades, 99
Demosthenes, 39-42, 44, 79, 97, 98, (Endnotes *passim*)

Dicæarchus, 7, 15, 16, 42, 55, 167 n.11, 169 n.11, 180 n.10
Dindorf, W. (Endnotes *passim*)
Dio Chrysostom, 192 n.25, 216 n.4
Diodorus, 125
Diogenes, 136
Dobree, P.P. (Endnotes *passim*)

Elmsley, P. (Endnotes *passim*)
Ennius, 63, 185 n.1
Epaminondas, 64
Epicurus, 129
Eubulides, 194 n.3 (XIX)
Euripides, 1, 2, 45, 51, 56, 60 ff., 82, 88, 102, (Endnotes *passim*)
Euthymenes, 64
Euthyphro, 94, 202 n.2

Fronto, 90, 198 n.7

Glycera, 145

Hadrian, 30, 85, 160
Hamilton, W.R., IV, 185 n.19, 204 n.10
Harmodius, 16, 93, 95, 184, 199 n.14
Harpocration Valerius (Endnotes *passim*)
Hegesias, 177 n.5, 190 n.10
Heliodorous, 60, 182 n.6
Herodes Atticus, 22, 128, 171 n.3
Herodotus, 16 (Endnotes *passim*)
Hesiod, 1, 137, 165 n.4, 183 n.10
Hipparchus, 101
Hippias, 101
Homer, 2, 74, 109
Horace, 190 n.11
Horatius, 53

Ictinus, 65

Jacobs, F.W., 83, (Endnotes *passim*)
Juvenal, 45, 180 n.11, 209 n.9

Keightley, T., 184 n.13
Klefts (robbers), 7, 29, 121, 143, 164, 173 n.15

Leake, W.M., IV, 31, (Endnotes *passim*)
Leptines, 79, 192 n.25
Livy, 1, 166 n.11 & 12, 199 n.13
Longus, 205 n.2
Lucian, 59, 98, 111

Mai, A., 91
Marcellinus Ammianus, 200 n.19, n.22, n.23
Marcus Aurelius, 90
Menander, 128, 145, 194 n.3, 202 n.8, 218 n.2
Micon, 46
Millingen, J., (Endnotes *passim*)
Miltiades, 26, 49, 79, 97, 170 n.12
Milton, 90, 201 n.29
Muller, K.O. (Endnotes *passim*)

Odysseus (General), 50, 51
Olympiodorus, 207 n.16
Otho, King of Greece, 2, 141, 142, 160, 180 n.11, 218 n.2

Paciaudi, P., 197 n.2
Pausanias, 9, 28, 35, 45, 61, 93, 94, 95, 129, 133, 150 ff., (Endnotes *passim*)
Peisistratus, 52, 131
Pericles, 23, 43, 44, 63, 96, 103, 104, 203 n.3, 204 n.8
Phidias, 46, 65, 67, 70, 188 n.12, 189 n.13
Philochorus, 189 n.6, 207 n.3, 208 n.7
Philostratus, 100, 154, 171 n.3, 179 n.2, 201 n.3, 202 n.12
Philip of Macedon, 99, 141
Photinus, 175 n.4, 195 n.5, 198 n.5, 203 n.4
Pindar, 87, 148, 168 n.16, 182 n.4, 195 n.9
Pittakes, K.S, 35, 164

Plato, 17, 34, 38, 55, 58, 87, 90, 91, 94, 97, 110, 111, 130, 132, (Endnotes *passim*)
Pliny the Younger, 183 n.10, 192 n.27
Plutarch, 43, 81, 143, (Endnotes *passim*)
Pollux, Julius, 175 n.2, 177 n.3
Polemon, 60, 182 n.6
Polybius, 199 n.12
Polydeucion, 22
Poussin, 24
Praxiteles, 79
Propertius, 103
Ptolemy, 145

Raffaelle (Raphael), 46
Reiske, J.J. (Endnotes *passim*)
Rose, H.J., 168 n.16, 180 n.7, 190 n.8
Ross, L., 157
Runkel, M. (Endnotes *passim*)

Simonides, 49
Society of Dilettanti, 172 n.5
Socrates, 5, 36, 78, 90, 91, 94, 180 n.9
Sophocles, 56, 78, 81, 96, 113, 118, 119, 133, 134, (Endnotes *passim*)
Spenser (Shepherd's Calendar), 83
S. Dionysius, 45
S. Paul, 45, 46
Steven of Byzantium, 170 n.14, 200 n.28, 207 n.4 & 5
Strabo, 4, 28, 59, (Endnotes *passim*)
Stuart, J, 208 n.2, 209 n.12, 217 n.3

Themistocles, 44, 79, 92, 146, 162, 176 n.17, 203 n.6, 218 n.5 & 6
Theophrastus, 175 n.4, 175 n.3 (X), 179 n.4, 192 n.28, 211 n.12, 214 n15, 219 n.9
Theocritus, 15, 169 n.4, 194 n.5, 205 n.2
Thirlwall, C., 173 n.14
Thirty Tyrants, The, 43
Thrasyllus, 53

Thucydides, 25, 97, 137, 167 n.18, 173 n.14, 202 n.12
Timon, 98
Tyrtæus, 16

Valckenaer, L.C., 173 n.14, 194 n.3, 215 n.4
Vassos, Captain, 12, 13, 128, 144, 217 n.4
Virgil, 33, 106, 117, 189, 202 n.10, 209 n.11, 219 n.14

Vitruvius, 186 n.11

Welcker, F.G. (Endnotes *passim*)
Wheler, G., 159
Wilkins, W., 190 n.8
Wolf, F.A. (Endnotes *passim*)

Xenophon, 19, 79, (Endnotes *passim*)
Xerxes, 46

Zosimus, 187 n.5